WORLD UNION
ON THE HORIZON

WORLD UNION

on the

HORIZON

The Case for
Supernational Federation

James A. Yunker

UNIVERSITY
PRESS OF
AMERICA

Lanham • New York • London

Copyright © 1993 by
University Press of America®, Inc.
4720 Boston Way
Lanham, Maryland 20706

3 Henrietta Street
London WC2E 8LU England

Library of Congress Cataloging-in-Publication Data

Yunker, James A.
World union on the horizon : the case for supernational federation /
James A. Yunker.
p.   cm.
Includes bibliographical references and index.
1. International organization.   I. Title.
JX1954.Y85   1993   321'.04—dc20   92–42458 CIP

ISBN 0-8191–9037–3 (cloth : alk. paper)
ISBN 0–8191–9038–1 (pbk. : alk. paper)

The paper used in this publication meets the minimum requirements of
American National Standard for Information Sciences—Permanence
of Paper for Printed Library Materials, ANSI Z39.48–1984.

To the Memory of

Immanuel Kant
(1724-1804)

author of "Eternal Peace"

CONTENTS

TABLES AND FIGURES

TABLES

FIGURES

PREFACE

The vision of pragmatic market socialism as a steppingstone to supernational federation occurred to me—with all the emotional force of a religious conversion—during the winter of 1961-62. At that time I was an undergraduate student at Fordham University in the Bronx. The chain of thought which culminated in the vision was initiated by a reading of *The Power Elite* by the noted sociologist C. Wright Mills. Once initiated, it proceeded very rapidly to its logical conclusion.

What it was about Mills's book that precipitated this revelatory experience is a question to which I can offer no conclusive answer. My family background was thoroughly conventional, and my various political and economic judgments had previously been entirely orthodox. To the extent that I had thought about such things as socialism and a world state at all, I had been firmly convinced that both concepts were not only infeasible but clearly undesirable as well. While C. Wright Mills was certainly left-liberal in his basic ideological orientation, he was by no means a genuine radical. The purpose of his book was hardly to preach the need for major social transformations, but rather merely to put the general population on its guard against excessive manipulation by the "power elite" of wealthy capitalists, corporation executives, and high military officers and government officials.

In my case, however, recognition of the possibility that my thinking may have been to some extent manipulated—and thereby tainted—by those with an especially strong vested interest in the status quo thoroughly disturbed me, and thoroughly dislodged my previously orderly structure of conventional political and economic judgments. For me, the late winter and spring of 1962 was a period of intense mental activity—an activity with deep emotional overtones. I never experienced anything like it either before or after. Although I do not believe that there is any such thing as direct divine intervention in human affairs, even so, use of the term "revelatory" to describe the experience seems apt and appropriate.

During the summer of 1962, I produced the first draft of a working manuscript with the grandiose title: "An Introduction to the New World." When I look at that manuscript today, I wince. It is too full of youthful enthusiasm, of dogmatic certitude, of anguish, rage, and hope. It is also very vague on many important practical questions. Nevertheless, it contains in embryonic form the fundamental thesis which I now put forward in this book, more than 30 years later, in a more finished and balanced manner.

Naturally the passage of 30 years calms the emotions, and it is also true that having encountered a great deal of skepticism and indifference toward these ideas during that period of time, my level of subjective assurance about them may have declined somewhat. Nevertheless, I still believe very firmly that supernational federation within the relatively proximate future is both possible and desirable, and that pragmatic market socialism might well provide the critical initial impetus to a progressive thrust by humanity toward such a federation.

The vision which unfolded before me in 1962 was that of an ideological convergence by the communist and noncommunist worlds on a common pattern of democratic market socialism. The communist nations would abandon central planning and oligarchic governance in favor of market reliance and multi-party democracy. The noncommunist nations would abandon private ownership of large corporations for public ownership—thus effectively abandoning capitalism for socialism. Upon the conclusion of the historic ideological conflict between communism and noncommunism, major disarmament agreements would become possible, freeing up large amounts of economic resources previously devoted to military uses. A large proportion of these freed-up resources would be utilized in a worldwide economic development program along the lines of the post-World War II Marshall Plan, only on a far larger scale.

Then and now, there are three major impediments to world government: ideological conflict, the economic gap, and nationalism. Then and now, democratic market socialism is a viable possibility for overcoming ideological conflict, and a worldwide economic development program is a viable possibility for overcoming the economic gap. This leaves nationalism as the only remaining impediment—and this particular impediment may be dealt with simply by means of an appropriate political design for the world government. Such a world government must be a relatively loose, federal form in which such rights as the right of secession would be perpetually guaranteed to the member nations.

This was the vision which crystallized itself in my mind 30 years ago in 1962—and the vision is still strong. Back in 1962, I dedicated my life to the task of promulgating the vision among humanity. This book is intended to be an important milestone in the performance of that task.

At a very early stage, I was forced to confront the fact that for whatever reason, my personal vision of supernational federation achieved through ideological convergence and worldwide economic development was not going to be easy to share. Wherever I turned, skepticism and indifference were the normal reactions. I soon abandoned all efforts to convey these ideas orally, in the hope that some day I would achieve a sufficient volume of published writing on them—a "critical mass," so to speak—that they would become known to a wide range of humanity, and would be given serious consideration by that wide range of humanity.

Over the years, I have published a considerable amount of material in the professional literature relating to the contents of this book. As a professor of economics, it has been easiest for me to focus on the economic aspects. By the mid-1960s, I had settled on the term "pragmatic market socialism" to describe the economic component of the democratic market socialist system on which the communist East and the noncommunist West might converge. Of the ideas contained within these pages, pragmatic market socialism is by far the most thoroughly examined in my previous article publications— approximately 15 articles deal with various issues and problems of this particular concept of market socialism. Of these, no doubt the single most comprehensive article is "A New Perspective on Market Socialism" (*Comparative Economic Studies*, 1988).

As for a worldwide economic development program, in the early 1970s I developed a small-scale model of a World Economic Equalization Program (WEEP) for purposes of numerical simulation on a computer. I clearly remember my feelings of wonder and excitement upon discovering strong indications in the computer output that almost unthinkable economic progress might be made in a relatively brief historical period—given a sufficient commitment by the rich nations. These results have been described in two articles in the economic periodical literature, the first published in the *Journal of Developing Areas* in 1976 and the second in *World Development* in 1988.

Although my training, experience, and efforts as an economist have not enabled me to develop the historical and political aspects of the plan in as great a degree of detail, I have nevertheless had occasion to publish one lengthy article which sets forth both the proposal for supranational federation and a most-probable scenario toward its foundation: "Practical Considerations in Designing a Supranational Federation" (*World Futures*, 1985). This book, *World Union on the Horizon*, is essentially an expansion and updating of "Practical Considerations."

Although the various articles mentioned above, in total, comprise a comprehensive exposition of the vision of supranational federation achieved through ideological harmonization and economic equalization, they are of course widely scattered through the professional literature, and for the most part they deal with very small parts of the overall concept. In this case, there would seem to be a great deal of validity in the adage that "the whole is greater than the sum of the parts." Therefore, I have from the beginning recognized the need to put the whole thing together in a substantial book, which would hopefully be read and appreciated by a sufficient number of people to achieve genuine significance in real-world human affairs.

The first effort along these lines was made in the early 1970s, in the form of a manuscript entitled *The Grand Convergence: Economic and Political Aspects of Human Progress*. The manuscript was never completed, but even so it attained approximately 950 pages of typescript. The various publishers whom I approached with the project declined interest on grounds of excessive length. But even I could see that there were other problems aside from length. Despite the fact that the concept had been gestating in my thoughts for a full decade, many of the practical details were still vague—and the writing was still marred by excessive youthful enthusiasm. And so I filed *Grand Convergence* away in order to concentrate my efforts on articles.

By the early 1980s, I felt that I was ready for another effort at a book. This manuscript was entitled *Pragmatic Market Socialism: An Economic and Political Appraisal,* and it comprised 1300 pages of typescript as of the time I approached the publishers in 1988. Again length was a problem. In addition to that, the advent of the reformer Mikhail Gorbachev in the Soviet Union promised to drastically revise the international situation. It was beginning to look as though pragmatic market socialism might not be required after all as a first step in the direction of supernational federation. Should the USSR and the other Eastern nations totally abandon communism and become fully democratic market capitalist nations, then ideological harmonization would have been achieved without benefit of pragmatic market socialism. Such an outcome would have seemed veritably miraculous only a few years ago, but now it is recognized by almost everyone as a very strong possibility.

In response both to the length problem, and to the radical transitions presently occurring in the world, I developed two successor manuscripts from *Pragmatic Market Socialism.* Material from the approximately 1150 pages on pragmatic market socialism was distilled into approximately 500 pages of typescript entitled *Socialism Revised and Modernized: The Case for Pragmatic Market Socialism.* That manuscript was published by Praeger in April, 1992. The material from the approximately 150 pages in *Pragmatic Market Socialism* on supernational federation was considerably expanded into approximately 375 pages of typescript—the present work: *World Union on the Horizon: The Case for Supernational Federation.*

Although *World Union on the Horizon* recognizes the possibility that ideological convergence may well be achieved on the basis of democratic market capitalism, the emphasis is still on democratic market socialism as the basis for such convergence. I still believe firmly that overall social welfare in the future would be somewhat higher under the "pragmatic" form of democratic market socialism described briefly herein and in greater detail in *Socialism Revised and Modernized,* than it would be under democratic market capitalism. And the turmoil and confusion within the communist nations, particularly within Russia and the other republics of the ex-Soviet Union, is still apparently a long way from full resolution. In the final analysis, until Russia itself has become fully, unequivocally, and indisputably a democratic market capitalist nation, pragmatic market socialism might still have a role to play as an ideological compromise solution.

But aside from the ideological question, this book offers a great deal of serious reflection on potential avenues toward supernational political unity. There is a very detailed proposal for a supernational federation tentatively designated the Federal Union of Democratic Nations. There is a very detailed proposal for a World Economic Equalization Program. There are kernels of thought here that may yet germinate and grow eventually into a powerful instrument for the assurance of human destiny. The work is visionary, to be sure, but at every step a sincere effort has been made to support the vision with realism and practical common sense. I can only hope that these ideas will awaken in some readers the same sense of awe and excitement which they awakened in me some 30 years ago.

1

A NEW PERSPECTIVE ON
INTERNATIONAL ORGANIZATION

A. WORLD UNION IN THE TWENTY-FIRST CENTURY?

Conventional opinion holds that at the present moment in human history, any speculation concerning the possible formation of a world state would almost certainly be premature. Much progress has indeed been made in the recent past in defusing the Cold War between the Western and Eastern blocs of nations and reducing ideological strife. Nevertheless, the remaining obstacles to world government—in particular, substantial residual ideological conflict, wide economic disparities, and entrenched nationalism—are deemed by many to be impermeable and insuperable, not only at the present time but indeed into the foreseeable future. Given the persistent divisiveness within the human race, the multiplicity of incentives to conflict, and the inherent propensity in human psychology toward hostility and aggression, it is all we can do to maintain peace among nations, and any thoughts at the present time toward a qualitatively higher form of international organization are merely a waste of intellectual resources. If humanity is fortunate, then in due course, after a prolonged period of favorable evolution, probably consisting of many decades or even centuries, humanity might at last be ready to inaugurate an effective, humane, and progressive world government. Until then, our best hope for peace and progress lies in the maintenance of a balance of power within the family of sovereign nation-states.[1]

This book poses a challenge to the conventional viewpoint on world government. The challenge is based on a specific proposal for a supernational federation tentatively designated the Federal Union of Democratic Nations. It will be argued that despite the fact that this concept of world government has not as yet been given serious consideration, either by the political leadership, the intelligentsia, or the general public, it is nevertheless a very straightforward, common-sensical, and intuitively appealing alternative. The Federal Union of Democratic Nations would be a political compromise: sufficiently loose and flexible to permit its inauguration in a world dominated by nationalism, and yet sufficiently active and substantial to form a viable focus for long-term, evolutionary processes of human integration and unification. In terms of authority, power, and responsibility, it would fall somewhere between the United Nations of today, which for the most part is an ineffectual assemblage of speech-making ambassadors, and the typical large contemporary nation-state such as the United States or Russia, whose state apparatus exercises substantial direct control over its respective citizen body.

The Federal Union of Democratic Nations would represent a legitimate state entity, a formally established government consisting of legislative, executive, and judicial branches, exercising powers of taxation, and armed with military forces. It would display the emblems and trappings of state authority: a flag, an anthem, a capital city, and so on. It would be actively involved, along with the lower levels of government at the national, regional, and local levels, in the management of human society. On the other hand, its power would be restricted both formally and informally. The supernational government would be superimposed upon the existing structure of nation-states; it definitely *would not supplant* this structure. Functions and responsibilities would be shared between the supernational government and the national governments; it would not simply be a matter of the national governments handing everything over to the supernational government and then disbanding. The rights of citizens and of national governments within the supernational federation would be constitutionally specified in considerable detail. Probably the single most important right retained by the various nation-states composing the supernational federation would be the permanent and inalienable right to free and unopposed secession from the union. This formal constitutional guarantee would be backed up by the additional right of member nation-states to maintain independent military forces of their own.

It will be argued herein that it would be possible to establish a meaningful and effective form of world government, the Federal Union of Democratic Nations, even though the Union would indeed be subject to extensive restrictions and limitations. The concept of a world state subject to "restrictions and limitations" of course runs counter to the conventional concept. The currently reigning concept of a "world state" in human imagination involves an extremely powerful, centralized, and totalitarian state entity. Such a state would have little regard for individual rights, and most of its energies would be devoted to the forcible suppression of nationalistic and/or ideological dissidence. Many if not most people imagine a potential world state as an instrument of evil and malevolence—as an alternative only to be seriously entertained if and when the sovereign nation-state system clearly demonstrates that it is incapable of averting catastrophic warfare.[2]

From whence has this negative perception of a world state emerged? One obvious factor is that the majority of humanity has felt itself threatened throughout the twentieth century by the possibility of being forcibly incorporated into militarily brutal and ideologically repugnant "world empires." First there was the prospect of a "Nazi world empire" dominated by Germany; this was immediately succeeded by the prospect of a "Communist world empire" dominated by the Soviet Union. The multiplicity, ubiquity, and ferocity of twentieth century conflicts has also perhaps generated a cynical, dog-eat-dog mentality concerning the role of government in human society, and this mentality elicits the intuition that in a world full of savage and ruthless sovereign nation-states, effective supernational control could only be gained and retained by a world state that was even more savage and ruthless than the worst of them. Finally, there is the terrifying prospect, with which mankind has been living for almost half a century, of a devastating nuclear world war. Such a war could instantly annihilate the majority of the human race, and sweep human civilization as we know it today into irretrievable ruins. Whenever the possibility of a world state is mentioned, it is almost invariably commented that the only plausible scenario for the establishment of a world state within the foreseeable future is in the aftermath of nuclear catastrophe. Of course, it seems obvious that amid post-apocalyptic chaos and retrogression, the only possible

world state would be one of complete totalitarian control and bar-
barian savagery. Such a world state might find support among the
survivors of a nuclear catastrophe on the basis that its alternative, the
continuation of the sovereign nation-state system, might soon bring
on a repetition of the catastrophe.

Thus in the contemporary mind, the notion of a world state carries
with it nightmarish, Orwellian connotations: human life in the
shadow of a world state would surely be miserable, and the only
possible argument for such a state might be that without it no life at
all would be possible.[3] This book will argue that the common
conception of world government as necessarily ruthless and
totalitarian is a serious misconception, and that indeed opportunities
presently exist for a liberal, tolerant, and progressive world government. Such a union could be formed peaceably and harmoniously,
without need of warfare, nuclear or conventional. Such a union could
thereafter make an important contribution to the further progress of
human civilization. The contribution would be in two distinct but
interrelated forms: (1) the existence of a world government would
permit significantly more beneficial control over and coordination of
certain political, economic, and social processes than can be achieved
through the contemporary nation-state system; (2) the existence of a
world government would foster a spirit of international fellowship
and cooperation which would significantly reduce the incidence and
destructiveness of warfare in future human history.

The case for supernational federation presented in this book com-
prises two major components. First, there is a relatively precise and
detailed proposal for a Federal Union of Democratic Nations. This
proposal is presented early in the discussion: in Chapter 2. The
proposal is designed to be sufficiently flexible that conceivably the
supernational federation could function successfully even in the
world as we know it today. The world as we know it today is a world
in which there are serious ideological rifts within humanity, in which
there are drastic disparities in the living standards of the various
nations, and in which nationalistic patriotism is extremely strong over
the entire spectrum of nations, from biggest to smallest, from richest
to poorest. Given that the Union would be basically a voluntary
association of nations (owing to the constitutional right of secession),

in the world as we know it today there would almost certainly not be full participation in the Union by all nations, even if the Union were to be extremely loose and politically feeble. But even under the present circumstances, there might be sufficient participation in a sufficiently cohesive Federal Union to make the Union an important progressive force in international politics.

The second component of the argument for supernational federation consists of the assertion that opportunities exist, so far mostly unexploited, to significantly reduce ideological and economic rifts within humanity over a relatively brief period of historical time. It will be argued that the ideological conflict situation between the communist and noncommunist blocs of nations could be effectively and permanently resolved within an extremely brief period of time, perhaps only a few years. Owing to the fact that the economic gap is based on something more tangible than the subjective judgments which have fueled the ideological conflict, the economic gap will inevitably require more time to be significantly reduced. But it will be argued that through the instrumentality of a coordinated world-wide economic development program, the current economic gap might be very substantially reduced within only a few decades. This would of course be much more likely to occur if the economic development plan could be supported by resources transferred from military expenditures consequent upon major arms reduction programs throughout the world. In turn, substantial arms reduction programs could be facilitated by diminishing ideological conflict. Thus ideological harmonization could be an indirect instrumentality toward the acceleration of world economic development.

The international conflict situation between the communist and noncommunist blocs of nations reached its zenith in the Cold War period following World War II.[4] With the development of nuclear weapons and long-range delivery systems by the superpowers during the 1950s and 1960s, the traditional balance of power was succeeded by a balance of terror. The capabilities of the superpowers with respect to a nuclear armageddon reached a rough plateau level in the early 1970s with the Strategic Arms Limitation Treaty (SALT). Despite the fact that almost every informed, sane individual in the world agreed that a nuclear war fought with existing stockpiles of strategic nuclear weapons would be unbearably costly, arms reduction remained an elusive goal. The development of mutual respect and trust between the superpowers was severely hampered by a longstanding, deep-rooted ideological conflict. The Soviet Union throughout its history vilified and excoriated the capitalistic economic system of the United States and the other Western nations as exploitative and inefficient. In response, the United States and the other Western nations vilified and excoriated the communist social system as politically undemocratic and economically inefficient.

The advent of Mikhail Gorbachev in the Soviet Union was almost universally recognized in the West as a very positive and optimistic development. Gorbachev proclaimed an era of economic and political reform, and the anticipated direction of reform would clearly reduce the distance between communist and noncommunist social systems. At the same time, Gorbachev expressed intense interest in arms reduction of all kinds, conventional and nuclear, strategic and local. Unfortunately, the initial efforts at economic restructuring (perestroika) produced such a degree of confusion and apparent productivity decline as to seriously endanger the reform process. At the same time initial efforts at political and social openness (glasnost) elicited strong separatist movements in several of the peripheral republics, as well as radical opposition to the historic authority of the Communist Party of the U.S.S.R. The rush toward regional autonomy and democracy has been extremely rapid, leading to the precipitous dissolution of the Soviet Union and the formal revocation of the traditional authority of the Communist Party. Such rapid and radical transformations obviously create the possibility of reaction and retrogression. At the present time, the situation within the various republics of the former Soviet Union, especially Russia, is very fluid and unpredictable. The first effort at a conservative coup in August of 1991 was unsuccessful, but there may be others. On the whole, it may be many years before the ultimate consequences of the developments initiated in the 1980s by Mikhail Gorbachev become clear.

At this point, there seems to be a substantial possibility that the ultimate outcome of the Gorbachev era will be a nearly total elimination of the ideological gap between the ex-Soviet Union and the West. The ex-Soviet Union may well emerge with a genuinely democratic political system and a market capitalist economic system. If this were to occur, quite possibly the People's Republic of China and the other communist nations would soon follow the same path. If they do follow this path, then the contemporary ideological conflict situation will have evaporated like snow before the spring sun. Some authorities on modern international relations believe that despite appearances to the contrary, ideological conflict was actually a relatively minor contributor to the post-World War II Cold War, and that the essence of the problem was a nationalistic conflict between an imperialistically minded Soviet Union and the Western alliance of nations informally lead by the United States. If this perception is correct, it implies that the abolition of ideological conflict will not necessarily, in and of itself, lead to genuine detente and significant arms reduction.

It is probably safe to say, however, that a majority of authorities would describe the ideological conflict situation as having been at least an "important" contributor to the nuclear arms competition between the Soviet Union and the United States specifically, and to international hostility and tension generally. Certainly this is the interpretation put forward in this book. Therefore it is presumed herein that were the various republics of the ex-Soviet Union, particularly Russia, and the other communist nations to adopt democratic market capitalist social systems comparable to those in the West, this would greatly enhance the prospects for genuine detente and significant arms reduction. While this outcome is certainly very much to be hoped for, it is by no means assured at this point in time. Therefore, another important possibility will be extensively considered herein: the possibility of ideological convergence, as opposed to ideological capitulation.

Ideological capitulation is the scenario widely envisioned in the West at the present time: the communist East abandoning socialism in favor of capitalism (i.e., public ownership of capital in favor of private ownership), central planning in favor of market allocation, and oligarchic Party control in favor of open, liberal democracy. This scenario anticipates the communist East surrendering all three of its historical distinctions from the standard Western social system. Considerable attention will be paid herein to an alternative possibility of ideological convergence by both East and West on a common pattern of democratic market socialism. Such a social system would incorporate from the standard noncommunist Western social system the principles of free market allocation and political democracy, while at the same time it would incorporate from the standard communist Eastern social system the socialist principle of public ownership of the capital means of production. Arguably this East-West hybrid would constitute a social system superior to that presently prevailing in either East or West. And it would avoid the need for complete ideological capitulation by the communist East. It would be psychologically easier for the peoples of the communist nations to admit past error with respect to the two issues of market versus planning and democracy versus oligarchy, if the peoples of the noncommunist nations make the conciliatory gesture of admitting past error with respect to the one issue of capitalism versus socialism. Mutual compromise by both parties to a dispute, as opposed to unilateral surrender by one party, is usually an essential feature of peaceful and permanent conflict resolution.

At the present time, of course, the overwhelming majority of the Western populations are highly skeptical of socialism, and especially so when the term "socialism" is taken in the strict sense as referring to public ownership of the capital means of production. But quite possibly this skepticism is based largely on an invalid presumption that any sort of socialist system must inevitably share some or all of the negative characteristics of communistic socialism: bureaucratic strangulation of the economy through an overly centralized economic planning system, excessive economic egalitarianism and an overly developed welfare state, and an oligarchic political system dominated by the Communist Party and severely deficient with respect to individual rights and personal freedom. The socialist economic system which will be proposed herein as a viable and attractive alternative to contemporary capitalism in the West is described by the term "pragmatic market socialism." It has in common with all plans of market socialism the features of market allocation, competition among firms, and consumer sovereignty. However, it is distinguished from the generic concept of market socialism through the specification that the basic motivation of publicly owned business enterprises would continue to be profit maximization. In practice, therefore, the economic processes of pragmatic market socialism would be virtually identical to those of market capitalism. The primary difference would be that capital property return produced through the business operations of corporate enterprise would be distributed to the population as a social dividend supplement to labor income rather than as a return on financial wealth. In other words, social dividend income would take the place of capital property income (dividends, interest, rent, and capital gains). This would eliminate the exploitative element perceived in modern capitalism by Karl Marx and the other principal architects of communist ideology, while at the same time retaining the market mechanisms and incentives which promote rational allocation and use of the capital means of production and overall economic efficiency.

A brief synopsis will be provided herein (Chapter 3, Section B) of the case for pragmatic market socialism, but it should be understood that the case for pragmatic market socialism is not an essential component of the case for supernational federation. Pragmatic market socialism is neither necessary nor sufficient for supernational federation. A supernational federation might be formed even if the hypothetical alternative of pragmatic market socialism were never realized in any nation; while at the same time even if every nation in the world were to adopt pragmatic market socialism, this would not necessarily lead to the formation of a supernational federation such as the proposed Federal Union of Democratic Nations. It is merely argued that pragmatic market socialism would be desirable for its own sake, and that moreover it offers a potential avenue toward ideological harmonization between the communist and noncommunist blocs of nation. This avenue would of course be rendered irrelevant if the communist nations do indeed settle upon democratic market capitalist social systems, because such a development would abrogate the ideological conflict situation, at least in its current form. At the current moment in history, most of the communist nations have entered a highly chaotic and unstable period, and it is too early for confident predictions that the present instability will resolve itself into democratic market capitalism. Until such time as democratic market capitalism is solidly established in the communist East, it remains true that democratic market socialism provides a plausible and attractive compromise on which to base genuine, permanent ideological harmonization.

The Federal Union of Democratic Nations proposed herein would quite likely be sufficiently loose and flexible to accommodate both the noncommunist social systems of most of the Western nations and the communist social systems of many of the Eastern nations—as they have existed until very recently—without modification of any kind. The Union Constitution, for example, would be quite explicit on the point that member nations could maintain either capitalist economies or socialist economies at their own discretion. At the same time, however, it is perfectly clear that the greater degree of homogeneity between the social systems of the various nation-states, the greater the probability of successfully founding and maintaining a supernational federation. Much the same holds true of economic differentials in terms of living standards as holds true of ideological differentials in terms of social institutions and processes. While the Federal Union of Democratic Nations, as envisioned, might be able to successfully accommodate the entire spectrum of nations from richest to poorest, obviously this is more likely to be the case if the spectrum from richest to poorest is not so great in an absolute sense as it is at the present time.

The basic Federal Union proposal incorporates the feature that member nations would be permitted to maintain the customary national restrictions on immigration which characterize the contemporary world. These restrictions have been almost universally adopted by nations to forestall floods of immigrants from poorer nations. The removal of these restrictions at the present time would lead to chaotic migrations as a consequence of which the economic living standards of the richer nations would almost certainly decline rapidly to levels which would be deemed intolerable by their populations. Just as allowance for different capitalist and socialist economic systems is essential for the feasibility of supernational federation in the short term, so also are the retention of immigration restrictions within the federation. But just as it is an important aspect of the case for supernational federation that major opportunities currently exist toward the amelioration of the ideological gap, so too it is an important aspect of this case that major opportunities also exist toward the amelioration of the economic gap.

An extremely important component of the overall argument of this book is the argument for a World Economic Equalization Program (WEEP) presented below in Chapter 4, Section B. Just as pragmatic market socialism, dealt with in Chapter 3, represents a presently unappreciated opportunity toward the reduction of ideological disharmony, so too the World Economic Equalization Program represents a presently unappreciated opportunity toward the reduction of the economic gap. Once again, it is important to understand the role of the Program in the overall case for supernational federation. A World Economic Equalization Program is neither necessary nor sufficient for supernational federation. Conceivably a Federal Union might be formed and might make a meaningful contribution to human destiny even if its official goals never encompassed international economic equalization; while at the same time even if a very high degree of international economic equality were attained, either through a formal Program or otherwise, this would not necessarily enable the formation and functioning of a supernational federation. It is merely argued that a World Economic Equalization Program would be desirable for its own sake, because it would quite likely significantly reduce international economic inequality within a relatively brief period of historical time, and that the Program would thereby significantly reduce an important impediment to viable and effective world government.

Ideological conflict might be terminated by means of ideological capitulation by the communist nations, i.e., their unconditional, unilateral adoption of democratic market capitalist social systems. It might also be terminated by means of ideological convergence by both communist and noncommunist nations on a common social system of democratic market socialism, either of the "pragmatic" variety or some other. Economic disparities may be reduced, either through unplanned processes of economic development, or through a systematic, coordinated effort such as the World Economic Equalization Program considered herein. Ideological harmonization and economic equalization would address two of the three major barriers to world government. The third major barrier, of course, is nationalism.

Complementing the ideological conflict situation and the economic gap is a sovereign nation-state system which assiduously cultivates concepts of national identity and superiority in the citizens of the respective nations. The nation-state system has been a major contributor to the frequency and ferocity of wars in the modern era, culminating in those ruinous bloodbaths of the twentieth century known as World Wars I and II. Thus far efforts to control the nation-state system by means of international law and international organization have been largely unsuccessful. The futility of the League of Nations, established after World War I, was demonstrated by its inability to control the forces which brought on World War II. The futility of the United Nations, established after World War II, was demonstrated by its inability to control the conflict between the communist and noncommunist blocs that had human civilization balanced precariously on the brink of a nuclear World War III since shortly after the end of World War II.

No doubt nationalism is a potent independent force in human affairs. One has only to observe the continuing controversies and difficulties encountered by the European Economic Community and the European Parliament in trying to achieve a higher level of integration and harmony among a set of Western European nations which display a high degree of economic and ideological homogeneity. (On the other hand, the potentialities that may exist for supernational federation may be suggested by the fact that many of these same Western European nations were locked in deadly, nationalistically inspired conflict only a few short decades ago.) But at the same time, it may plausibly be argued that nationalistic senti-ment is significantly enhanced and inflamed by ideological and economic considerations. For example, the intense nationalism of the United States population may be largely explained by the fact that the nation is perceived as the main line of defense—if not the sole line of defense—against both the ideological horrors of communistic socialism, which would have been imposed on the population by the Soviet Union and the other communist nations but for the military establishment of the national government, and also the economic horrors of mass poverty, which would come about through massive immigration were it not for the barriers established and enforced by the national government. If it were not for the communist nations and the poor nations of the world, the U.S. population would feel less threatened and would be less prone to nationalistic patriotism. If the United States population could look out at a world that contained only nations such as Canada and France, it would not be nearly as nationalistic as it actually is.

Ideological and economic considerations also exacerbate the negative attitude of the United States population toward the concept of world government. In the United States (as is true in most other nations), the term "world state" tends to conjure up an image of a very highly centralized, tightly organized, and extremely powerful state entity, essentially the equivalent of the nation-states currently existent in the world today. It is typically envisioned that the distribution of relative power and authority between the world government and the various national governments would be analogous to the distribution of relative power and authority between, say, the federal government of the United States and the various individual state governments, such as those of Illinois and Iowa. Such a vision, together with the ideological conflict and the economic gap which characterize the contemporary world, suggests to most U.S. citizens that they would quickly become the victims of intolerable oppression by a potential world state. The world state would (it is imagined) quite likely impose some inferior form of socialism on the U.S. economy, and would also almost certainly impose confiscatory taxation on the U.S. citizenry to finance a "world-wide welfare state" designed to benefit the impoverished masses of Asia, Africa, and Latin America. A disarmed United States would be powerless to resist these brutal impositions by the world state, just as the populations of Illinois and Iowa would be powerless to resist what they might regard as brutal impositions by the federal government of the United States.

However, to imagine that the establishment of a world state would necessarily lead to this unfortunate outcome for the citizens of the United States, is exactly analogous to imagining that the establishment of socialism in the United States would necessarily lead to exactly those forms and procedures which characterized Soviet-style communism. As argued below in Chapter 3, pragmatic market socialism represents a socialist alternative that would avoid the undesirable characteristics of Soviet communism and which would represent a superior form of economic organization for the citizens of the United States and the other capitalist nations. Similarly, the plan developed below in Chapter 2 for a Federal Union of Democratic Nations represents a world state alternative that would avoid undesirable characteristics of over-centralization and inadequate guarantees of the interests of the populations of the member nation-states. The forms and procedures proposed below for the Federal Union of Democratic Nations represent a plan of world government which combines the legitimate human aspiration toward a shared authority higher than that of the national governments, with a desirable system of guarantees for the rights and privileges of member nation-states. The Federal Union alternative casts new light on the issue of a world state versus national sovereignty, and greatly enhances the case to be made for a world state and against national sovereignty.

In the long view of human history, the nation-state has been a powerful force for unity and cooperation among mankind. The great contemporary nation-states maintain a reasonably harmonious and mutually supportive condition over immense expanses of territory encompassing populations in the tens of millions, even hundreds of millions. This is not to say that unalloyed social bliss is achieved within nation-states; they are all beset, to a greater or lesser degree, with various forms of disharmony ranging from violent crime through to intense political controversy. But one only has to look far enough back into history to see what dramatic progress has been made. The nation-states of today, great and small, maintain a high level of peace and stability among numerous regional, religious, ethnic, and other sub-groups which would otherwise assuredly be engaged in continuous violent strife. Be this as it may, the time may now be at hand for mankind to proceed beyond the sovereign nation-state system as we know it today.

History has demonstrated that the peaceful cooperation enforced upon the internal population by the existence of a nation-state generates a tremendous amount of power and capability. This power and capability may, under favorable conditions, be used to develop a high level of material welfare among the population. Under less favorable conditions, this power and capability may be used mainly to develop a strong military force. When nations go to war, the collision of strong military forces on the battlefield normally produces tremendous death and destruction. This is even more apparent in the contemporary world owing to the remarkable advances of science and technology. Just as the nation-state has a positive side and a negative side, so too does scientific and technical knowledge. Science and technology has given mankind the means of significantly lengthening and improving individual human existence. At the same time, it has given us the means (in particular, nuclear weapons and long-range delivery systems) of quickly terminating much of individual human existence, and of sharply immiserating the remainder of individual human existence.[5]

The development of nuclear weapons and long-range delivery systems lends new urgency to longstanding concerns regarding the sovereign nation-state system. The idea of a world government is a natural progression beyond the idea of national government. Just as the national government has been an historical means of ameliorating and controlling regional and local conflicts, so too a world government could be a future means of ameliorating and controlling national conflicts. World Wars I and II in the twentieth century, not to mention a host of lesser conflicts, have demonstrated the fearsome destructiveness of modern "conventional" armament. We can only guess at the transcendent destructiveness of nuclear weapons employed in an unlimited war.

Some argue that the transcendent destructiveness of nuclear weapons has rendered world government needless and superfluous. Mutual Assured Destruction (MAD) is regarded by some strategists as the most effective guarantee of peace ever devised by mankind. No nation, it is argued, is likely to initiate unlimited war when the consequences of unlimited war almost certainly include nuclear catastrophe. There may be an element of wishful thinking, of aversion to hard reality, in this benign perception of the impact of nuclear weapons on the future prospects of human civilization. One may indeed grant that the balance of terror has thus far maintained its stability and even that it promises to maintain its stability for a prolonged period. One may indeed grant that the probability of unlimited nuclear war over the next five years, or the next ten years, seems comfortingly small. None of these stipulations are sufficient to abrogate the long-term peril represented by the existence of nuclear weaponry. Probabilities accumulate, and even though the probability of unlimited nuclear war over the next five or ten years may be quite small, over a sufficiently long period the cumulative probability of nuclear war will become very substantial.[6]

Indeed, it is widely agreed among authorities on international relations that "sooner or later" something will have to be done—or something will have to happen—to profoundly and qualitatively alter the present international situation, if the human race is to be spared the horrors of nuclear war. But the typical viewpoint is also that mankind will have to "evolve" slowly away from the present dangerous predicament, and that there is nothing of very great importance which can be done at the present time (such as the formation of a world government) to hasten this evolutionary process. As indicated at the outset, this book intends to challenge this pessimistic and passive viewpoint. It will be argued herein that humanity may indeed initiate a viable and effective world government in the very near future, that this government may gradually become a stronger and more positive force in human affairs as time proceeds, and that this government may in fact provide the decisive extra insurance needed by humanity against the threat of nuclear disaster, as well as other less immediate and dramatic—but still potentially deadly—threats, such as explosive population growth and accelerating environmental degradation.

It should be understood that what is intended here is a conservative case for world union. No allegations are made that without a world union mankind will inevitably encounter apocalyptic disaster, or that with a world union mankind will assuredly evade apocalyptic disaster. The argument is simply that with a world union there would be a *higher probability* of evading apocalyptic disaster, and of achieving a generally higher rate of economic and social progress, than there would be in the absence of a world union. Moreover, no predictions are put forward herein concerning the future course of human history. In particular, no assertions are made that the courses of history and science are converging in such a way as to "force" world union on the human population. It is merely argued that science (specifically in terms of transport and communications) has made world union possible, and that history has made it desirable. As to whether or not the possibility and desirability of world union will be recognized by a majority of the human population and acted upon accordingly, this is a question which will only be answered with the passage of time.

Despite the conservative nature of the case for world union put forward in this book, it is to be expected that some individuals will unthinkingly dismiss this case as a mere utopian fantasy. Even under the most propitious historical circumstances, mankind has displayed a great deal of caution and skepticism concerning change of any kind, and particularly concerning social change. The unimaginative and obstructionist element in human mentality has been greatly augmented by the various disasters and adverse developments of the twentieth century. The first half of the twentieth century was blighted by two catastrophic world wars; and the second half of the twentieth century has been blighted by the imminent prospect of an even more catastrophic nuclear world war. During the twentieth century, ideology and idealism have produced horrifying periods of totalitarian repression. The Bolshevik Revolution, intended to liberate mankind from the shackles of capitalism, brought on the Stalin dictatorship in Russia; while the National Socialist concept of national pride and regeneration led to the Hitler dictatorship in Germany. We have also become conscious, during the twentieth century, of explosive population growth and its attendant severe environmental degradation. We have become aware of a tremendous gap in the economic welfare of the populations of the various nation-states: even if ideology can be surmounted as the primary source of divisiveness within humanity, the economic gap stands ready to take its place. Understandably enough, all this has severely eroded the attitude of optimism and belief in progress which characterized human thinking during the nineteenth century. It has fostered an extremely short-sighted, egotistical and excessively conservative attitude among the populations of every nation, and particularly among those of the richer nations. Such an attitude, obviously, is scarcely conducive to a careful and objective consideration of the possibility of world union.

But it may be that the worst depths of negativism and despair are now behind us. As the twentieth century comes to a close, there are many positive signs. The ideological conflict between communism and noncommunism definitely appears to be winding down. A certain amount of apparent economic progress is being registered even in the poorest nations of the world. There is evidence that the rate of population growth has declined slightly in the recent past. Some progress is being made in the area of environmental quality. Science and technology continue to make extraordinary advances, continually expanding the capabilities and prospects of mankind. Among other things, modern transport and communications have totally abrogated the various practical problems of integration and coordination which impeded territorially extensive states in the distant past.

On the whole, it must be acknowledged that humanity appears to be gaining a higher degree of positive control over its own destiny at the present time. A supernational federation such as the Federal Union of Democratic Nations could consolidate and enhance these positive trends. It would be a serious mistake to view a world government as a revolutionary departure from the status quo as it stands today. Although it is commonly believed at the present time that a world state would require enormous social alterations of all kinds, the fact is that an appropriately designed world state would be a very direct and natural progression from the current status quo, and would indeed require only relatively minor transformations in present-day institutions and attitudes. Such a state would indeed be an "evolutionary" development and not a "revolutionary" development. Therefore its viability and attractiveness should not be underestimated. The reader is urged to give serious and thoughtful consideration to the case for supernational federation put forward in this book. The first decisive steps toward this potentially magnificent human achievement will be taken in the reader's own mind.

B. OUTLINE AND SYNOPSIS

The case for supernational federation put forward in this book is both multifaceted and extremely controversial. It is important that the reader possess at the outset a good idea of the structure and nature of the argument. Therefore this section of Chapter 1 will provide a concise narrative outline of the remainder of the book, broken down by chapter and section. Another reason for providing such an outline is to assist reference to specific parts of the argument. Different readers will have different ideas as to which aspects are more important and which aspects are less important, and the availability of a narrative outline will facilitate concentration on those aspects considered more important.

Chapter 2: A Proposal for Supernational Federation

2A. The Federal Union of Democratic Nations. The prescriptive content of contemporary writing on international organization is quite small, and what prescription exists is normally in the form of a few vague and sketchy recommendations tacked on at the end of elaborate recitals of problems and difficulties. The position motivating this work, on the other hand, is that "world problems" are sufficiently well known to the informed reader as not to require elaborate exposition, and furthermore, any useful consideration of the questions of whether or not a world state is possible at this stage of human history, and whether or not a world state would have a positive impact on future human development, presupposes a relatively precise and detailed understanding of exactly what sort of world state is being proposed. Therefore the proposal for supernational federation is presented at the outset of the discussion.

The Federal Union of Democratic Nations would be a legitimate, full-fledged state entity with the power to promulgate and enforce laws, the power to levy taxes and engage in public works, and the power to raise and maintain military forces. Its leaders would be directly elected by the citizens and its administrative apparatus would be substantial and in constant operation. It would have a capital city, regional offices, and the standard symbols of state authority: a flag, an anthem, emblems, and so on.

At the same time, there would be numerous restrictions on the power and authority of the supernational federation in order to forestall tendencies toward oppressiveness and totalitarianism. In the first place, as suggested by its name, the Federal Union would be a federal rather than a unitary state. That is, it would supplement—not replace—the national states taking membership in it. These member nations and their respective governments would not merely be formal

entities within the supernational federation; they would retain substantial degrees of sovereignty, autonomy, and independence. Key
restraints on the supernational state would include the following: (1)
member nations would retain the right to raise and maintain military
forces; (2) member nations would retain the right to withdraw
(secede) from the supernational federation at their own unilateral
discretion; (3) a dual voting principle would be employed in the
legislative assembly; (4) special budgetary provisions would be
enacted to prevent legislative deadlocks from freezing the operations
of the federation.

Established by a Federal Union Constitution, the Federal Union of
Democratic Nations would comprise the standard three branches of
government: (1) a legislative arm called the Union Chamber of
Representatives; (2) an executive arm guided by a Union Chief
Executive; (3) a judicial arm called the Union High Court. All three
would be directly elected by the population: Union Representatives
would have terms of five years, the Union Chief Executive a term of
ten years, and Union Justices terms of 25 years. Component branches
of the executive arm would include the following: Ministry of the
Interior, Ministry of Finance, Ministry of Justice, Ministry of Science,
Education, and Culture, Ministry of Planning, Ministry of External
Development, Ministry of Security, Ministry of Non-Union Affairs,
and World Development Authority.

The institutional proposals are developed in the light of the various
perceived problems and hazards inherent in the concept of a world
state. The first and foremost of these is the possibility that a world
state would attempt to impose upon member nations uncongenial
social systems (e.g., communism). Second to this but still extremely
important is the possibility that a world state would attempt quick and
drastic redistribution of income and wealth from the richer to the
poorer member nations. This potential policy is referred to herein as
"Crude Redistribution," and it is sharply contrasted to the preferred
policy of "Common Progress" (by which living standards in *all*
nations would increase, but the *rate* of increase would be higher in
the poorer nations than in the richer nations). The position taken
herein is that a supernational federation will only be feasible and
viable if the supernational government completely, totally, and une-

quivocally renounces Crude Redistribution in favor of Common Progress. Many specific proposals are designed to allay fears and apprehensions based on the possibility of misguided social activism and/or Crude Redistribution.

The single most fundamental proposal which would militate against the world state becoming an instrument of oppression is the right of secession. This right would be reinforced by the right of member nations to maintain independent military forces. It is proposed that all military forces of the Union, whether maintained by the member nations or by the Union itself, wear the same uniform, have similar weaponry, and be considered formally as components of the overall Union Security Force. But in the event of fundamental and irreconcilable conflict between the Union and a particular member nation, the nation would have both the formal authority and informal means (i.e., its own military) of resuming its independence from the Union.

Secession would be a drastic step and, if widely prevalent, would threaten the viability and existence of the Federal Union. There are certain key proposals designed to forestall the emergence of such serious conflicts between the Union and its member nations that secession would be contemplated. Among the most important is the dual voting system in the Union Chamber of Representatives. According to this system, any proposed measure would have to be passed by a 60 percent majority on two bases: the population basis and the material basis. In the population vote, a Union Representative's voting weight would be the proportion of the population of the entire Union represented by the population of his or her own Union District. In the material vote, that same Union Representative's voting weight would be the proportion of the overall revenue of the entire Union represented by the revenue raised in that Representative's Union District. Thus the richer nations, as providers of most of the Union's revenues, would retain more power in the legislature than would be the case if voting weight were based exclusively on population represented.

Although much attention is devoted to the "negative" issue of impeding undesirable policies and activities by the supernational federation, some attention is also devoted to the "positive" aspects of supernational federation. For example, concentration of the space exploration effort within a single political entity encompassing a very large proportion of the human population might lead to a more vigorous and successful effort. The same is true of the Union's pursuance of a World Economic Equalization Program under the guidance of the World Development Authority—with the understanding that this program would be conducted along the lines of Common Progress and not Crude Redistribution.

The psychological importance of the Union as a symbol of human unity and solidarity is emphasized, and this importance dictates, among other things, that the capital city of the Federal Union must be a very impressive and attractive location. In addition to the usual imposing public buildings, the capital city should contain numerous superior tourist attractions: museums, theaters, a botanical garden, a zoo, and a major amusement park along the lines of Disneyworld. In short, the capital city should be made into one of the great tourist meccas of the world.

Other important practical issues are discussed in this section. For example with respect to immigration, it is conceded that although free movement of goods and capital within the Union should be pursued, the elimination of the present national barriers to immigration will have to await the success of the World Economic Equalization Program. With respect to a common language, the argument is made that that there should be only one official language within the Union, and that this language should be English.

2B. Scenarios toward Foundation. According to predominant conception at the present time, in all probability a world state would be a ruthless and totalitarian political entity. Therefore the only plausible scenario through which such a state could be established is in the aftermath of a horrific nuclear world war which would reduce humanity to terror and desperation. This particular scenario toward the formation of a world state is not given any serious consideration here. This lack of consideration is not based on a presumption that nuclear war is extremely improbable. Even though the diminution of the Cold War between East and West has reduced the immediate threat, very substantial nuclear stockpiles—and the resolution to use them if circumstances require such use—will continue to exist for a very long time into the future. The lack of consideration is rather based on the judgment that a postnuclear-armageddon world would be so radically unlike anything we are familiar with—indeed so radically unlike anything in human history—that speculation is futile and useless. It would seem that amid such complete destruction and chaos, a retrograde movement toward political dissolution would be equally as likely as a progressive movement toward political integration.

In any event, the argument of this book is that a properly designed supranational federation with adequate safeguards for national and individual rights would not be ruthless and totalitarian, and therefore its establishment does not require horrific and desperate circumstances. The basic world state proposal being put forward herein envisions a world state sufficiently loose, tolerant, and flexible that conceivably it could be a benign and productive force even in the world as we know it today—a world in which significant ideological conflict persists, in which there are very large economic disparities between rich and poor nations, and in which the psychological attitude of nationalism is extremely prevalent and deepseated. Of course to the extent that ideological conflict, economic disparities, and nationalism become less important, the possibility of a viable and useful supranational state is thereby proportionately enhanced. The present section considers various possibilities (or "scenarios") toward the amelioration of these three basic impediments to supranational government.

The prevailing view at the present time is that all three of these impediments to a world state must be reduced to negligible proportions before a world state would become feasible. But this prevailing view is based on the misapprehension that a world state must necessarily be as unified and tight-knit as are the nation-states of today. The present proposal for supranational federation is rather based on the idea that if it is sufficiently tolerant, flexible, and limited, a world state could be established in the relatively near future, and that once established the world state would itself become an instrument for the reduction of ideological, economic, and nationalistic impediments to a higher level of harmony and cooperation within humanity.

Each of the three impediments to supranational unity has its own special character. In principle, the ideological impediment is the most amenable to rapid diminution in the short term because ideological viewpoints are mental and judgmental rather than physical and objective, and under some circumstances are subject to rapid transformation. The economic impediment, on the other hand, is more concrete and substantive, and even under the most favorable circumstances will require many decades to overcome. Nationalism is a manifestation of a primitive tribal instinct implanted in humanity by natural selection; as part of "basic human nature" it might seem the least amenable to diminishment. However, there are two important points to be made about nationalism: (1) nationalistic sentiment is exacerbated by ideological controversy and economic disparity, so the reduction of the latter two impediments to supernational unity will automatically reduce the nationalistic impediment; (2) the basic tribal instinct manifested by nationalism did not preclude the development of large and populous nation-states, therefore this same instinct need not preclude an even larger and more populous supernational state.

Each of the three impediments to supernational unity is analyzed and assessed in the following three chapters of the book: Chapter 3 deals with ideology, Chapter 4 with economics, and Chapter 5 with nationalism. The remainder of this section of Chapter 2 succinctly previews the discussion to follow in the context of providing scenarios toward the foundation and development of a world state.

At the present time, prospects for a high level of ideological harmonization within a relatively short period seem auspicious. There are strong indications that the most powerful communist nations are in the process of adopting the noncommunist position on all three aspects of ideological conflict: they seem on the verge of abandoning socialism for capitalism, central planning for market orientation, and Party oligarchy for multi-party democracy. If all three abandonments actually take place, complete ideological capitulation will have transpired, and the intense ideological conflict that has characterized most of the twentieth century will be no more. Clearly this outcome is much to be desired, as it would greatly improve international relations, substantially reduce the military burden, and significantly enhance the possibility of supernational federation.

But at the present time, the complete ideological capitulation by the East so much anticipated by the West has not yet been completed. The West should perhaps not be excessively complacent about this matter. Complete ideological capitulation of the sort desired is not an easy matter: psychologically it will be very difficult for the people of the East to admit total error in the past, to concede that every aspect of communist ideology and practice has been misguided and perverse. Therefore primary attention is devoted herein to an alternative "convergence" scenario toward ideological harmonization that would not require total ideological capitulation by the East.

According to the ideological convergence scenario (as opposed to the ideological capitulation scenario), East and West would converge on a form of democratic market socialism known as "pragmatic market socialism." This system would incorporate public ownership of large-scale, established business enterprise (i.e., socialism), but at the same time the publicly owned business enterprises would be profit-maximizers operating in a competitive market environment. Their profits would be distributed to the entire population, since under socialism the entire population is considered to be the legal owners of the capital stock employed by business enterprise. In its day-to-day operations, the pragmatic market socialist economy would be practically indistinguishable from the market capitalist economy which has achieved such a high level of performance in the advanced industrial nations. The political system complementary to the pragmatic market socialist economic system would be the standard multi-party democratic system common to the advanced industrial nations.

Thus the proposal is that the West abandon capitalism for socialism, and at the same time the East abandon planning for the market, and oligarchy for democracy. A compromise middle position could be reached between traditional communist ideology and traditional noncommunist ideology, a position that would not necessitate total ideological capitulation by the communist nations. If there seems to be a reasonable possibility that the ideological convergence scenario described above could be achieved within a relatively brief period (say 10 to 15 years), then the foundation of the supernational federation might be postponed until it has actually been accomplished.

But it is emphasized that ideological harmonization, whether through capitulation or convergence, is not necessarily essential to the foundation of a world state. The proposed federation would be sufficiently tolerant to permit both capitalist economies and socialist economies in the member nations, and it might also admit member nations whose political systems are appreciably less democratic than the standard attained by the advanced industrial nations. A high degree of ideological harmonization would be desirable and helpful, but it is not vital. Just as the contemporary world has achieved a high level of toleration of religious diversity, so too the future world might achieve a high level of toleration of diversity in basic social institutions.

Beyond the ideological gap lies the economic gap. Of the two gaps, the economic is probably the more formidable long-term impediment to a world state. But this does not mean that the formation of a world state should await the closing of the economic gap. The recommended scenario is that a Federal Union of Democratic Nations be formed in the near future, and that one of its primary purposes during its first decades of operation be to close the economic gap by means of a massive World Economic Equalization Program (WEEP), supported largely by resources reallocated from military uses via the arms reduction programs made possible by reduced tension consequent upon ideological convergence. The proposed institutional features of the Union would be such as to render very unlikely any major deviation in the conduct of the WEEP by the Federal Union from the desired principle of Common Progress. While it is unlikely that the WEEP could be transformed into an instrument for Crude Redistribution, nevertheless, owing to the democratic influence of the populous poorer nations in the Federal Union government, the Union would no doubt become a powerful force for the continuation of the WEEP to its successful conclusion.

The purpose of worldwide economic equalization is more likely to be achieved if the Federal Union of Democratic Nations does exist, than if it does not exist. At the same time, it is conceded that the goal of worldwide economic equalization may indeed prove to be unattainable. If this turns out to be the case, then quite possibly a permanent, effective supranational government may also be unattainable. The position taken in this book is not that such objectives as worldwide economic equalization and supranational government are *definitely attainable*, but that there is a *sufficiently high probability* that they are attainable to merit a serious, resolute, and determined effort to attain them.

It is argued here that the force of nationalism, in and of itself, would not be so strong as to abrogate the possibility of effective world government—particularly if the ideological gap can be appreciably reduced through ideological harmonization and the economic gap can be appreciably reduced through a World Economic Equalization Program. Although nationalism is often described as an "irrational" and "unreasoning" state of mind, the fact is that in the modern world nationalistic sentiment has been greatly aggravated by ideological and economic factors. For example, citizens of the United States tend to be intensely nationalistic because they perceive the nation to be their main line of defense against the horrors of the communist social system and the miseries of mass poverty experienced in the Third World nations. The argument is made that basic nationalistic emotions are not so overwhelming within most people as to preclude a rational and objective consideration of the possibility of supranational government.

Chapter 3: Prospects for Ideological Harmonization

3A. The Problem of Ideology. An ideology may be defined as a relatively comprehensive and systematic set of perceptions, ideas, and preferences concerning individual human behavior and/or social organization. Although the term "ideology" normally refers to the social ideologies of the modern era (liberalism, egalitarianism, socialism, communism, fascism, libertarianism, and so on), it may reasonably be extended to the religious ideologies of earlier eras. If religious distinctions are accepted as fundamentally ideological, then it may be said that humanity has accumulated a vast amount of experience with ideology throughout all recorded history. The fundamental characteristic of an ideology is that its validity cannot be fully established by means of logical reasoning and objective empirical inquiry. As a result, multiple ideologies tend to arise, and sometimes their various components are in serious disagreement.

Ideological differences tend to exacerbate friction and conflict. Throughout history, people have been made uncomfortable by the knowledge that other people possess belief systems very different from their own. These alternative belief systems implicitly cast doubt on a person's own belief system, implicitly suggest the possibility of error and mental incapacity. Thus they are fundamentally troubling and irritating, and they enhance the possibility that generalized hostility will boil over into violent conflict with those holding these alternative belief systems.

Opinions differ as to the practical significance of divergent belief systems in the generation of conflict and war in human history. Some wars have been fought between groups with very similar belief systems—even with virtually identical belief systems. At the same time, peaceful relations have been maintained for prolonged periods between groups with very different belief systems. It is clear that discomfort over divergent belief systems is not the only incentive to conflict. There are material grounds for conflict which have nothing to do with psychological belief systems. Subjugation of another group through military conquest may enhance a certain group's wealth, power, and self-esteem. Considerations of this sort have led some to the conclusion that ideological divergences are relatively minor and unimportant incentives to armed conflict.

Nevertheless, it is probably safe to say that to most informed individuals, the overall historical record—which includes numerous dramatic episodes of prolonged and intensive conflict seemingly exacerbated by ideological divergences, such as the Islamic wars of expansion, the Crusades, the wars of the Protestant Reformation, the Napoleonic wars, the two world wars of first half of the twentieth century, and the Cold War of the second half—this historical record suggests strongly that ideological conflict can frequently be a very significant contributor to both the probability and the severity of warfare. Ideological divergences interact with the material incentives (wealth, power, etc.) to augment propensities toward conflict and war. There is a natural resentment toward those who hold opposed viewpoints—one feels impelled to punish them for their mental incapacity or hypocrisy in espousing such erroneous ideas. At the same time, there is what might (in certain lights) be perceived as a commendable impetus toward assistance: one desires to conquer other people with opposed viewpoints in order to "rescue" them from their error, to enable them to see for themselves the invalidity of their belief systems. Thus conquest may actually be in the long-term self-interest of these other people—it may be "for their own good."

An important example of the intermixture of material and ideological incentives to warfare in modern history was the 1941 invasion of the Soviet Union by Nazi Germany. No doubt Hitler was veritably obsessed with the notion of incorporating the vast natural and human resources of the Soviet Union into a Germanic world empire. But this obsession was closely allied to his deep contempt for communism as a social system. The invasion could be—and indeed was—rationalized and justified on grounds that it would be freeing the Russian people (and the other nationalities of the Soviet Union) from the intolerable barbarity of Bolshevism. Without this extremely important ideological overlay on the basis of Germanic national self-interest, it is very doubtful whether both Hitler and the entire German people would have mustered the resolution to undertake the 1941 invasion of the Soviet Union.

A still more important example of the interaction between national and ideological interests has been the contribution of the confrontation between the communist and noncommunist ideologies to the post-World War II Cold War which had humanity poised perilously on the brink of nuclear catastrophe for the better part of half a century. The more cynical Western interpreters of twentieth-century Russian history have deprecated the Russian ideological objective of worldwide socialization as a crude form of dissimulation and camouflage of its true motivation: the establishment of a Russian world empire. Support for the hypothesis that Russian national interest has always been the primary impetus to Soviet behavior— rather than the liberation of the world from the shackles of capitalism—is alleged to reside in various apparent historical inconsistencies, such as, for example, the Nazi-Soviet Non-Aggression Pact of August, 1939. However, close examination of this episode suggests strongly that from the Soviet standpoint the Pact was not at all inconsistent with a *long-term* objective of aiding and abetting worldwide socialist revolution. On the whole, it would appear that espousal of the cause of socialist revolution by the Soviet leadership has always been *directly contrary* to the national interests of Russia, at least as these interests may be interpreted in any rational light. This espousal has isolated Russia from the rest of the world both economically and culturally, and it has brought with it a crushing military burden and heightened apprehensions of invasion and conquest. During the last half of the twentieth century, espousal of socialist revolution has put the Russian nation at dire and continuous risk of nuclear devastation.

The development of nuclear weapons and long-range missiles, and the accumulation of tremendous arsenals of these and other weapons among the superpowers, has dramatically increased the potential destructiveness of another world war along the lines of World Wars I and II. For several decades, the United States, the Soviet Union, and other nations have been striving to contain the accumulation and proliferation of arms. Progress toward arms control and reduction has been limited, however, owing to the virulent ideological conflict between communism and noncommunism. This conflict has strongly militated against the degree of trust and mutual respect needed to implement major arms limitation agreements.

During the latter part of the 1980s and into the 1990s, the efforts of Mikhail Gorbachev and his successors to effect fundamental transformations in the Soviet Union have significantly reduced the level of ideological controversy. A natural consequence of this reduction has been the very promising Strategic Arms Reduction Treaty (START) of 1991. This treaty supports the expectation that further reduction in ideological controversy would yield better international relations and further progress in nuclear and conventional arms reduction. Therefore we should seek actively for additional means and courses toward ideological harmonization.

One such possibility is that of ideological convergence on a uniform pattern of democratic market socialism, the economic component of which would be the pragmatic market socialist system discussed in Section B of this Chapter. Although the dominating hope and expectation at the present time in the Western world is that of full ideological capitulation by the communist East, this hope and expectation has not as yet been fully borne out. Until it is fully borne out, pragmatic market socialism might have a role to play in the furtherance of ideological harmonization. Clearly it would be psychologically easier for the Eastern world to abandon central planning for the market and oligarchy for democracy, if the Western world undertakes a parallel abandonment of capitalism for socialism. This would avoid total ideological capitulation by the communist nations, and would represent genuine compromise—which is nearly always an essential component of permanent, peaceful conflict resolution.

3B. Socialism in the West. Karl Marx's nineteenth century critique of capitalism comprised a static and a dynamic component: respectively the surplus value theory of exploitation, and the theory of recurring and worsening business depressions. Although the exploitation mechanism rendered capitalism inequitable and morally unworthy (in Marx's view), the instrument of capitalism's eventual collapse would not be exploitation per se, but the immiseration of the proletariat through ever-worsening business depressions. Nineteenth century mainstream economists complacently dismissed Marx's thinking: they believed that business cycles were a relatively minor problem, and that in any event socialism would be economically unworkable.

A great turning point in the history of capitalism occurred in the 1930s. Western capitalism was assailed by the Great Depression, a depression of unprecedented severity, and at the same time the great industrialization campaign in the socialist Soviet Union was forging ahead, suggesting that socialism was not as economically unworkable as had previously been thought. Under such urgent circumstances, the capitalist socioeconomic system in the West underwent dramatic transformation. Traditional laissez faire thinking went into eclipse as the Keynesian proposal for activist government anticyclical policy came to the fore. After World War II, the Great Depression failed to reemerge, and for nearly half a century none of the economic recessions which have occurred have even remotely approached the severity of the Great Depression. Marx's prediction of the ultimate collapse of capitalism amid the chaos and despair of a catastrophic business depression seems to have been definitively refuted.

But even if Marx's dynamic critique of capitalism is proven invalid, this still leaves the static critique: the exploitation theory. Marx's fundamental position was that the institutional developments of modern capitalism have made capital property income (dividends, interest, and so on) into *unearned income*. Aside from the question of business cycles, these institutional developments (the technological concentration of physical capital into large production units, the concentration of financial capital ownership, the separation of ownership and control) have continued apace into the contemporary world. To many individuals—even if they have no conscious or explicit sympathy with socialism—capital property income does in fact *seem* to be unearned. Marx used the term "exploitation" to describe the process by which capitalists appropriate capital property income, but this term may connote an unrealistically active process. It is perhaps more plausible that the contemporary capitalist is a *passive rentier* rather than an *active exploiter*.

Several important arguments have been offered in defense of capitalism, ranging from capital property income as an earned return to capital management effort and/or the sacrifices of saving, through the people's capitalism thesis, to the political argument against socialism that it is inconsistent with genuine democracy. However, none of these arguments are particularly compelling when subjected to careful scrutiny. In the final analysis, capital property income is indeed very unequally distributed under contemporary capitalism, and it presents itself prima facie as an unearned income.

But even if we granted, for the sake of argument, that contemporary capitalism suffers from the apparent inequity of highly unequal distribution of unearned capital property return, there remains the question of whether there exists a socialist alternative that would be superior. The history of Soviet socialism, and of socialism in the several other communist nations, suggests that while socialism clearly possesses fundamental economic viability, it is nevertheless very substantially inferior to capitalism in terms of economic efficiency— at least as capitalism currently functions in the advanced industrialized nations. At the same time, however, there are a number of features of communistic socialism—in particular the central planning system—which are not necessarily required by socialism in and of itself (i.e., defining "socialism" simply as public ownership of the capital stock).

Indeed, the concept of *market socialism* has been widely recognized in Western economics as an explicit alternative to the *central planning socialism* of the Soviet Union ever since the influential seminal work of Oskar Lange in the 1930s. Although the specific marginal cost pricing proposal offered by Lange is perhaps too theoretically oriented to be taken very seriously, there are in fact several other possible variants of market socialism with greater intuitive appeal. Among these are service market socialism, cooperative market socialism, and pragmatic market socialism.

Special emphasis is placed on the pragmatic market socialist proposal because it would be the most similar in actual operation to the contemporary market capitalist system—thus minimizing the possibility that it would be significantly less efficient and effective than capitalism. Pragmatic market socialism would retain private ownership of capital in some specific categories of business enterprise, the most important of which are small business and entrepreneurial business. Public ownership would apply to large, established corporations—of the sort which dominate economic life under modern industrial conditions. Executives of publicly owned corporations would be responsible to agents of a Bureau of Public Ownership (BPO) rather than to boards of directors elected by stockholders, but they would continue to conduct their operations according to the objective of maximizing the long-term rate of profit. Executives of specific corporations would be independently evaluated on the basis of their own earned profits, and the economic market would therefore be just as competitive as it is under capitalism. Capital property income earned by publicly owned corporations would go into a social dividend fund, and be distributed to individual citizens in proportion to their respective earned labor incomes. In addition to its greater equity owing to a more equal distribution of unearned capital property income, the pragmatic market socialist economic system would in all probability be at least as efficient as contemporary capitalism—and possibly somewhat more efficient.

The "internal" case for pragmatic market socialism are those benefits (definitely greater equity and possibly greater efficiency) unrelated to the international situation. The "external" case takes into account the possible role of pragmatic market socialism in achieving a reliable and permanent resolution of the ideological conflict situation between the communist and noncommunist nations. Pragmatic market socialism constitutes a system that would be recognized as genuine socialism even by traditional communist ideologues, but which at the same time might well be acceptable to the populations of the noncommunist nations. It could therefore provide a basis for ideological harmonization through convergence rather than through the more psychologically difficult route of capitulation.

Should the communist nations completely abandon socialism, then the external benefit of pragmatic market socialism would be rendered null and void. But such an abandonment has not yet taken place in the two most important communist nations, Russia and China. And it is by no means inevitable that it will take place. The basic socialist complaint against modern capitalism as exploitative and inequitable has proven extremely resilient over the last century and a half. Consideration of a socialist alternative such as pragmatic market socialism suggests a possible reason for this resilience: that there do in fact exist socialist alternatives—not yet implemented—that would be superior to contemporary capitalism.

3C. Reform in the East. The socialism versus capitalism issue is only one of the three main components of the ideological controversy between communism and noncommunism. However, it has always been the most critical and fundamental component. The other two issues, Party oligarchy versus political democracy and central planning versus market orientation, are derivative issues of far less consequence.

None of the communist nations had achieved stable democratic systems prior to their transitions to communism, and so the absence of democracy merely continued a historical tradition rather than being a consequence of the implementation of socialism. After their transitions to communism, any tendencies toward democracy were hindered by extreme internal polarization owing to the failure to pay any compensation whatsoever for socialized property, and by the external hostility of the outside world which remained mostly capitalistic. From the beginning, the communist nations have been characterized by a fortress mentality according to which the ordinary controversies, indecisiveness, and governmental instability of political democracy have been regarded as unaffordable luxuries.

It is highly significant that the communist ideological critique of Western-style democracy has never advanced the fundamental criticisms about the effectiveness of democracy which were advanced by the fascist ideologues of the interwar period. Rather Western-style democracy ("bourgeois democracy" in the communist lexicon) has been chastised as false and misleading—as sufficiently influenced and controlled by capitalist interests that the democratic implementation of socialism is virtually impossible. This line of argument would of course be completely irrelevant if applied to a socialist commonwealth.

With respect to the issue of planning versus market, even at the height of the Stalin era, the Soviet central planning system displayed some market features. Since the death of Stalin in 1953, the decentralization of economic authority and the amplification of individual autonomy and responsibility have been continuing themes in Soviet economic thinking. Some progress in these directions has been made, despite the proven resistance of the traditional Stalinist central planning system to fundamental change. It can be stated, as a general principle, that just as communist ideology has no *fundamental* quarrel with political democracy, so too it has no *fundamental* quarrel with the market economy.

In recent years, the rate of transition in the Soviet Union and the Eastern European communist nations has accelerated dramatically. Very significant progress has been made toward the implementation of Western-style multi-party democracy. At the present time, the economic systems of these nations are in a condition of flux and disarray, but it seems very likely that the stated objective of full transition to a market economy will eventually be achieved. With respect to the abandonment of the core concept of socialism (i.e., the privatization of all or most publicly owned industrial enterprise), this has been promulgated even in Russia, which throughout the twentieth century has been the world's foremost champion of socialism. But the Russian industrial economy has not as yet been significantly privatized and capitalized, and the attainment of this end in the near future is not lightly to be predicted.

Neither Western-style political democracy nor a high degree of market orientation are fundamentally contradictory to core communist ideology as developed by Lenin on the foundation of Marx. But the reestablishment of capitalism by means of privatization of the industrial economy would indeed be fundamentally contradictory to this ideology. Considering the remarkable success of this ideology in the past, the capitalization of Russia will be a difficult task. But as far as worldwide ideological harmonization is concerned, it is *not a necessary task.* Pragmatic market socialism would be a compromise middle ground comprising socialism from the communist ideology and the market from noncommunist ideology. It represents another possibility, a possibility which—if conditions warrant—may indeed come to the fore in the future.

Chapter 4: Prospects for Economic Equalization

4A. The Economic Problem. Looking beyond the ideological gap, we perceive what is probably an even more ominous impediment to the development of international amity and supernational government: the economic gap. In contrast to the ideological gap, the economic gap is not simply a matter of different opinions about proper social organization. The economic gap is rather based on concrete, tangible differences in capital resources, natural resources, and human resources. It cannot be overcome merely by adjustments in mental attitudes.

There are some hopeful signs: population growth in the Third World of Africa, Asia, and Latin America has tapered off somewhat over the past few decades, and some measurable progress in individual living standards has been made over the same interval. But against this we must consider the facts that the absolute gap in living standards as between the Third World nations and the advanced industrial nations remains very substantial, that this gap seems to be slowly widening, and that population growth throughout the world, but particularly in the less developed countries (LDCs), is still legitimately described as "explosive."

It is very doubtful that the problem of worldwide economic disparity will "cure itself" in any reasonable period of historical time.

At least two factors were operative during the rise of the advanced economies which cannot be replicated in the future for the benefit of the Third World economies: the incorporation of the tremendous natural resources of the North American landmass into the world economy at a critical point in its development, and the intensive exploitation of a stock of nonreplenishable fossil fuels during the same period.

The economic gap is a serious problem because of the natural psychological consequences of severe economic inequality: envy and resentment on the part of the "have-not's" and jealousy and suspicion on the part of the "have's." Although the theory of economic imperialism (according to which the advanced nations owe a large part of their economic prosperity to their exploitation of the poorer nations) is dismissed contemptuously by the economists of the advanced nations, the existence and prevalence of this theory, as a rationalization of the natural hostility of the poor against the rich, is only to be expected. What problems will be caused by this hostility in the future cannot be predicted with any precision. However, it seems clear that complacency is unwarranted. Nuclear proliferation proceeds apace, and in the future more and more poor nations will possess the means to vent their hostility in an effective manner.

The idea of undertaking a massive "worldwide Marshall Plan" to combat the problem of world poverty has been prevalent ever since the economic gap became a major area of concern in the post-World War II era. Many have lamented the allocation of tremendous economic resources to the arms competition, when these same resources allocated to international development may have made major inroads into world poverty. Many others, however, have arrived at the conclusion that massive international development aid—even if it were to be given—would be ineffective as a means of increasing economic productivity in the Third World nations and raising their living standards. In general, a spirit of bleak pessimism has taken strong hold in the advanced nations, and for the most part the LDCs are being left to their fate.

It is argued here that this spirit is morally wrong—that it is a shallow rationalization of short-sighted selfishness. The deescalation of the Cold War is freeing substantial economic resources from military uses, and a large proportion of these resources should be devoted to a massive effort designated herein the World Economic Equalization Program (WEEP). The Program would be along the lines of the post-World War II Marshall Plan, and would embrace the entire community of nations, rich and poor. Up to this point in modern history, a WEEP has never been tried, and until it is tried, predictions of its inevitable failure are purely speculative and highly presumptuous. Possibly a WEEP would in fact be a failure, but the only way to be sure of this is to try it and see. If after a reasonable period of time the Program is manifestly failing to achieve its objectives, it would be discontinued. If that were to happen, then the populations of the rich nations would be easy in their consciences that they had at least made the effort to help their fellow human beings in the poor nations.

4B. A World Economic Equalization Program. Some relevant published research work by the author is discussed in this section. This work is based on a simple computer simulation model of a potential World Economic Equalization Program. The theoretical relationships of the model are based on conventional economic theory and the numerical parameters of the model are based on standard data sources. The model focuses on large-scale transfers of "generalized capital" from rich nations to poor nations. Generalized capital includes not only physical capital such as plant and equipment but also human capital in the form of education and training. The principal criterion of welfare employed by the model is per capita consumption.

Results of the benchmark simulation of the model are very encouraging. The model suggests that at the cost of a relatively minor retardation in the growth rate of per capita consumption in the rich regions of the world over the planning interval of 35 years, very dramatic growth in the per capita consumption of the poor regions could be achieved. This progress would be so dramatic that within 35 years, living standards in the poorest regions might rise to as much as 80 to 90 percent of those in the richest regions. The direct cost of the Program to the richest regions would be in the neighborhood of 3 to 4 percent of Gross National Product, but it must be emphasized that this cost is not inconsistent with continued rise in per capita consumption in these regions. These extraordinary results may be attributed to a very basic economic principle as applied to generalized capital: the principle of diminishing marginal product of a factor of production.

Results from the benchmark simulation suggest the feasibility of achieving worldwide equalization on the basis of Common Progress within a relatively brief period of historical time. But at the same time it is conceded that these simulation results are far short of conclusive proof that a World Economic Equalization Program would be successful. Alternative simulation results based on different numerical parameter values are presented in the technical appendix to Chapter 4, and these results clearly demonstrate the possibility of failure. Nevertheless, the favorable results from the benchmark simulation support the position that a World Economic Equalization Program is sufficiently likely to succeed to justify the effort.

4C. Functioning of the Program. Some thoughts are provided in this section on the actual functioning (as opposed to the sheer scale) of a potential World Economic Equalization Program. Perhaps the most critical principle is that the resource transfers from rich nations to poor nations should be composed entirely of generalized capital: production machinery and equipment, education, and training. There should be no transfers whatsoever of consumption commodities. The purpose of the program is not to directly augment current consumption in the poorer countries; it is rather to augment their long-term productive capacity.

Some other important principles of the WEEP are as follows: Specific contributing nations would provide credits for the purchase of production equipment, education, and so on, from suppliers within those same nations. This provision will significantly enhance the political feasibility of the Program by making it an instrument for the prosperity of various firms and institutions in the contributing nations, rather than a continuing source of balance of payments strain. A substantial proportion of the contributed resources would be allocated on commercial criteria to reduce tendencies toward inefficiency. Finally, the Program would be accompanied by a major effort to reduce the rate of population growth within all participating nations—and particularly within the poorer nations. These and other principles will augment the success probability of the WEEP. While of course it cannot be absolutely guaranteed that the Program would be a success, there is a sufficiently high probability that it would succeed to make the endeavor a virtual moral imperative.

Chapter 5: State and World State

5A. The Problem of Nationalism. There is a certain school of thought which is so impressed by the concept of nationalism as an emotional force beyond the pale of reason and rationality that it would deny the possibility of supernational federation even if very substantial progress were made toward closing the ideological gap and the economic gap. This school of thought, however, attributes too much weight to tribalistic instinct as a force against political unification. Just as tribalistic instinct did not in the past preclude the formation of nation-states extending over large territories and encompassing large populations, so too in the future tribalistic instinct will not necessarily preclude the formation of a supernational federation extending over an even larger territory and encompassing an even larger population.

In assessing nationalism as an impediment to world government, two central factors must be taken into account. First, there are reasonable grounds for anticipating significant reductions, within the relatively proximate future, in both the level of ideological controversy and the extent of economic disparity in the world. Both of these factors have had a strong aggravating effect on nationalistic sentiment in modern history generally, and particularly during the twentieth century. Second, the proposed Federal Union of Democratic Nations would represent a relatively weak state entity, at least during its initial phases. The Union obviously would not possess the same degree of power and authority as is currently possessed by the largest nation-states of the contemporary world. It is not being proposed that the supernational federation displace its component nation-states, but rather that it complement them.

Although the twentieth century has witnessed a horrifying episode of the pathological overdevelopment of nationalistic pride in the history of Adolf Hitler's Nazi Germany, in long-term historical perspective the force of nationalism has largely been a unifying and harmonizing force. The spirit of nationalism helps to maintain peaceful and cooperative conditions within the very large and diverse populations of today's nation-states. Just as a healthy degree of individual self-esteem is not inconsistent with a person being a conscientious and productive member of a larger society, so too a healthy degree of nationalistic self-respect is not necessarily inconsistent with a nation's meaningful participation in a supernational federation along the lines of the proposed Federal Union of Democratic Nations.

Consideration of modern history shows nationalistic spirit to be associated with three major conditions and motivations: (1) religious and ideological ideas and aspirations toward the general reform and progress of human civilization; (2) desires for political unification and territorial expansion; (3) desires for liberation from governments perceived to be remote and oppressive. Some historical episodes show a relatively simple pattern: for example, the British revolutionary period from 1640 to 1688 witnessed an intensification of British nationalism almost exclusively on the basis of the first motivation.

The genesis and development of American nationalism in the United States from its inception through the early twentieth century, on the other hand, shows a more complicated pattern involving all three motivations. The immediate impetus to the American Declaration of Independence and the Revolutionary War was the desire for liberation from the British imperial government in London—a government perceived by the colonists to be remote and oppressive. But the American founding fathers quickly supplemented this immediate motivation with a vision of a new and improved democratic political commonwealth, based upon the natural rights of man and eschewing the aristocratic distinctions and the religious activism of the state which had characterized Europe through its long and difficult history. Finally, American nationalism was further intensified throughout the nineteenth century by the "manifest destiny" of westward territorial expansion toward the Pacific Ocean. The interaction of these three basic correlates of nationalism—in various permutations and combinations—may be observed in numerous other historical episodes: the French Revolution and the Napoleonic Wars, the consolidation of Italy and Germany, the decline and ultimate collapse of the Ottoman and Austro-Hungarian empires, the ideological and military conflicts of the twentieth century involving fascism and communism, the dissolution of the colonial empires of Britain, France, and other European nations after World War II.

The key point which emerges concerning nationalism as an impediment to world government is that out of the three motivations to nationalism, only one tends to be in direct conflict with such a government: the motivation toward liberation from remote and oppressive governance. With respect to the other two motivations, these might easily be perceived as favorable to world government. Just as in the past nations have been perceived by their populations as instruments toward the advance of worldwide human civilization, and as instruments toward unification and expansion, so too in the future the Federal Union of Democratic Nations could be perceived as an instrument toward these same ends.

Quite aside from the problem of nationalism, it goes without saying that in order to be viable, the Federal Union must not be perceived by any substantial proportion of its population as remote and oppressive. The advance of transport and communications technology has of course greatly diminished the potential problem of remoteness, relative to a century ago or to still earlier times. As for oppressiveness, the democratic character of the Federal Union would militate against this, as would the various institutional safeguards incorporated into its design. In summary, while it must be conceded that nationalism does in fact constitute a serious impediment to supranational federation, it is by no means an insuperable obstacle, bearing in mind the nature of the proposed federation, and also the nature and role of nationalistic sentiment in modern history.

5B. The Concept of State Organization. The previous section of Chapter 5 argued that nationalism, considered as an emotional force, does not constitute an insuperable obstacle to supranational federation. The present section argues that the related concept of national sovereignty, considered as a political principle, equally does not constitute an insuperable obstacle to supranational federation. The supranational federation being proposed here would be sufficiently tolerant and flexible that it could fairly be said that its component nation-states would retain considerable sovereignty. There would by no means be the "total abrogation" of national sovereignty envisioned by most of the casual thinking about world government that has been done up to this point in time—such thinking being muddled and fallacious.

An analogy is drawn between the concepts of personal freedom and national sovereignty. Both concepts express ideals and aspirations, but to be properly appreciated, their various practical limitations and constraints must be taken into account. By general consensus we refer to a citizen of a prosperous, democratic nation such as the United States as being "free"—even though physical constraints prevent that individual from flying like a bird or living forever, even though financial constraints (probably) prevent that person from living a life of ease and luxury, and even though social constraints (probably) prevent that person from exercising more than vestigial personal influence on the determination of government leaders and on the formulation of public policy. In the same way, we could legitimately characterize a member nation-state of the Federal Union of Democratic Nations as being "sovereign"—even though that nation-state would be subject to certain reasonable restraints and limitations by virtue of its membership in a larger political organization. Indeed, even in the contemporary world, a world in which a supranational government does not yet exist, the national sovereignty of nation-states is already subject to very significant internal and external constraints. Any national government which chooses to ignore these constraints will quickly become embroiled either in domestic revolution or foreign war.

Emphasis is placed on the fact that the supranational federation is intended—as the designation indicates—to be a *federal* form of government rather than a unitary form. The practical operations of unitary and federal forms of national government do not always correspond to the logical distinction: there have been examples of highly decentralized unitary nations, and there have been examples of highly centralized federal nations. Nevertheless, it may certainly be said that the formal provision for federal institutions of government in the design of the Federal Union of Democratic Nations expresses an explicit intention toward the decentralization of governmental power, and this expressed intention will significantly enhance the likelihood that de facto decentralization will actually be attained.

The practical objective is to achieve a proper allocation of governmental authority and functions as between the supranational entity and the various component national entities such that all the entities involved will clearly fit the criterion of statehood, and such that all entities will be properly characterized as sovereign in their respective areas of authority. No doubt the specific details of this allocation will always remain controversial. The perennial arguments between liberals and conservatives regarding the proper activity of the national government in relation to that of lower-level governments will be repeated in the context of supranational government in relation to national governments. But just as such arguments at the national level manifestly do not imply the infeasibility of national governments, so too such arguments at the supranational level would not imply the infeasibility of a supranational government.

The notion of world government is hardly unheralded in human thought. The ancient and medieval empires, though obviously deficient in terms of modern concepts of freedom, democracy, and toleration, manifested a natural human aspiration toward political universality. The more successful of these empires were not entirely brutal and despotic; at certain times and places some of them achieved a sufficient degree of humane civilization and benign governance as to somewhat foreshadow—or at least to suggest—the world state presently envisioned. Two major efforts have been made so far in the twentieth century toward a qualitatively higher form of international organization: the League of Nations was founded in the aftermath of World War I, and the United Nations was founded in the aftermath of World War II. While both of these efforts have fallen short of being genuine states and have clearly been disappointments in terms of their basic purposes, the passing of the Cold War—an episode that in a psychological sense at least has been almost as harrowing as the two world wars—may now be presenting humanity with a third opportunity. It is an opportunity which can and should be exploited through the foundation of the Federal Union of Democratic Nations.

5C. Purposes of a World State. Some indications are provided in this section of the purposes of a world state, organized according to the well-known four-part categorization of the purposes of state entities: (1) maintenance of security against external threats; (2) peaceful resolution of internal conflicts between citizens and groups; (3) provision of public goods and services, and regulation of the economy; (4) protection of political and social rights of citizens.

As to external security, it is of course hoped that in the long term all nations will take membership in the Federal Union, so that the purpose of protecting member nations against invasion by nonmember nations will be rendered obsolete. However, owing to the strict condition of voluntary membership in the Federal Union, it is quite possible that a number of nations will eschew membership, and this particular purpose of the supernational state might in fact remain relevant for some considerable period of historical time. Even if all nations eventually do become members of the Union, it is anticipated that some level of military force will be maintained indefinitely against the possibility—however remote that possibility might seem—of conflict with intelligent nonhuman species. Although the intergalactic warfare featured in some varieties of science fiction clearly verges on the preposterous, there is perhaps a sufficient kernel of plausibility in this particular long-term threat to merit at least a modest permanent military establishment.

Turning to internal security, clearly the single most important practical purpose of world government is to reduce the probability of catastrophic nuclear warfare in the future history of human civilization. Realism demands recognition of the fact, however, that even if a supernational state is established and becomes an important part of human civilization, the threat of catastrophic nuclear war will probably never be completely eliminated. One of the most obvious dangers is that of a nuclear civil war between the Federal Union and various nation-states attempting to withdraw from the Union. The establishment of a supernational state might create hopes and expectations that will prove unrealizable. Despite the formal provision for free and unhindered secession in the Union Constitution, when the time comes for the dissolution of the Union, supporters of the Union might regard the prospective secessions as treasonable defections to be forcibly resisted with every means available.

An example of the danger is provided by the United States Civil War from 1861 to 1864. Several decades after the formation of the

United States, relations between the Northern states and Southern states had degenerated into a rancorous controversy over free trade and slavery. The effort by the Southern states to secede from the Union was forestalled by means of four years of bitter and bloody civil war. It is argued here that had the U.S. Constitution explicitly recognized the potential issue of secession, either to allow it or to forbid it, in all probability the U.S. Civil War would never have been fought. In general, we must balance the potential role of a supernational federation in forestalling international warfare between fully sovereign nations against the potential risk that such a federation would set the stage for equally destructive civil wars. On the whole, taking into account the explicit allowance of secession in the Union Constitution, it would seem that the supernational federation would almost certainly have a diminishing net impact on the threat of catastrophic nuclear war in the future.

In the area of economic participation and regulation, the Federal Union should take a sufficiently active role to maintain a high level of visibility and status. It is important to understand that the purposes of the Union are not purely practical and utilitarian in a narrow, short-run sense—they also encompass the general, long-term objective of increasing the solidarity and cohesiveness of the entire human race. This suggests that the supernational federation should perhaps be allowed to take over certain functions, even though they are arguably handled effectively at the national or lower levels, just in the interest of furthering this long-term objective

This is not to suggest that there are not a number of important matters on which coordinated effort by a supernational government is likely to be more effective and successful than the uncoordinated efforts of a host of independent and fully sovereign nation-states. For example, population control and environmental preservation are two interrelated objectives on which determined action by individual nations is deterred by the reality that the problems being addressed are world problems rather than mere national problems, so that potential energetic efforts of some nations to address these problems would be ineffective if all or most other nations are failing to undertake such energetic efforts. A more positive natural area of activity by the supernational federation is that of space travel and exploration, an area in which concentration of most efforts under the aegis of the Federal Union would probably yield substantial economies of scale and a higher rate of progress.

Finally, the Federal Union could be an effective instrument for the pursuit and preservation of individual human rights. Through its direction of the World Economic Equalization Program under the auspices of the World Development Authority, the Federal Union would make a determined effort to implement the proposed right to a decent standard of living. As its name indicates, the Federal Union would have a fundamental predisposition in favor of individual freedom and political democracy, and it would endeavor to make these concepts a reality for the great majority of the human population. At the same time, the Federal Union must not become over-enthusiastic in its pursuit of human rights, lest it come to be regarded as an instrument of oppression by a substantial number of individuals and groups. The watchword on this matter, as on others, must be patience. The World Union must pursue its objectives in a flexible, gradualistic manner. Presuming that it does so, its potential positive contribution to the future destiny of humanity is likely to be substantial.

Chapter 6: Summary and Conclusion

6A. The Case for Supernational Federation. The case for supernational federation is succinctly summarized in this section. At this point in the historical evolution of human civilization, a world state has become both attainable and desirable. The ideological conflict between communism and noncommunism which has bedeviled the last half of the twentieth century is definitely on the wane. Even if the present hopes for total ideological capitulation by the communist East were to be disappointed, there exists another possibility for fundamental, permanent ideological harmonization through convergence by both East and West on a common economic pattern of pragmatic market socialism. The pragmatic market socialist economy would incorporate the basic socialist principle of public ownership of large-scale productive enterprises with the basic market principle of decentralized economic decision-making by a multiplicity of independent, profit-maximizing firms. At the same time, pragmatic market socialism would be fully compatible with

Western-style, multi-party political democracy. Just as pragmatic market socialism might be an effective means of overcoming the ideological gap, so too the World Economic Equalization Program, a massive program of development assistance along the lines of the post-World War II Marshall Plan, might be an effective means of overcoming the economic gap. With the ideological gap and the economic gap both in recession, nationalistic sentiments would also recede—quite possibly to the point where a world government would become a definite possibility.

It is emphasized that for a world government to be feasible, it would have to be a relatively loose, limited, tolerant, and flexible type of government. The model for such a government cannot be the large, tightly unified and integrated nation-states of today. The specific proposal set forth here for a Federal Union of Democratic Nations incorporates a number of important checks and balances for safeguarding individual and national rights. Nevertheless, the Federal Union would manifest the basic characteristics of a state, and it would in all probability exercise sufficient power and authority to make a positive contribution to the future development of human civilization. It would reduce the threat of catastrophic warfare by means of fostering and facilitating attitudes of amity and mutual support within humanity. At the same time, it would be an effective tool for the pursuit of such critical objectives as population control, environmental preservation, and space exploration.

The case being put forward in this book toward world government is a very cautious and conservative case. The envisioned world government would be a legitimate state entity, and would therefore constitute a definite qualitative advance over previous efforts at international organization (the League of Nations and the United Nations). At the same time, however, the envisioned world government would be sufficiently limited in its scope and constrained in its operations that it may reasonably be viewed, in the long-term historical perspective, as an evolutionary development and not a revolutionary development. There are no aspirations toward utopian conditions in the short term. The purpose of the Federal Union of Democratic Nations would rather be to establish political conditions which will foster and facilitate the long-term progress of human civilization over the course of future decades, centuries, and even millennia.

6B. The Question of Implementation. Even if it were to be stipulated, for the sake of argument, that the objective case for supernational federation appears to be quite formidable, there is still one more very consequential skeptical point to be made. This is the point that despite its objective attractiveness, it will be totally impossible to establish a supernational federation because of the enormous and immovable prejudice against the concept in contemporary thinking and attitudes. While it is clearly the case that unreasoning opposition to change is a fundamental human predisposition and has played an important role in human history, human history also demonstrates that humanity is extremely intelligent and creative. Therefore human civilization has been evolving and developing—and progressing—throughout all recorded history. This process will certainly continue into the future—and the process may well include the formation of a world state.

At the moment, of course, there exists no appreciable movement anywhere in the world toward the foundation of a world state, and this fact clearly suggests the improbability of a world state at any time in the foreseeable future. Nevertheless, the position taken here is that a world state is becoming increasingly feasible and attractive, and all that is needed is to achieve recognition of this by a sufficiently large majority of humanity. The twentieth century has been a difficult century for mankind, but as we approach the end of this momentous century, the future prospects for human civilization are brightening. Contemporary human civilization is equipped with an extraordinary communications network, and a tremendous capacity for rapid transformations, both psychological and institutional. If and when a movement toward supernational federation is initiated, it might well develop at a rapid rate.

Obviously it would be premature to endeavor to provide a detailed tactical plan for a potential future movement to found the Federal Union of Democratic Nations. However, some very broad guidelines for such a movement seem relatively self-evident. What is needed is a very good-humored and low-keyed campaign of information and persuasion. It must be strongly and continuously emphasized that the Federal Union proposal is a very cautious, sensible, and evolutionary step toward supernational political unification. The position taken is not that the Federal Union of Democratic Nations would definitely and inevitably be a positive step. It is rather that there is a *sufficiently high probability* that it would be a positive step to merit the endeavor. If the venture is unsuccessful, then it could and would be discontinued—either through the secession of individual nations or the dissolution of the entire Union. But to merely *assume* that the Federal Union of Democratic Nations would be a failure is inconsistent with the finer qualities of humanity—such an assumption, quite simply, would be morally unworthy.

Humanity will not be frightened or intimidated into founding a world government. Therefore restraint should be exercised in invoking such catastrophic possibilities as nuclear warfare and environmental breakdown. Greater emphasis should be placed on the positive aspects of mutual support and progress. The movement should totally eschew the usual disruptive and confrontational tactics of the "demonstration" in favor of a quieter and more benign type of public manifestation known as the "gathering." The campaign toward supernational federation would be conducted as an effort in information dissemination and friendly persuasion, an effort coordinated by an international pressure group called the Human Interest Society. Branch offices of the Society would operate in the various nations, and membership would be open to all those with a positive interest in supernational federation.

Would such an effort be successful? And if so, how much time will be required to achieve success? Only the passage of time will be capable of answering these questions definitely. Success might require many long decades of difficult effort. Success might never be achieved, despite the heroic efforts of a great many individuals. Nevertheless, the case for supernational federation is sufficiently cogent, and the possibility of success is sufficiently nonnegligible, that there exists a strong moral imperative toward action.

NOTES

1. The conventional dismissive attitudes toward the concept of a world state among international relations authorities at the present time are indi-

cated by the following representative quotes:

Inis Claude (1962, p. 208): "I do not propose to deal extensively with the question of the feasibility of world government in the present era, or in the foreseeable future. This abstention is in part a reflection of my conviction that the answer is almost self-evidently negative; if I must plead guilty to dismissing this question summarily, I do so in the belief that there is little point in belaboring the obvious."

Richard Falk (1975, p. 245): "In other words, there is no credible transition path to be followed over the next several decades that could lead reliably toward world government of a benevolent character."

Roger Hilsman (1975, pp. 574): "The truth of the matter is that the only proposal for abolishing war that is logically persuasive is the creation of a world state. Since war has been effectively abolished over whole continents that are controlled by stable, well-established states, it seems logical that war could be effectively abolished throughout the entire planet by establishing a stable, well-established state governing the whole world. But like the proposal for ending the Nazi submarine menace in World War II by boiling down the oceans, the policy is easy to lay down, but implementing it is something else again..."

Hedley Bull (1977, pp. 261): "There is not the slightest evidence that sovereign states in this century will agree to subordinate themselves to a world government founded upon consent. The idea of a world government brought about by social contract among states has always rested on the argument that the need for it will create the conditions that make it possible; that what must be if order is to be brought about in world politics, will be. However, the fact of modern international politics has always been that states do not recognize any such need..."

Carl Friedrich von Weizsacker (1978, pp. 110): "The third level, hope for a liberally organized world state, is wholly utopian as a road toward peace. Who will create it?"

2. In Chapter 18 of the 1971 edition of *Swords into Plowshares*, Inis Claude subjects the notion of world government to a much more thorough critique than it usually receives in the international organization literature. Claude's argument may be summarized as follows: World government would either be useless or it would be intolerable. If it were such a weak federation that it could not suppress wars among member nations, or between members and nonmembers, there would be no value in it. On the other hand, if it were given enough power to suppress wars among nations, it would almost certainly constitute an intolerable tyranny. The latter is seen as the more serious defect, and the point is stated as follows (p. 430): "The problem of power looms large with respect to any governmental system

adequate to cope with the elements of disorder and discord in the international community. If a global regimen is to have sufficient power to fulfill its task, questions of profound gravity arise: who will exercise and control the force of the community, in accordance with what conception of justice, within what constitutional limits, with what guarantees that the limits will be observed? These are not questions that can be readily answered, but they are crucial for the threat of global tyranny lurks in unsatisfactory answers. In terms of Western liberalism, the problem is not to get just any kind of world government—Hitler and Stalin were only the most recent of a long series of leaders who would have been glad to provide that—but to get a system of world order that is compatible with the political ideals of the democratic heritage." Claude states that the proponents of world government to date have not provided satisfactory answers to the rhetorical questions posed in this passage. It is the argument of this book, of course, that satisfactory answers do in fact exist to these questions.

3. For the benefit of those readers who may be unfamiliar with George Orwell's novel *1984*, it is an intellectually and emotionally devastating expression of post-World War II angst and apprehension. Essentially a well-conceived and well-expressed science fiction story which extrapolates from the totalitarian regimes in Hitler's Germany and Stalin's Russia, the plot centers around the elimination of a small group of dissidents who are resisting the gross physical and mental manipulation and repression of a militaristic police state in a Great Britain of the future. Not the least horrifying element of the story is that the regime, noxious though it obviously is by all civilized standards, has nevertheless succeeded, by means of intensive propaganda through the mass media, in winning the unquestioning obedience and loyalty of the overwhelming majority of the population. The profoundly disturbing impact of Orwell's vision is suggested by the abundance of serious literary and political commentary inspired by *1984*: for example, Samuel Hynes (1971), William Steinhoff (1975), Irving Howe (1983), W. F. Bolton (1984), and Shlomo Sholam and Francis Rosenstiel (1985).

4. Since the dawn of the nuclear age in 1945, a very substantial literature has developed on the nuclear war threat. Early reactions to the reality of nuclear weapons include Bernard Brodie (1946) and William Laurence (1951). Herman Kahn (1960, 1962) analyzed possible scenarios leading to a nuclear war. Tom Stonier (1963) assessed the blast, thermal, and radiation effects of a single detonation. In 1979 the Office of Technology Assessment of the U.S. Congress issued a study on the potential consequences of a major nuclear missile attack on the United States. The United Nations issued an analogous report on nuclear weapons in 1980. In 1984, Paul Ehrlich and

Carl Sagan, eminent figures from the realm of popular science, contributed to a book which adds to the already recognized hazards the possibility that a major nuclear war would raise up a cloud of dust so thick as to create a permanent, frigid twilight. The nuclear threat has inspired a survivalist literature: for example, Pat Frank (1962), and Ronald and Robert Cruit (1982). It has also inspired a number of eminent intellectuals to express their dissatisfaction with the situation: Linus Pauling (1958), C. Wright Mills (1958), Norman Cousins (1961), Bertrand Russell (1962), Carl Friedrich von Weizsacker (1978). Sometimes more or less specific proposals have been put forward for reducing the threat: Quincy Wright et al (1962), Walter Millis and James Real (1963), and Jonathon Schell (1982). The usual idea is to engage in a certain amount of limited unilateral disarmament in hopes of setting off "escalation" in disarmament. A few representative general assessments of the nuclear war threat include Herbert York (1970, 1987), Nigel Calder (1979), Edward Zuckerman (1979), Robert Scheer (1982), Arthur Macy Cox (1982), Lawrence Freedman (1986), Henry Shue (1989), Edward Rhodes (1989). Specialized assessments of the nuclear proliferation issue include Walter B. Wentz (1968), C. F. Barnaby (1969), George Quester (1973), William Epstein (1976), Ashok Kapur (1979), Joseph A. Yager (1980), Edward J. Markey and Douglas C. Walker (1982), Joseph F. Pilat (1985), Jozef Goldblat (1985), Jed C. Snyder and Samuel F. Wells (1985). There is even a market for what might be called "decorative" books on nuclear war: Shelford Bidwell (1978), William J. Koenig (1981), John Bradley (1982), and Charles Messenger (1984).

5. There is such a nightmarish unreality about the nuclear threat that the human mind experiences great difficulty in directly confronting this awful fact. Here are a few typical statements:

Nigel Calder (1979, p. 5): "In the middle range of H-bombs, the superpowers nowadays possess thousands of bombs and missile warheads with an explosive force of about 1 megaton, each eighty times more powerful than the Hiroshima bomb. For a single 1-megaton bomb bursting on the ground, the region of 'burnout,' or near-total destruction, extends at least 2.6 miles in all directions. Within this region the blast, wind, and innumerable fires started by the heat of the explosion smash and burn virtually all civilian structures. Closer in, within half a mile of the explosion, the destruction is beyond comprehension: the blast pounds the strongest buildings like a giant hammer and bursts people's lungs, the radiant heat consumes flesh, and the nuclear radiation is a thousand times the fatal dose. Thus citizens in the inner region are killed in three ways at once. The crater, where everything is vaporized, is about the size of a football stadium. Particles of soil laced with radioactivity are blown by the wind to settle as dangerous fallout over hundreds of square miles. If the attacker chooses to explode his 1-megaton bomb high in the air as an 'airburst,' there is no crater and no local fallout, but the area of burnout is nearly three times greater—60 square miles. That is for an unremarkable nuclear weapon—standard issue, one might say, and weighing only half a ton or thereabouts."

Office of Technology Assessment, U.S. Congress (1979, p. 94): "This case discusses a massive attack that one normally associates with all-out nuclear war. The attack uses thousands of war-heads to attack urban-industrial targets, strategic targets, and other military targets. The number of deaths and the damage and destruction inflicted on the U.S. society and economy by the sheer magnitude of such an attack would place in question whether the United States would ever recover its position as an organized, industrial, and powerful country."

Martin Laurence (1973, p. 11): "The strategic nuclear balance between the two Superpowers, the United States and the Soviet Union, dominates, directly or indirectly, all other contemporary military affairs. With the nuclear arsenals they have created, these two powers could virtually destroy each other as modern industrial societies and, in doing so, inflict immense damage on the whole world environment."

V. Kortunov (1982, p. 17): "Nobody can foresee all the consequences of nuclear war, either in its global or in its 'limited' version. However, no man with a sound mind will ever deny the fact that these consequences would be disastrous in either case. Every time specialists familiar with the subject, whether military historians, medical scientists, or ecologists, who base their conclusions on real facts, raise the curtain, as it were, on the possible scenario of a rocket-and-nuclear war, people find themselves facing a truly fearful chasm the extent of which no human mind can grasp."

Michael Haas (1974, p. 4): "The ever-present possibility of World War III haunts us all."

6. Even though the probability of an event occurring in any one period may be extremely small, the cumulative probability of the event occurring over a prolonged period of time could become quite substantial. If p represents the probability that a nuclear war will occur in one year and P represents the probability that nuclear was will occur over a period of n years, then the formula relating the latter to the former is as follows:

$$P = 1 - (1-p)^n$$

Using this formula, it may be determined, for example, that if the probability of a nuclear war occurring within 1 year is 1 in 1000, then the probability of a nuclear war occurring within 100 years is almost 1 in 10. Consideration of this formula suggests that if mankind is to be preserved indefinitely from nuclear war, the short-term probability of nuclear war must eventually be reduced to an extremely low level. Awareness of the "increasing cumulative probabilities" phenomenon is often expressed implicitly in the literature. Some examples follow:

Erich Weede (1983, p. 251): "While I believe that I have produced some evidence in this article...that extended deterrence reduces the risk of war, I do not believe that extended deterrence rules out war, or at least nuclear war, between blocs forever. Given the nuclear capabilities for destruction and an inherently unstable arms race, some reduction in the risk of war is unlikely to suffice in the long run."

Ronald Clark (1980, pp. 297-298): "Less unlikely than such calamities is the much prophesied nuclear exchange, either between the two super-powers or at least on such a scale between less well equipped countries that the world would be left a diminishing archipelago of radioactive debris. Of course no one in his right mind would allow it to happen; but accidents occur, misjudgments are made, and pulling down the pillars could be the aberration of crazy rulers. The odds that Hitler, marooned in his bunker, would not have pressed the button had it been available, seem rather low. Since 1945 there has been more than one forecast that the holocaust would come before a named date that has now already passed. There should be little comfort in this. The more frequently the ball stops in a black, the greater the chance of a red; nuclear war tomorrow may be unlikely, but the odds shorten with time."

Carl Friedrich von Weizsacker (1978, p. 106): "The Third World War is likely. It is likely because the compulsion to engage in hegemonic competition in a system of sovereign major powers which has always led to major wars in history continues to exist today, without abatement, and with the identical structural consequences."

Richard Barnet (1977, pp. 172-173): "The war that no one wants will come by miscalculation. It will spring from the conviction that it cannot be avoided... The threat of unintended war is growing.. The technological nightmare into which we have entered is an environment that chokes rational thought."

2

A PROPOSAL FOR
SUPERNATIONAL FEDERATION

A. THE FEDERAL UNION OF DEMOCRATIC NATIONS

It is perhaps symptomatic of the relatively rigid and unimaginative contemporary mindset concerning international relations and international organization that the prescriptive content of the social scientific literature in these areas is virtually nil. The authorities are agreed, of course, that the populations of all nations should strive to maintain a cosmopolitan outlook, and should be tolerant, sympathetic, and flexible toward the populations of all other nations. It is also agreed that national governments should be nonaggressive, supportive and cooperative toward other nations, and that they should be moderate and unassuming in their interpretations of their own national interest in relation to that of other nations. No doubt these are essential positive principles, but in and of themselves they hardly illuminate, let alone resolve, the myriad practical policy questions with respect to everything from international treaty negotiations and international law to the institutions and procedures of international organization.[1]

At the present time, serious writing on international law and organization tends to be elaborately descriptive. Of course the authors are always under some pressure to derive at least a few prescriptive "implications" from their descriptive analyses. These are usually delivered in the form of some highly superficial and virtually meaningless generalities half-heartedly tacked on to the very end of the work. The notion which apparently underpins most conventional work is that by describing the "problem" in immense detail, one might intuitively generate the appropriate "solution." Judging from the literature, this notion, at least applied to the larger problems, may well be invalid—that is, unless it is assumed that the current policy status quo (at least in broad outline) is in fact the optimal solution to the present international situation. Obviously the present work is based on quite a different notion, as follows. The international "problem" is sufficiently well known by now that elaborate descriptions of it are not necessarily very helpful. Moreover, the current policy status quo is not in fact the optimal solution to the present international situation: the inauguration of a supernational federation would improve upon the current policy status quo. However, this proposed "solution" to the problem must be developed in some detail before it can possibly be judged whether it does effectively address the problem. Finally, to properly judge how effective the proposed solution might be to the problem, it is necessary to look at the problem in the light of the proposed solution. In other words, the problem and the solution must be considered jointly rather than separately.

Therefore, this work will definitely not consist of a sketchy proposal for a supernational federation tacked on to an elaborate recital of the problems and perils confronting mankind—problems and perils such as ideological and nationalistic hostility, and the possibility of nuclear catastrophe or environmental breakdown. The reader of this work will normally already know as much about these things as it is necessary to know. It is not necessary to persuade the reader that these things are problems; it is rather necessary to persuade the reader that supernational federation might be a partial solution to these problems. Since the notion of a "world state" is so prejudicially misunderstood at the present time, the supernational federation proposal is presented near the beginning of the work, rather than at the end, and also the proposal is described in a reasonable amount of detail. Once the proposal itself is understood, a more accurately focused discussion will be possible of the two essential questions: how such a federation might come about; and what sort of a positive role it might play in the future history of human civilization.

What is desired is a sufficiently active, powerful, and influential supernational government authority to provide efficient international administrative services, and to constitute a meaningful deterrent to armed international conflict. At a minimum the supernational federal government envisioned here would possess the standard state powers of passing and enforcing laws, of levying taxes and engaging in public works, and of raising and maintaining military forces. It would possess a substantial administrative apparatus in continuous operation. Its leaders would be directly elected by the citizen body rather than being elected or appointed by national government leaders. The supernational government would possess the standard symbols and trappings of state authority: a flag, an anthem, an oath of allegiance, emblems, formal protocols, a capital city, and so on and so forth.

At the same time, the supernational government must be restrained from engaging in certain policies (for example, the imposition of socialist or capitalist economic systems on member nations, or of ruinous taxation on member nations) to which a substantial proportion of its citizens would be adamantly opposed. Key restraints on the power and authority of the supernational government would include the following: (1) member nation-states would maintain control of their own military forces; (2) member nation-states would enjoy a perpetual and inalienable right to withdraw from the supernational federation at their unilateral discretion; (3) a dual voting principle would be employed in the legislative assembly; (4) special budgetary provisions would be enacted to prevent legislative deadlocks from freezing the executive and administrative activities of the federation. Although such limitations as these are not customary with respect to present-day national governments in their relationships with subsidiary regional and local governments, nevertheless they are not fundamentally contradictory to the concept of state authority. In other words, the supernational federal government, even though operating under various restraints and restrictions, would still constitute an authentic, legitimate state entity, and as such it would possess a reasonable chance of realizing the positive purposes for which it is intended.

Let us commence our consideration of a potential supernational federation with some fundamental matters of descriptive nomenclature and formal organization, in the understanding that these are purely tentative suggestions designed merely to foster practical and concrete conceptualization of the special problems and potentialities of this type of government. Many of these details might well be revised or amended in the future in accordance with further thought and study. The proposed name of the federation would be the Federal

Union of Democratic Nations (FUDN). The Federal Union of Democratic Nations would be a supranational government founded on the basis of the Federal Union Constitution.

The Federal Union Constitution would comprise five principal sections: (1) nature and purposes of the Union; (2) the three branches of government (legislative, executive, and judicial); (3) powers and responsibilities of the supranational government; (4) rights and responsibilities of citizens and national governments; (5) a Transitional Codicil to remain in effect for the first 50 years of operation of the Federal Union. The regional components of the Federal Union would comprise between 100 and 200 Union Districts, of roughly equivalent population. The Union Districts would have no administrative significance, but would merely be regions from which legislators are elected. Some large nations would contain several Union Districts; on the other hand, several smaller nations might be needed to comprise a single Union District. Union elections would be held every five years. Each Union District would elect a single Union Representative to the Union Chamber of Representatives every five years. The entire population of the Union would elect a Union Chief Executive, the head of the executive branch of the supranational government, every 10 years. Finally, the elections of the 25 Union Justices serving on the Union High Court (the judicial branch of the supranational government) would be staggered: the term of office of a Union Justice would be 25 years, so that one fifth of the members of the Court would be elected in each quinquennial election.

The principal functions of the Union Chamber of Representatives would include the following: (1) to debate and vote on permanent legislation or policy directives proposed internally or by the Union Chief Executive; (2) to debate and vote on major personnel appointments by the Union Chief Executive, including all Cabinet positions; (3) to debate, amend and vote on the budget presented by the Union Chief Executive; (4) to impeach and remove members of the legislative and/or judicial arms of the government who are found guilty of serious criminal or Constitutional offenses. Passage of any legislation, directive, approval, or sanction by the Union Chamber of Representatives would require at least a 60 percent majority on two bases: the population basis and the material basis (these bases are explained below). As indicated in the previous paragraph, the Union Chamber of Representatives would comprise between 100 and 200 members and it would be a unicameral legislative body. Both the small size of the legislative arm and its unicameral nature are justified by the objective of maintaining a relatively close, personal, friendly, and collegial attitude among the legislators. This is especially important in view of the natural divisiveness to be expected within the legislature, owing to traditional nationalistic and other prejudices. Bicameralism is the rule rather than the exception among contemporary governments, based on the need for checks and balances. But there would be an ample sufficiency of other checks and balances in the supernational government envisioned here, so that bicameralism is not required for this purpose.

Perhaps the single most important of these formal checks and balances within the supernational government would be the dual voting principle. According to this voting principle, the vote of each Union Representative on a particular matter would be weighted in two different ways in two conceptually distinct votes. In the population vote, the weight of each Union Representative's vote would be equal to the proportion of his/her Union District's population to the total population of the Federal Union. Thus, if the population of a given Union District is 1/97th of the total population, the vote of that District's representative would be weighted as 1 in 97 in the population vote. In the material vote, the weight of each Union Representative's vote would be equal to the proportion of total Federal Union revenues raised in his/her Union District during the previous budgetary period. Thus, if 1/5th of the Federal Union's total revenues were raised in a particular Union District in the previous budgetary period, then the vote of that District's Union Representative would be weighted as 1 in 5 in the material vote. Passage of any measure would require a 60 percent majority in both the population and the material vote.

The dual voting mechanism combines two intuitively appealing principles: the traditional one-person-one-vote principle underlying universal suffrage in the modern Western democracies, and the reasonable principle that those who pay more to support a government's activities should have a proportionately larger say in determining that government's activities. The obvious short-term motivation for the dual voting principle is to impede possible efforts by populous poorer nations to impose radical redistribution on rich nations. If the World Economic Equalization Program is successful, then the proportion of Union revenues raised in a given District would tend to become equal to the District's population, and this particular motivation would become irrelevant. In the meantime, the provision provides some of the benefits of bicameralism, without incurring the ponderous unwieldiness and inherent divisiveness of bicameralism. With respect to the budgetary allocations needed to maintain the Federal Union's executive branch activities, if the 60 percent majority approval on both the population and material basis cannot be achieved on the budget proposal submitted by the Union Chief Executive, the budget utilized in the previous budgetary period would become operative. This provision would protect against the possibility that legislative deadlocks in the Chamber of Representatives would paralyze the regular activities of the Federal Union. The initial Federal Union budget would be specified in the Transitional Codicil section of the Federal Union Constitution.

The executive arm of the Federal Union of Democratic Nations would be guided by the Union Chief Executive, an official elected by majority vote of the entire population of the Union every other quinquennial election for a term of ten years. If the Federal Union achieves its desired objective, this individual would ultimately be acknowledged as the paramount political leader of the entire human population. It is clear that a major factor determining the success of the potential Federal Union of Democratic Nations would be the energy, determination, intelligence, patience, and good judgment of its Chief Executives. The function of the executive branch of the Federal Union would be to enforce legislation passed by the Union Chamber of Representatives, and to administer the various agencies of the supernational government in conformance with policy directives passed by the Chamber, and in conformance with the best judgment of the Union Chief Executive. As one aspect of administration of the executive arm, the Union Chief Executive would supervise the preparation of proposed legislation, and of a proposed federation budget to be submitted for approval to the Chamber of Representatives.

The activities of the Federal Union would be organized under nine agencies, whose directors, nominated by the Union Chief Executive and approved by the Chamber of Representatives, would comprise the Cabinet. The nine agencies would be as follows: (1) Ministry of the Interior; (2) Ministry of Finance; (3) Ministry of Justice; (4) Ministry of Science, Education, and Culture; (5) Ministry of Planning; (6) Ministry of External Development; (7) Ministry of Security; (8) Ministry of Non-Union Affairs; (9) World Development Authority. Some indications of the kinds of activities in which these agencies would engage will be given in the following.

The judicial branch of the Federal Union of Democratic Nations, the Union High Court, would have as its primary functions the following: (1) deciding on the validity of legal challenges to various legislation or administrative policies of the Federal Union brought by individuals or national governments on grounds that such legislation or policies violate either the letter or the spirit of the Federal Union Constitution; (2) ruling on challenges to national and lower level legislation and policies on grounds that such legislation or policies violate individual rights guaranteed by the Federal Union Constitution; (3) adjudication of disputes between national governments. According to conventional opinion, it is desirable that a high court enjoy a substantial degree of continuity and stability, so that its concern for tradition and basic principle might serve as a beneficial restraint on the legislative and executive branches, since the latter branches are often perceived as more susceptible to the forces of short-term political expediency. The provision of a 25-year term for elected Union Justices should render them more or less immune from considerations of short-term political expediency. Such immunity might be still further enhanced by stipulating that Union Justices may serve one term only.

The ultimate objective of the Federal Union of Democratic Nations would be to achieve a high degree of political unity among all humanity. Quite obviously, for there to be any possibility of achieving this objective, the Federal Union must be a very tolerant, liberal, and flexible government. It goes without saying, for example, that the

Federal Union must be absolutely neutral toward religion, now and for all time. Although social ideologies and economic disparities have become the primary focus of concern in the modern era, history amply demonstrates the enormous potential for conflict inherent in differing religious belief systems. Moreover, it seems almost unimaginable that mankind will ever settle on a common religion. The difficulty is that religious faith is not subject to the normal dictates of logic and reason. The controversies of social ideologies are, at least in principle, resolvable by means of empirical observation and logical deduction. Economic disparities may be addressed, at least in principle, by shifts in resources. But religious belief is beyond empirical observation, logical deduction, resource shifts, or any other mundane considera- tion. Fortunately, the world's great religions share certain significant commonalities: they all preach some degree of resignation, selfless- ness, toleration, and charity. These commonalities may, under favorable circumstances, lead to a strong spirit of ecumenicalism and mutual respect. The Federal Union must be completely neutral toward specific religions, and must confine itself solely to the effec- tive implementation throughout the Union of the individual citizen's Constitutional right to free and unrestrained religious expression.

Religion is by far the most important example of permanent diversity within the Federal Union, but there are other examples of cultural and ethnic diversity to be permanently maintained and respected. The question of political and economic diversity may be more difficult. It is proposed that the Federal Union Constitution guarantee to each citizen of the Union two natural rights which could have significant political and economic implications: (1) the right to democratic control over the political leadership; (2) the right to a decent standard of living. These rights may imply a higher degree of long-term political and economic homogeneity within the Union than could be managed in the short term.

Looking first to the political issue of democratic control over the leadership, the very name of the federation (the Federal Union of *Democratic* Nations) expresses a fundamental aspiration toward democracy.[2] Ultimately the objective is to have all elections within the Union be completely free and open, and to have a high degree of freedom of speech and press throughout the Union. In other words, the democratic ideal of the advanced Western nations, such as the United States and the nations of Western Europe, is the long-term objective. It may be possible, however, to accommodate within the Union for a prolonged period many other nations, such as the remaining traditional communist nations as well as numerous quasi-fascist right-wing dictatorships in the Third World, whose political institutions are quite different from those of the advanced Western democracies. Almost without exception, these other nations proclaim themselves democratic in the fundamental sense that the government enjoys the support of a majority of the population, and that it endeavors to govern in the best interests of the population. In many cases there is a degree of truth in these protestations, even though it is also obviously true that the objective of governance in the interest of the people is better served, over the long term and on the whole, by regularly scheduled, free and open elections. At least at the present moment in history there is a high level of agreement on terminology: even the most centralized and oligarchic governments usually proclaim themselves basically democratic. It is proposed that the supernational government be reasonably tolerant of various restrictions on political democracy within component nation-states, and that it work to reduce these restrictions in a unhurried, gradualistic manner relying mostly on persuasion and exhortation rather than threats of force.

Looking now to the economic issue of the standard of living, the specification of a Constitutional right to a "decent standard of living" may reasonably be interpreted as implying a high level of economic welfare throughout the Union: a standard of living comparable to that now enjoyed by the richer nations of the world. This interpretation of the Constitutional right suggests a high level of homogeneity at a high standard of living, and this interpretation of the right should indeed be pursued so long as the World Economic Equalization Program appears to have at least a reasonable chance of achieving its goal. Obviously, however, even if the Program is quite successful, a relatively prolonged period would be necessary to close the economic gap. In the meantime, the Union would have to be tolerant of economic disparities. If the Program is unsuccessful and is finally abandoned, the Constitutional right to a "decent standard of living" would have to be permanently downgraded to something along the lines of "basic needs": enough food and shelter to permit physical survival and comfort plus some rudimentary amenities such as literacy. Conceivably the Federal Union could function even though it had abandoned the economic equalization goal, at least as an explicit short-term policy objective. At the same time, it is obvious that the prospects for permanent operation of the Federal Union would be greatly enhanced by the successful completion of a World Economic Equalization Program. This critical issue will be further addressed at various appropriate points in the following.

Another potentially divisive issue relating to the economic standard of living involves capitalism versus socialism. Much will be said on this particular issue in the following, particularly in Chapter 3. Suffice it to say that the available evidence at this point in history seems to indicate that both capitalist and socialist economic systems are basically viable: that both of them are capable of providing at least a "decent standard of living" over the entire range of the population from most well-endowed to least well-endowed. No doubt it is true that under a perfectly controlled experiment, one system could be scientifically proved superior to the other. However, it also seems quite probable that there will never occur even an imperfectly controlled experiment to this end, let alone a perfectly controlled experiment. And even if a positive determination of the superiority of one system over the other could be achieved, it is fully possible that the numerical difference would not be particularly large. Given that both systems are basically viable and that one system will probably never be scientifically proven superior to the other, the Federal Union should remain neutral on the issue and should be fully tolerant of both capitalist and socialist economic systems in member nations. There may or may not ultimately be a convergence by all nations on either the capitalist or the socialist economic form, but this is a matter from which the Federal Union government should remain entirely aloof. It should make no policies affecting the matter, and individual members of the government should, insofar as possible, exercise great restraint even in expressing personal opinions about it.

Central to the functioning of any state entity are two critical issues: military power and financial funding. These would obviously be very sensitive issues in the context of a supernational federation. Whether or not such a federation is feasible depends to a large extent on whether acceptable, practical arrangements can be worked out in these areas: arrangements which would strike a satisfactory balance between the competing objectives of supernational unity and national security. Therefore, before continuing any further in our description of a potential Federal Union of Democratic Nations, let us consider specifically how these two critical matters might be handled.

Military Power. One of the important purposes of a nation-state is to deter armed conflicts between subsidiary governments representing component localities. Thus, for example, the national government of the United States would not allow the states of Iowa and Illinois to go to war with one another. If necessary, the United States military forces would be employed to physically suppress such a war. But to those who are personally familiar with life in the contemporary United States, the notion that the state governments of Illinois and Iowa would contemplate making war on one another is simply inconceivable. The ideal of national unity has become so strongly rooted in the United States that state leaders never in their wildest dreams imagine using armed force to resolve various disputes and controversies with other states. It is simply taken for granted that these disputes and controversies will be resolved peacefully by some type of negotiation, arbitration, or adjudication. This psychological attitude is possible because the citizens of the United States harbor very little emotional allegiance to their respective states: rather their emotional allegiance is almost entirely bestowed upon the nation. Thus, armed conflicts between states are not so much deterred by the existence of the United States military forces which would forcibly suppress such conflicts were they to occur (although such forcible suppression would indeed be inevitable); rather they are principally forestalled by the absence of emotional allegiance in citizens to their respective states.

The long-term goal of the Federal Union of Democratic Nations would be to achieve an analogous situation in the international sphere: that is, to bring about a condition under which the citizens of the Union would harbor very little emotional allegiance to their respective nations, but would rather bestow such allegiance almost entirely upon the Federal Union. The lengthy process of evolution by which such a condition might eventually be achieved would involve a complex interplay between real factors (such as the supranational federation's military forces) and psychological factors (the important symbolic impact of the very existence of the supranational federation). We are concerned at this point with one particularly crucial real factor: the military force of the Federal Union.

It is customary that state entities possess military forces: these military forces protect the citizen body from outside aggression and they also deter (at least potentially) the citizen body from engaging in warfare among itself. It is therefore proposed that the Federal Union of Democratic Nations possess a military force, to be designated the Union Security Force, which would be administered by the Ministry of Security. The Union Security Force would comprise land, sea, and air forces, and it would be armed with the entire range of weaponry from small arms through to strategic nuclear weapons. Every effort would be made to maintain this force in an effective fighting condition and in a high state of readiness. Both potential functions just mentioned would be served by such a force: to deter outside aggression, and to forestall armed internal conflict. With respect to outside aggression, the ultimate objective of the Federal Union would of course be universal membership by all the nations of the earth, and were this objective to be eventually achieved there would be no danger of outside aggression by other nations.

However, numerous writers of science fiction have warned us of the possibility that, even if the human race were to achieve complete political unity, it would still have to confront the possibility of conflict with nonhuman species emanating from other planets. Although most of this science fiction speculation seems patently preposterous, there is perhaps enough substance to these visions to postulate a Ministry of Security and a Union Security Force as permanent components of the supranational state, even were complete participation in the Union and perfect internal harmony to be achieved. In the near term, however, such a force might more plausibly be necessary to deter aggression against member nations by nonmember nations. It is of course fairly probable that not all nations of the earth will join the Federal Union upon its formation. Moreover, member nations of the Federal Union would be guaranteed the right of secession from the Union, so that some nations might withdraw from the Union at some point after initially joining it. Until the goal of universal membership has been achieved, the threat of aggression by nonmember nations against member nations would continue to exist, and this threat would justify a Union Security Force.

It is proposed that any and all military forces financially supported by national governments at their own discretion be formally considered units of the Union Security Force. In addition, the supranational federation would financially support some Union Security Force units of its own. The uniforms, insignia, code of conduct, and basic weaponry would be the same across all units of the Union Security Force, including those supported by national governments and those supported by the supranational government. This would be in the interest of promoting psychological feelings of unity and common purpose among both military personnel and the general civilian population. It would hopefully make it easier to mobilize the entire Union Security Force as an effectively unified military instrument to confront potential threats of aggression against particular member nations by outside forces.

At the same time, in the absence of such common dangers, the units of the Union Security Force supported by a particular nation, which would be composed almost entirely of its own citizens from the rank and file up through the highest level of officers, and which would be stationed on its own territory, would serve as guarantees of independent action by the nation should it decide to secede from the Federal Union because it deems certain Union policies or actions to be intolerably prejudicial to its national interests. Of course, the possibility would exist that if a particular nation announced its secession from the Union, the supranational government would ignore the formal guarantees of the right of secession contained in the Union Constitution, and would send its units of the Union Security Force into battle against the nation's own military units. In this case, a nuclear civil war might well ensue.

Lest this possibility be taken as an important argument against supranational federation, it ought to be recognized and appreciated that the threat of nuclear war will almost certainly forever exist in human affairs. Even the formation of a Federal Union of Democratic Nations would not entirely eliminate this threat. It seems plausible, however, that on the whole, the formation of a supranational federation along the lines of the FUDN under discussion here, would reduce the threat of nuclear war by an appreciable margin. This is because a nuclear international war between perfectly sovereign nation-states seems more likely than a nuclear civil war between nations which were, or which had been at one time, members of a supranational federation. This critical issue will be considered at greater length in Chapter 5 below.

Financial Funding. The supranational government would possess three revenue sources: (1) taxation; (2) bond issues; (3) directed contributions. A permanent restriction on the power of taxation in the Union Constitution would be that tax rates must be uniform over all nations. Thus, for example, different tax schedules could not be set for rich member nations and for poor member nations. In addition, some important restrictions would be imposed by the Transitional Codicil, a supplementary article of the Union Constitution to remain in effect over the first 50 years of the Union's existence. Two provisions of the Codicil relating to taxation would be as follows: (1) the only tax that may be imposed by the Federal Union is a proportional personal income tax, to be collected from the national governments, of a maximum of five percent of personal income at the initiation of the Union, with the maximum percent thereafter rising by one percent per decade to a maximum of ten percent of personal income at the end of fifty years; (2) of the amount of tax revenue raised by the Federal Union in a particular Union District, at least 50 percent must be returned to that District in the form of supranational government expenditures directly benefiting the citizens of that District.

These two restrictions would not be relevant for revenues raised from bond issues or from directed contributions. Bond issues are well-known from contemporary government finance, but the concept of a "directed contribution" is novel. A directed contribution would be a voluntary donation made by a national government to support a specific supranational agency, program, or activity designated by the national government. For example, the national government of the

United States might make an annual directed contribution to the World Development Authority to support the World Economic Equalization Program. Quite possibly directed contributions would be the main source of support for the WEEP.

It will be argued in the following Section B of this chapter that on the whole, it would be preferable to inaugurate the Federal Union of Democratic Nations prior to, rather than after, the successful completion of the World Economic Equalization Program (WEEP). Of course, the obvious danger in forming a supernational federation before the economic gap has been overcome is that the poor nations would endeavor to use the federation as an instrumentality toward Crude Redistribution. The use of capital letters here is well-advised, because if and when the contemporary ideological conflict has been fully controlled, the greatest remaining obstacle to successful supernational government and permanent world peace would be the conflict between the directly competing policy concepts of "Crude Redistribution" versus "Common Progress."

The basic idea of Crude Redistribution is that world-wide economic equalization should be brought about very quickly at a standard of living somewhere between the presently very high standard in the rich nations and the presently very low standard in the poor nations. If a resolute effort were ever made to implement the policy of Crude Redistribution, in all probability the rich nations would fight desperately in defense of their wealth and high living standards, and almost certainly they would not flinch from the use of nuclear weapons. The outcome would very likely be immense death, destruction, and chaos, involving rich and poor nations alike. Even if the policy of Crude Redistribution could be implemented peacefully, the available economic evidence suggests strongly that very drastic reductions in the standards of living of the rich nations would be necessary to achieve very marginal increases in the standards of living of the poor nations. This is because the same mechanisms which create the so-called equity-efficiency tradeoff with respect to transfers within nations would continue to hold with respect to transfers between nations.

Therefore the only possible way in which the rich nations would ever voluntarily enter a supernational federation along with the poor nations would be if the supernational federation formally, explicitly, categorically, and unequivocally renounces the policy of Crude Redistribution. The World Economic Equalization Program must be officially founded on the preferred alternative policy: the policy of Common Progress. The basic idea of Common Progress is that living standards in all nations would continue to rise, but the rate of increase in the rich nations would be slightly lower so that the rate of increase in the poor nations could be considerably higher. The objective of Common Progress is graphically illustrated in Figure 4.2 in Chapter 4 below, which depicts the rapid convergence of per capita consumption in all areas of the world toward a higher level. Whereas Crude Redistribution suggests a redistribution of final output from rich nations to poor nations, Common Progress implies the transfer of a part of new productive resources from rich nations to poor nations. As will be emphasized, the World Economic Equalization Program envisions no transfers whatever of final consumption goods, rather only of productive inputs such as plant and machinery, and education and training.

Many of the specific provisions being outlined herein for the Federal Union of Democratic Nations have as their obvious purpose the creation of difficult obstacles and problems for a potential supernational government tempted to stray from the true path of Common Progress in the direction of Crude Redistribution. To begin with, it would be difficult for a Union Chief Executive to devise a budget seriously tainted with Crude Redistribution objectives in the face of the limitations on the power of taxation imposed by the Union Constitution, and particularly those of the Transitional Codicil. And when such a budget was presented to the Chamber of Representatives, it would assuredly not be approved by the material vote, even though it might be by the population vote. If somehow these obstacles were surmounted, and a Crude Redistribution budget were adopted as Federal Union policy, the rich nations would simply secede from the Union.

Such a mass defection by the rich nations might be opposed by the remaining poor nations by means of civil war. But the poor nations would have as little chance of achieving their economic objectives via war as they would have at the present time of militarily conquering and economically despoiling the rich nations. Crude Redistribution is currently forestalled by the military power of the rich nations, and it would be similarly forestalled within the context of a supernational federation such as the one under consideration here. And so in fact it would not be to the advantage of a Union Chief Executive (even if he or she were personally in favor of Crude Redistribution) to prepare a budget incorporating Crude Redistribution objectives, and it is reasonable to expect that he/she would be sufficiently wise and realistic to recognize the fact. It is quite possible and even probable that some Union Chief Executives would be from poor nations and would thus be very determined that the policy of Common Progress be pursued steadily and vigorously through the World Economic Equalization Program administered by the World Development Authority. But in all probability the Union Chief Executive would adhere strictly and conscientiously to the Common Progress policy, as the best hope of achieving the economic equalization goal in the long run.

If a Federal Union of Democratic Nations were to be established in the near term, before the successful completion of the World Economic Equalization Program, then clearly the successful prosecution of the WEEP would be the major item on its agenda for many decades. This would undoubtedly generate some political friction between representatives of poor nations and representatives of rich nations within the supernational government. It is to be hoped that the Federal Union would be able to survive this friction. But there are many other important programs and activities that might be inaugurated and/or guided by the supernational government, which would not be so inherently sensitive and controversial. These other programs and activities would enhance the visibility and status of the supernational government, and would gradually build up a spirit of shared endeavor and supernational patriotism among the citizens of the supernational federation. Let us briefly consider some such projects and activities which might be carried on under the aegis of the Federal Union of Democratic Nations.

If we look far ahead into the future, to a time when the frustrating and perilous predicaments, entanglements, and complications which presently plague the human race will hopefully have been consigned forever to history, we recognize in the illimitable expanse of outer space which envelops our small planet Earth, an immense horizon beckoning insistently to humankind. The first tentative steps venturing out into the unbounded ocean of space have already been taken: most notably NASA's manned spaceflights to the moon between 1969 and 1975. The modern study of astronomy has revealed that the sun which warms our planet is only one medium-size star out of myriad billions of stars stretching away across millions of light-years (a light-year being roughly equivalent to 6 trillion miles). It seems quite likely that many other stars possess solar systems similar to our own. The possibility exists of exploration, colonization, and trade with intelligent races living on other planets. But the immense distances between stars, coupled with the upper limit on velocity first discerned by Albert Einstein (the speed of light: 186,000 miles a second), confronts the possibility of interstellar travel by human beings with serious obstacles—obstacles which may or may not eventually be overcome. In the work of many science fiction authors, it is of course assumed that these obstacles have long since been overcome ("overdrive" being a standard term to describe the technology), and that the human race has moved out vigorously unto the interstellar stage—a stage which dwarfs the cramped confines of the planet Earth which presently constrain us.

Perhaps these dreams of interstellar expansion are doomed never to be achieved. But it is one of the ineffable characteristics of humanity to undertake any great task which appeals to the imagination. Only the most narrow and limited sort of human mentality can fail to be inspired by the prospect of interstellar travel and expansion by the human race. Therefore the Federal Union of Democratic Nations should sponsor a vigorous program of research and development aimed at achieving practical means of manned space travel. The initial objective would be manned interplanetary travel to explore the other planets of our own solar system. But the long-run goal would be manned interstellar travel to other stars and solar systems. One of the Ministries mentioned above, the Ministry of External Development, would be assigned exclusively to this purpose. Although individual member nations would be free to undertake space exploration on their own account, it is to be hoped that most space exploration would be centralized under the aegis of the Ministry of External Development. This seems to be an area in which duplication of effort might be particularly costly, and in which important economies of scale would be operative. Another reason for centralizing the effort would be to put the Federal Union at the center of attention in an exciting and inspiring area of human endeavor.

To return to more mundane matters, it is a conventional policy of a modern nation-state to maintain a free trade area within the nation's boundaries. The close economic ties which this policy forges between all parts of the nation facilitate psychological feelings of unity, cooperation, and shared purpose. Therefore a primary task of the Ministry of the Interior during the early years of the Federal Union should be to oversee the dismantling of various national impediments (such as tariffs, import quotas, and so on) to the free flow of physical commodities and financial capital between member nations. The Ministry of the Interior might also participate in the processes of travel and trade by building and/or maintaining international highways and railroads, as well as airports and seaports.

Unfortunately, the immigration barriers established by the rich nations to restrain the flow of migrants from the poor nations must be kept in force until the successful completion of the World Economic Equalization Program. It is an almost universal opinion among the economists of the rich nations that the abolition of immigration restrictions under the current condition of wide economic disparities between nations would lead to a massive wave of migration from the poor nations to the rich nations, and that the probable result of such a massive wave would be a drastic reduction in the living standards of the rich nations.[3] In other words, it is believed that the effects of free migration would be equivalent to those of Crude Redistribution. Thus the elimination of barriers to human mobility within the Federal Union must await successful completion of the WEEP.

However, existing barriers to commodity mobility and capital mobility should be removed as quickly as possible. Economists generally believe that the elimination of such barriers would be beneficial to all parties in the long run, even though the realization of these benefits may impose substantial hardships and costs on some individuals and groups in the short run. The incentive to undertake these hardships and costs within the context of supranational federation would not merely be to capture relatively narrow economic benefits, but in addition to further the cause of supranational unity, in the expectation that the triumph of this cause would yield very substantial economic and psychological benefits over the long-term future course of human development.

The pursuit of a common market within the Federal Union would undoubtedly cause many short-term difficulties and frictions. But it is reasonable to expect that most of these difficulties and frictions might be surmounted within the first two or three decades. There is another objective which would, if achieved, immeasurably assist the spirit of supranational unity and patriotism. Unfortunately, pursuing it may well cause even more severe difficulties and frictions than would pursuit of a common market. Indeed, it may require literally centuries before these difficulties and frictions are fully surmounted. This objective is the attainment of a common language throughout the Federal Union.

History has clearly demonstrated that a common language is a powerful force in support of political unity; it has equally demonstrated that different languages are frequently a potent divisive force: more often than not, the curse of separatism is linguistically based. Although as a speaker of English, the author's judgment may be biased on the matter, it is certainly arguable that in view of the present widespread dissemination of the English language throughout the world, there are compelling arguments of practicality and convenience in favor of the adoption of English as the official language of the Federal Union of Democratic Nations. Whatever language is selected, that language should be the *sole* official language. Once a second official language has been allowed, the arguments would be endless for a third, a fourth, and so on and so on. The operations of the Union would be in peril of bogging down in a multilingual morass.

A possible compromise to facilitate the adoption of English as the sole official language of the Federal Union might be to require schoolchildren in English-speaking nations to study some other language to the same extent and intensity that schoolchildren in other nations study English. According to the proverb, "Misery loves company": thus the knowledge that schoolchildren in English-speaking nations were being subjected to the mental strain and anguish of studying another language no less than their own children, might provide a sufficient amount of psychological solace to non-English speakers to induce them to accept English as the sole official language of the Federal Union of Democratic Nations. The Ministry of Science, Education and Culture would be the logical repository for the responsibility of directing the long-term Federal Union program toward a common language.

There are some other objectives and areas of activity for a supernational federation that would not be as financially and/or psychologically costly as those discussed above. For example, certain organizational and regulatory functions pertaining to international transport, commerce and communications, and environmental protection—some of them already well developed at the present time—could be taken over by appropriate ministries of the Federal Union. It should not be excessively difficult to establish a common currency within the Union, under the aegis of the Ministry of the Interior. The Ministry of the Interior could also engage in the collection and dissemination of economic and social statistics pertaining to the member nations. Among the projects of the Ministry of Science, Education, and Culture might be the support of several elite universities, newly founded by the Federal Union at various locations throughout the federation. The Ministry of Planning would have nothing to do with direct economic planning of the sort that was long favored in the Soviet Union and some other communist nations. Rather it would operate as a permanent, large-scale "think tank," which would carefully analyze and evaluate various policy concepts and proposals emanating in embryonic form from legislators and executives in the supernational government. Its reports would then become inputs into practical decision-making by these legislators and executives. The idea is that the Ministry of Planning would be entirely divorced from day-to-day legislative and executive processes, so that its personnel would be able to examine various policy questions in a calm, deliberate, informed, and objective manner. These and many other possibilities exist for increasing the visibility and influence of the supranational federation in human affairs in ways that are not unduly objectionable and controversial.

Another important project to be carried out under the aegis of the Ministry of the Interior would be the development of a capital city for the supranational federation. The capital city should not merely be a locus for the operations of the various branches of the supranational government; in addition to that it should be developed into one of the great tourist attractions of the world. To assist this purpose the Union capital should be located fairly close to a major existing city that is already an important tourist attraction. This should also be a city of fairly central location (in a world sense), and it should be a city possessed of major historical and cultural significance. One obvious candidate by these criteria would be Athens, Greece.

The Federal Union complex should be developed on the remote outskirts of the selected city, in order that its development not be excessively constrained by existing structures. To begin with, the government buildings should be large and impressive, and should incorporate interesting and aesthetically pleasing architectural designs. They should be grouped around an expansive, park-like mall, ornamented with many fountains, ponds and canals. Also around this mall should be situated several large-scale museums, covering various aspects of human endeavor from the fine arts to space exploration. Not far away from the mall should be two additional attractions much favored by tourists. One would be a large zoo and botanical garden; the other would be a major theme park such as Disneyworld. The tourist trade should be assiduously cultivated by means of luxurious hotels and fine restaurants, as well as by theaters, concert halls, opera houses, markets, shopping centers, and so on and so forth. In other words, every effort should be exerted to make the Federal Union capital city into one of the most important tourist meccas in the world. As the capital city would be filled, from one end to the other, with a plethora of flags, emblems, and other symbols of the Federal Union of Democratic Nations, it would hopefully inspire its many visitors with the humane and civilizing spirit of supranational unity. If the capital city is developed in a competent manner, it might become one of the most effective instruments of all toward the development of supranational patriotism.

In the first decades of the Federal Union of Democratic Nations, it is quite possible that many visitors to the capital city will be citizens of nonmember nations. It is essential that these visitors be favorably impressed, and that they return home as supporters of entry into the Union. The reader may have noticed above that one of the proposed ministries of the supernational federation is the Ministry of Non-Union Affairs. This Ministry would handle diplomatic relations between the Union and nonmember nations. This point brings to mind once again the fact that the envisioned supernational federation would be a voluntary association. This means that the Federal Union should absolutely abstain from the use of armed force or direct economic pressure to induce nonmember nations to enter the Union, or to deter member nations from seceding from the Union. At the same time, the Federal Union must always stand ready to welcome new member nations at any time these nations express a voluntary desire to enter the Union. Strict adherence to this "open door" policy must always be maintained, although such adherence will almost certainly impose heavy short-term practical and psychological burdens on the Union.

If the Federal Union of Democratic Nations develops successfully, nonmember nations will experience increasing incentives to join the Union. To begin with, participation in the Federal Union free trade area would represent very tangible economic benefits. Moreover, the poorer member nations would receive preferential treatment in the World Economic Equalization Program. Member nations of the Union would also enjoy more security against the threat of foreign invasion by nonmember nations. But aside from these practical matters, there would be the extremely important, albeit intangible, psychological element in Union membership. The history of nation-states and nationalism, among other things, demonstrates the attractiveness to individual human beings of being part of large-scale social undertakings. Human beings are social animals, and they derive a high degree of comfort and encouragement from active participation in society. All other things being equal, they prefer being part of larger organized social groups than smaller organized social groups. Perhaps it is a matter of some fundamental, primitive impulse toward risk-sharing: the larger the group sharing the risk, the less risk to each individual member of the group. Also no doubt there are considerations of power and capability. In general, larger organized social groups possess more power and capability than do smaller organized social groups, and to some extent at least larger group power and capability tend to translate into tangible benefits to the individual member of the group. The expectation of these benefits in the future creates a psychological incentive to participation, even if the current benefits of participation are not particularly obvious or dramatic.

Of course, the incentives of nonmember nations to join the Union will be greater to the extent that the Union's citizenry maintains a relatively high level of unity and harmony. This is not to say that a utopian condition of beatific bliss is either possible or necessarily desirable. It goes without saying that there will inevitably be a great deal of vigorous, even acrimonious, political discussion and debate within the Federal Union into the foreseeable future. But such discussion and debate should be conducted within a context of deeply shared purpose and mutual respect. Political issues should generally be regarded as temporary problems and difficulties which will eventually be surmounted by the Federal Union, not as permanent liabilities which call into serious question the fundamental value and very existence of the Federal Union. This positive attitude toward political debate would be facilitated by the development of what might be termed "supernational patriotism."

The capital city described above would be one instrumentality toward supernational patriotism. But there are other important avenues that should be vigorously pursued. Primary school educators should be urged to impart a positive viewpoint on the Federal Union to their students. This is not to imply mindless enthusiasm for and celebration of the Union. The problems and difficulties should be clearly recognized and acknowledged, but the children should also be told that unless there emerges incontrovertible evidence to the contrary, they should assume that the Federal Union is on the whole making a positive contribution to human welfare. The Federal Union flag should be hung in elementary school classrooms, and the children should join in the daily recitation of an oath of allegiance along the following lines: "I pledge my allegiance to the principles of the Federal Union of Democratic Nations: to freedom and justice for all; to health and happiness for all; and to the solidarity and friendship of all people." Such an oath might be accompanied by an oath of national allegiance, although hopefully the supernational oath will eventually supplant the national oath.

There are other areas in which supernational and national recognitions might for a while occur simultaneously, with the expectation that in the long term the supernational recognition will eventually supersede the national recognition. At sports events and other public occasions, the playing of the supernational anthem may eventually supplant the playing of the national anthem. The supernational holiday celebrating the foundation of the Federal Union may eventually supplant various national holidays such as Independence Day, Bastille Day, and Guy Fawkes Day. Representatives of the supernational government may eventually be accorded social primacy at various state functions attended also by representatives of national governments. Caution and patience must obviously be exercised in these matters: trying to push too far too quickly could lead to a reaction which might jeopardize the continued participation of important nations in the Federal Union. Much depends on the wisdom of the proponents of the supernational federation in knowing when and how to push for certain advances, and also when to refrain.

There is a subtle interplay between "real factors" and "psychological factors." The real factor in this case is the existence of the Federal Union of Democratic Nations, its physical substance in terms of buildings and people, its active participation in the governance of society. The psychological factor is the impact upon human mentality of the Federal Union, of its provision of a higher focus of loyalty and allegiance than the focus presently provided by the national government. The more successful the Federal Union is in terms of its practical operations, the more rapidly will the psychological attitude of supernational patriotism grow and progress. At the same time, the more developed becomes the spirit of supernational patriotism, the more successful the Federal Union will tend to become in its practical operations and endeavors. The objective is the simultaneous, interactive development of both real and psychological factors in a kind of snowballing process toward a very high level of effectiveness and unity. It should not be anticipated that progress will be continuous and linear. No doubt there will be setbacks, periods of retrogression and apprehension, disappointments and defeats. But this has indeed been the history of humanity throughout all past ages. Despite all the tragic reverses experienced by humanity through its long history, the general trend has definitely been upward. Supernational federation now offers us the opportunity of consolidating, continuing, and accelerating the upward trend established by human history up to the contemporary age.

B. SCENARIOS TOWARD FOUNDATION

Conventional judgment at the present time perceives only one serious possibility through which world government might be achieved within the foreseeable future: in the aftermath of a nuclear war.[4] This possibility will not be extensively considered herein. It is not that nuclear war is so very unlikely. We endeavor to reassure ourselves with the thought that since the effect of unrestrained nuclear war would no doubt be catastrophic, the probability of such a war is exceedingly small. But there may be an element of wishful thinking in this reasoning.

The Strategic Defense Initiative (SDI) which has been such an important part of military thinking in the United States during recent years demonstrates that the notion that nuclear war need not be catastrophic—to the properly prepared side—is still quite viable even in the face of massive offensive nuclear arsenals. It must also be recognized that many large-scale wars do not come about "deliberately." That is, often both sides threaten to go to war if their demands are not met, not in the expectation that war will definitely occur, but in the hope that the other side, faced with a resolute opponent and the likelihood of war, will submit to their demands and war will thereby be avoided. Miscalculated brinkmanship of the sort which launched World War I and World War II could just as easily launch a nuclear World War III. While provocative behavior might to some extent be deterred by the terrible costs of nuclear war, it might at the same time to some extent be encouraged by the thought that these same terrible costs will tend to make the other side more readily submit to provocative behavior.[5] And finally, the idea that fear will forever deter the human race from engaging in nuclear war seems to discount two salient characteristics of humanity: mortality and emotionalism. Every individual human is going to die someday anyway—whether there is a nuclear war or not. And most human individuals recognize a whole range of outcomes as being "worse than death," even though logically these outcomes may in fact offer reasonable levels of physical well-being and psychological happiness. Thus there are many artificial lines which have been drawn in the world today such that if the other side ventures to cross these lines, nuclear weapons will be unhesitatingly employed. Hopefully the optimists who confidently predict that "it will never happen" will be proved correct. Nevertheless, it would be rash to proceed on the basis of the assumption that "it *cannot* happen."

Therefore the major reason for dispensing with the possibility that nuclear war will precipitate world government is not that nuclear war is itself highly unlikely—but that it is highly unlikely that nuclear war would precipitate world government. Conceivably a very limited nuclear war between the superpowers which would be halted after a few counterforce exchanges, or a regional nuclear war in the Mideast or some other unstable area, might so shock humanity as to make the formation of a world government possible. On the other hand, an initial experience with a successfully limited nuclear war would encourage belief in the inherent feasibility of limited nuclear war. This in turn could encourage additional experiments with nuclear war, and one of these exchanges could blossom out into unrestrained nuclear war. Of course it is doubtful whether humanity will get away with even one limited nuclear war. Given the deeply ingrained propensities in humanity toward self-righteous rage and hostility, it is easy to imagine that just one mushroom cloud—particularly if a city lies under that cloud—will be quite enough to precipitate rapid escalation toward unrestrained nuclear warfare.

Amid the postapocalyptic ruins and chaos following an unrestrained nuclear war, it seems rather unlikely that a successful movement toward a higher form of international unity could be mustered among the survivors.[6] More likely, the breakdown of transport and communication, and the fury of each particular surviving populace against their various surviving enemies, would generate a political retrogression toward the type of regional independence, autonomy, and self-aggrandizement that characterized Europe during the medieval period. Under the prevailing viewpoints and moods of postnuclear-armageddon human civilization, those proposing world government would quite likely be speedily executed as treasonous renegades trying to gain through deceit the victory which the enemy was not able to gain through military means. But in the final analysis, it is pointless to speculate at great length on the political thinking and propensities that might ensue upon the conclusion of an unrestrained nuclear war. All that we really know is that mankind will be subjected to unprecedented suffering and stress. Whether this suffering and stress will "shock humanity to its senses," or will lead to a "rapid descent to barbarism," simply cannot be predicted with any degree of confidence.

Therefore this book will leave the consideration of a possible world government in a post-nuclear world to those who may be alive to consider it. Instead this book will consider the possibility of world government in the world as it is today—a world which has thus far been spared the nightmare of nuclear catastrophe. Certainly it is generally recognized by most informed individuals at the present time that world government is at least potentially a means of greatly mitigating the possibility that nuclear catastrophe will befall mankind in the future. At the same time, it is widely believed that world government is not at this time a practical and feasible means to this end, however attractive that end might be. To some extent this belief is based on the erroneous assumption that a world government must be at least as tightly unified and organized as are the great nation-states of today. In the previous section, a proposal was outlined for a Federal Union of Democratic Nations—a form of supernational government which would obviously not be as tightly unified and organized as are the great nation-states of today, but which at the same time would be a viable state entity with good prospects for favorable future evolution toward a higher level of unity and organization. Hopefully, this proposal, in and of itself, will respond to some of the perceived problems with world government. But aside from misperceptions and misunderstandings as to the necessary characteristics of a world government, there is at this time a very acute consciousness among informed individuals of the sources of divisiveness within humanity. This consciousness accounts for the widespread belief that absolutely no form of international organization more ambitious than the United Nations can be envisioned in the contemporary world. This section of the chapter will complement the previous section on the Federal Union of Democratic Nations by considering the primary obstacles to a higher level of international organization, and by speculating on some potential means by which these obstacles could be significantly reduced within the relatively proximate future. That is, we shall be concerned with some potential scenarios toward the formation of a supernational federation along the lines of the Federal Union of Democratic Nations. The ideas sketched out in this chapter provide an entry point into the following three chapters, concerned respectively with ideological conflict, economic disparities, and nationalism.

As just suggested, therefore, we may discern three major obstacles to supernational federation of the sort proposed herein: (1) ideological conflict; (2) economic disparities; and (3) nationalism. According to the currently prevailing view among mankind, it would be necessary to reduce all three of these obstacles to virtually negligible proportions in order to achieve a level of homogeneity and cosmopolitanism adequate to support world government. Since it seems inconceivable that these three problems will be reduced to virtually negligible proportions within the foreseeable future, the impossibility of world government within the foreseeable future is thereby indicated. Quite a different view is propounded here. According to this alternative view, world government *may itself* be a means of overcoming the obstacles to world government. More precisely, the formation of a world government in the near future—in the understanding that it would initially be a relatively weak and ineffective type of government—could tend to gradually overcome the obstacles to a powerful and effective world government in the long run.

An adequate comprehension of this alternative can only be achieved if the reader will recognize and appreciate that there can be wide variations in the practical cohesion and effectiveness of various state entities which are all properly describable as "governments." So long as an individual cannot imagine a "government" in any terms other than those properly pertaining to the present-day governments of, for example, the United States and Russia, then that individual will not be capable of perceiving either the feasibility of the Federal Union of Democratic Nations outlined in the previous section of this chapter, or the feasibility of the various scenarios toward its formation outlined in the present section. But once it is recognized that a spectrum of possibilities exists rather than a single possibility, then the sensibility of the following discussion becomes apparent. The degree of homogeneity and toleration achieved prior to the formation of the supernational federation will affect the initial degree of cohesion and effectiveness of the federation. To the extent that there is less homogeneity and toleration, the initial cohesion and effectiveness will be less. But it is argued that we should be satisfied with an initially small degree of homogeneity and toleration because the future development of homogeneity and toleration would be more rapid with a supernational federation in existence than under the present-day sovereign nation-state system.

At the the present time, proponents of world government tend to be complacently dismissed by conventional authorities as utopian dreamers. At the same time, these conventional authorities often concede the desirability of world government in the remote future. What may in fact be a utopian dream is not so much the formation of a world government in the relatively near future, but rather the expectation that under the present-day nation-state system, homogeneity and toleration will tend to gradually increase until finally, in the remote future, the feasibility of a world government will become obvious even to the most conservative and nationally oriented mentalities. Were such a degree of serenity and harmony among sovereign and independent nations as envisioned by conventional authorities in the remote future actually to be achieved, then there would be *no need* for world government. Indeed, what actually makes world government so desirable at the present moment in world history is its potential role in fostering serenity and harmony among nations.

As often reiterated in these pages, there are three principal obstacles in the contemporary world to serenity and harmony among nations: ideological conflict, economic disparities, and nationalism. Each of the three has its own special characteristics. Behind the ideological conflict are opposed opinions concerning relatively precise and well-defined issues of social organization. In principle at least, these issues are resolvable through experiment and empirical observation. Also in principle, opinions may, under certain circumstances, be subject to rapid transformation. These considerations suggest that ideological conflict may be relatively tractable, and capable of rapid diminution under the right circumstances. Economic disparities, on the other hand, are based on objective differences in the economic resources (human, capital, and natural) available to any given national population. These differences are not a matter of opinion, they are not subject to resolution by empirical testing, and they are not amenable to rapid diminution—at least to the same extent as the opinions underlying ideological conflict. On the other hand, the psychological overtones and consequences of economic disparities are very similar to those of ideological conflict. Both ideological conflict and economic disparities generate anger, intolerance, hostility, and a strong propensity toward quarrels and violence.

Nationalism is, like ideology, basically a belief system, but unlike an ideological belief system it is relatively imprecise, nebulous, and nonrational. Ideologies involve specific beliefs about specific social forms (e.g., public ownership of capital versus private ownership), and there is usually a reasonably plausible body of rational argumentation to substantiate the specific belief. Nationalism, on the other hand, amounts to little more than a generalized belief that *our* people and *our* leaders tend to be good, wise, and modest, while *their* people and *their* leaders tend to be bad, foolish, and grasping. Needless to emphasize, the belief itself, when subjected to cold rationality, is inherently invalid and perverse, and so also is the heavily selective anecdotal evidence, based mostly on various real and imagined historical grievances, which is used to substantiate the belief. Nevertheless, in practice nationalism seems to be well beyond "cold rationality." It apparently speaks to some potent, primitive, tribal instinct implanted in humanity by Darwinian natural selection. The tribal instinct has no doubt been a primary factor in the evolutionary success of the human race. The mutual support and cooperativeness within the group fostered by this instinct has been responsible for the magnificent achievements of human civilization throughout history. On the other hand, the adverse side of the tribal instinct is that it tends to foster hostility and conflict between different human groups. In one sense, the political progress of humanity has been the gradual redefining of the tribal instinct operative within each individual person to encompass larger and larger groups spread over wider and wider territories. The final step is to incorporate the entire human race within each person's tribal instinct.

Throughout the evolution of mankind, tribalistic sentiment has been intensified by threats to any particular human group presented by other human groups. Thus in the modern era, nationalistic sentiment has become intensified to the extent that a particular nation has felt itself threatened by other nations. In the twentieth century, important new ideological and economic elements have been added to these perceived threats. The communist nations have (until very recently) been promulgating social transformations which much of the human population perceives as hateful, dreadful, and appalling. The gap between the living standards of the richest nations and those of the poorest nations has significantly widened. Many people in many nations feel threatened by these realities: of being forced into socialism against their will, and/or of having their living standards reduced by confiscatory taxation or other varieties of economic despoilation. As the nation is perceived to be the primary safeguard against these degradations, nationalistic spirit has been enhanced and inflamed. Of course, nationalism was an important factor long before the emergence of communism and the economic gap. The point is not that these new ideological and economic threats have *created* nationalistic enthusiasm, but merely that they have *enhanced* it.

There is not much to be done about nationalism, in and of itself. It is of course agreed by most rational individuals that nationalistic spirit is capable of overdevelopment into perverse chauvinistic attitudes, and it is generally recommended that parents and educators exercise proper restraint and moderation in the inculcation of nationalism in the young, and that they endeavor to balance healthy nationalism with an equally healthy cosmopolitanism. But what precisely constitutes "proper restraint and moderation" in this matter is a very difficult and nebulous question. Under present circumstances, generalized exhortations to the population to adopt less nationalistic and more cosmopolitan attitudes, and to impart these new attitudes to the young, may have some role to play in the advance toward supernational federation, but it is probably a very limited role. Therefore we should not focus on the possibility of reducing nationalism, per se, but rather on the possibilities for reducing two major contributors to nationalism in the modern world: ideological conflict and the economic gap.

No doubt the greatest opportunities at the present time for a relatively rapid and decisive improvement in the prospects for world government reside in the area of ideology. Grounded as it is in mental attitudes rather than objective reality, ideological conflict is, at least potentially, subject to rapid diminishment. The three most important components of the overall contemporary ideological conflict between the communist and the noncommunist nations are: (1) socialism versus capitalism; (2) planning versus market; (3) oligarchy versus democracy. In very rough terms, communism prescribes oligarchic planned socialism, while noncommunism prescribes democratic market capitalism. One scenario of development over the next one to two decades is that the communist nations will change their position on all three of these central components: they will abandon socialism for capitalism (i.e., they will privatize all or most state-owned property); they will abandon planning for the market (i.e., by either abolishing or drastically altering such central planning agencies as Gosplan in the Soviet Union); and they will abandon oligarchy for democracy (i.e., by permitting the organization of political parties other than the Communist, or by implementing authentically democratic determination within the Communist Party, or by a combination of the two).

The above scenario is designated the "ideological capitulation scenario" herein. As of 1970 or 1980, this scenario would have been deemed more or less preposterous by the large majority of students of contemporary communism. However, as of the early 1990s, owing to the major transitions brought about by such historic leaders as Mikhail Gorbachev in the Soviet Union and Deng Xiaoping in the People's Republic of China, the plausibility of this scenario has been greatly enhanced. Most of the communist nations have already

implemented reforms which significantly reduce the distance between communist societies and noncommunist societies; and there is
much speculation about even more dramatic reforms in the near
future. At the moment of writing, the situation appears very fluid. But
a conservative estimate would be that at least several years will have
to elapse before the final outcome of the current reform movement
in the communist world will be clearly discernible. This reform
movement may indeed ultimately result in the ideological capitulation hoped for by the West. But the probability of such capitulation
ought not to be exaggerated. It will be very difficult for the populations of the communist nations to admit complete and total past error
with respect to all three essential components of communist ideology
(socialism versus capitalism, plan versus market, and oligarchy versus democracy)—which is exactly what they will have to do if the
capitulation scenario is to be achieved. It is a psychological fact that
people are very adverse to admitting any error at all, let alone total
error.

Thus considerable attention will be devoted here to an alternative
scenario toward the rapid diminishment of ideological conflict, an
alternative which would not impose such a giant strain on the pride
and self-esteem of the peoples of the communist nations. This will
be termed the "ideological convergence scenario," and it would
involve a complementary movement by both the communist and the
noncommunist nations toward a common pattern of democratic
market socialism. The communist nations would abandon planning
for the market, and oligarchy for democracy; while the noncommunist nations would abandon capitalism for socialism.[7]

The specific socialist economic system envisioned in the convergence scenario is designated by the term "pragmatic market
socialism." The economic institutions and operations of pragmatic
market socialism would be very similar to those of contemporary
capitalism in the economically advanced nations of the United States,
Western Europe, and so on. The system would incorporate the same
principles of market allocation, consumer sovereignty, and material
incentives to effort which are deemed by Western economists the vital
underpinnings of economic prosperity and progress. Public ownership would extend to most large-scale, established business corpora-

tions, but the motivation of publicly owned business enterprise would remain the same profit-maximization objective currently operative under capitalism. The only difference would be that the profit-maximization objective would be enforced on the executives of publicly owned business enterprises by a public ownership agency rather than by private stockholders. Profits, interest, and other forms of property income generated by the business operations of these enterprises would be paid over to this public ownership agency, and the great preponderance of this income flow (upwards of 95 percent) would then be distributed by the public ownership agency to the general population as a social dividend supplement to earned labor income. It seems quite likely that such a socialist system would possess the same high level of economic efficiency as does the contemporary capitalist system in the advanced, industrialized Western nations.

Although a transition to the above-described economic system must be described as a transition from capitalism to socialism as these terms are customarily defined in dictionaries, it need hardly be emphasized that the envisioned system bears little or no relationship to certain concepts of socialism which are currently quite prevalent in human thinking. Some of these notions are highly pejorative and are held mainly in the Western noncommunist nations: socialism as "strait-jacket planning," as a "giant bureaucracy," as a "vast welfare state," and so on and so forth. At the present moment, the concept of pragmatic market socialism is little known in the West. But should this concept become better known and understood, the prospects for the implementation of this form of socialism might become appreciable. Pragmatic market socialism does indeed respond effectively to the usual litany of "arguments against socialism," and it would be deemed far more attractive by the typical individual in the Western nations than the numerous better-known concepts of socialism on which adverse opinions about socialism are normally based. At the same time, pragmatic market socialism is definitely a form of "socialism" by any reasonable standard of definition, and it would therefore quickly be recognized as such by even the most traditionalist mentalities in the communist nations were it to become an important factor in the noncommunist nations.

Should pragmatic market socialism be inaugurated in the West (or at least in several of the more important Western nations), this would amount to an implicit admission of past error on the issue of capitalism versus socialism. Such an admission by the West would make a parallel admission of past error by the East, on the issues of planning versus market and oligarchy versus democracy, far less psychologically stressful. The pragmatic market socialist system is an economic system rather than a political or a social system. In principle, it could operate whether the political system were oligarchic or democratic, or whether the social system were, say, elitist or egalitarian. But the idea of pragmatic market socialism, at least as an explicit and detailed policy proposal, has arisen in the West, in the context of a highly democratic political system and a relatively egalitarian social system. Indeed, an important part of the case to be made for pragmatic market socialism is that it is fully consistent with political freedom and democracy as they currently exist in many Western nations. To those in the West interested in pragmatic market socialism, the concept is therefore definitely considered a form of democratic market socialism. In fact, it is arguable that under pragmatic market socialism, Western democracy would attain a higher level of purity, owing to the elimination of the excessive influence in social decision-making of a class of extremely conservative wealthy capitalists. Thus pragmatic market socialism may be perceived in the West as possessing political virtues as well as virtues of economic efficiency and equity.

The pragmatic market socialist system provides an attractive model for the communist nations. While it incorporates the essential core of communist ideology—socialism—at the same time it incorporates a market oriented economic system and it is fully consistent with a democratic political system. Although there has been much discussion within the contemporary communist reform movements of reestablishing capitalism through the privatization of government-owned capital, it would seem at this point that a much higher degree of consensus has been reached as to the desirability of greater market reliance in the economic sphere and greater freedom and democracy in the political sphere. Pragmatic market socialism offers a means of achieving the most important elements of the reform program without abandoning that which has always been the sacrosanct core of communist ideology—socialism. In short, pragmatic market socialism could provide a viable middle ground between the present-day social systems in the Western noncommunist nations and the present-day Eastern communist nations. The salient advantage of this middle ground is that it may be reached without need of full ideological capitulation by either side. The pragmatic market socialist alternative, and the overall possibilities for ideological convergence, will be examined in greater detail in Chapter 3 below.

The detailed discussion of ideological convergence in Chapter 3 should not be construed as indicating that ideological convergence is a necessary prerequisite for the formation of a supernational federation. The ideal of peaceful coexistence has long since been formally embraced by all communist and noncommunist governments, and potentially this ideal could be made a reality literally at any time. The clearest evidence that coexistence has become a permanent reality would be the implementation of major disarmament agreements by the superpowers. Such agreements are always a possibility, even if—in the final analysis—there were to be little or no significant alteration in the social systems of either the communist or noncommunist nations. The Federal Union of Democratic Nations is intended to be sufficiently flexible to incorporate both capitalist and socialist economies, and it has been specified that the federation government should take no stance as to which type of economy is preferable.

On the other hand, clearly the psychological impediments to supernational unity would be less to the extent that there is greater objective homogeneity among various national economic, political, and social systems, and to the extent that ideologies are explicitly similar. Certainly if there is any reasonable hope of making a major advance in terms of ideological unity within a reasonable period of time, the formation of the supernational federation should be postponed until that hope has been exhausted. For example, at the moment of writing, the possibility of ideological capitulation by the communist nations appears to be at least "reasonable." But if this possibility has not been realized within an appreciable period of time (say ten years), it would not be sensible to further postpone the formation of the supernational federation until such time as such capitulation is achieved. If the possibility of ideological convergence (as opposed to ideological capitulation) were to emerge through the development of a reasonable amount of interest in the West in the pragmatic market socialist alternative (or some other similar alternative), then once again an appreciable period might be allowed to elapse in hopes that this interest would generate a tangible advance. But if at the end of this appreciable period, ideological convergence were to seem no more likely than ideological capitulation, then the formation of the supernational federation ought to proceed. The existence of the Federal Union might facilitate future ideological developments. Although the Federal Union government would take no official position on capitalism versus socialism, a section of the Ministry of Planning could be assigned a permanent task of carefully and objectively evaluating the performance of the two systems. Possibly its efforts would bring to light far more compelling evidence on the matter than exists at the present time.

Beyond ideological conflict there lies the economic gap, a reality which is perhaps even more threatening and ominous because it is not amenable to termination through the relatively simple expedient of opinion shifts. Under some circumstances it might be reasonable to propose that we wait for ideological harmonization before forming the world union (i.e., if a significant degree of harmonization appears likely within a few years), but the position taken here is that we should definitely *not* wait for economic equalization prior to forming the union. The reason is that it is virtually inconceivable that a significant degree of equalization could be achieved within a few years. Economic equalization, even if successfully achieved, would probably require at least 50 to 100 years. Particularly if important steps are made toward ideological harmonization and consequently support for the idea of world government is on the increase, the enthusiasm of the moment should be exploited before it peters out. Although the economic gap is clearly a major impediment to the effectiveness of world government, the existence of a supernational government would greatly enhance the probability that a World Economic Equalization Program would be inaugurated and carried out successfully, so that this impediment is removed.

Thus the most favored scenario is that of simultaneous formation of the Federal Union of Democratic Nations and commencement of the World Economic Equalization Program at the same time, in the relatively proximate future. Another somewhat more conservative scenario would call for the commencement of the World Economic Equalization Program and its operation for a reasonable period of time (say 10 to 20 years) prior to a decision on the supernational federation. Arguably 10 to 20 years would be sufficient to gauge whether or not the WEEP will be successful, and also it is arguably a sufficiently brief period as not to entail the dissipation of an evolving movement toward world government. If the Program is in fact proceeding successfully so that it appears that the economic impediment to supernational unity will be duly eliminated (even though it might require 50 to 100 years to do so), then the federation could be formed under better auspices. On the other hand, if the Program is not working (i.e., not making discernible progress toward economic equalization), that might suggest the unviability of supernational federation: the federation would not be formed and thus would be avoided the disappointment of false hopes.

The problem with this scenario is that a World Economic Equalization Program not supported by a Federal Union of Democratic Nations might not be sufficiently comprehensive and vigorous to get the job done. If the Federal Union were operating, there would be a better chance that the WEEP would be effective enough to have a major impact on the problem. The WEEP would be given a fairer chance for success. If the pessimists are correct and even a very comprehensive and vigorous WEEP is not perceptibly closing the economic gap, then the Program could be terminated and (if desired) the Federal Union could also be terminated (via the withdrawal of most of the large nations). On the whole, it would appear that the danger of disappointed false hopes is not as great as the danger that without a Federal Union of Democratic Nations to support it, the WEEP effort would be too small-scale, restricted, and halfhearted to achieve success. The question of economic disparities and prospects for economic equalization will be discussed in Chapter 4 below.

To summarize the primary scenario advocated herein, the communist and noncommunist nations would converge, more or less simultaneously and over a relatively brief period, on a form of democratic market socialism known as "pragmatic market socialism." This convergence would virtually abrogate the ideological conflict situation as we know it today. This advance would be acknowledged and consolidated by means of a major arms reduction agreement. An alternative scenario toward ideological harmonization is that of ideological capitulation by the communist nations, through which they would adopt social systems essentially equivalent to those of the Western noncommunist nations. As before, the authenticity of ideological harmonization would be demonstrated by a major arms reduction program. Finally, there is a scenario of "genuine coexistence" in which neither side would make any important alterations in its respective internal social system, but the significance of the distinctions would be downgraded to a point permitting significant rapprochement and major arms reduction.

However it is achieved, the arms reduction agreement would be quickly followed, within a very few years, by the simultaneous foundation of the Federal Union of Democratic Nations (FUDN) and the commencement of the World Economic Equalization Program (WEEP). A considerable proportion of the economic resources released by the arms reduction agreement would be channeled into support of the WEEP. An alternative scenario would be the commencement of the WEEP approximately 10 to 20 years prior to the anticipated foundation of the FUDN. Only if the WEEP seems to be achieving its objectives would the FUDN actually be established.

The various scenarios discussed in this section of Chapter 2 may seem to some skeptics to be evading what is the most essential issue: by what means (or "scenarios") are the *mental attitudes* of the population to be modified in such a way that supernational federation becomes a possibility. These skeptics, of course, tend to assume that these mental attitudes are in fact incapable of transformation, and thus the whole prospect of supernational federation is no more than an unrealizable utopian dream. Such an assumption, of course, simply begs the question. Some suggestions are offered below in Section B of Chapter 6 ("On the Question of Implementation") on the specific tactics of persuasion to be used in a movement toward world government. But the above skeptical question goes deeper than the practical matters considered there.

The operative assumption herein, of course, is that various objective, real-world factors and considerations underlie the currently prevalent mental attitudes concerning a world state. For example, the populations of the affluent Western nations generally fear a world state because they are afraid of oligarchic planned socialism such as has been observed in the communist world, and because they are afraid of grinding mass poverty such as is currently observed throughout the Third World. At the same time, people in the communist nations may harbor residual fears that a world state might prove an instrumentality for the reestablishment of capitalistic exploitation, and people in the Third World nations tend to worry that it might prove an instrumentality for the reestablishment of colonial exploitation. Such fears as these may be reduced through some form of ideological harmonization and through a World Economic Equalization Program. As for the notion that nationalism, in and of itself, creates an "unreasoning" opposition to world government which is beyond any sensible issues of ideology or economics, it is sheer speculation that this type of opposition would be sufficient to abrogate the possibility of world government despite any progress being made in the areas of ideology and economics. It is a speculation, moreover, which seems not only to display a poor appreciation of human political development throughout history—a development which has generated the large contemporary nation-state, a polity which dwarfs in size and scale the polities of earlier periods—but which also seems to display an unseemly contempt for the basic rationality of the individual human being.

Needless to emphasize, the present advocacy of a Federal Union of Democratic Nations is based on a degree of confidence in this basic rationality of mankind. It is assumed that *if* a sensible case can be made for world government, then there is a reasonable probability that mankind will perceive the validity of the case and move toward the formation of a world government. Surely it is the worst kind of negativism to assert that regardless of the sensibility of the case for world government, human rationality is too dense and/or inflexible to appreciate the case. The focus of this work is on a specific plan of supernational federation, and on various scenarios toward its formation, which together constitute a case for world government. The reader's attention ought to be focused on the specifics of this case—it should not be distracted by unduly pessimistic proclamations of the irretrievable irrationality of humankind on this particular question.

NOTES

1. Particularly since the end of World War II and the dawning of the nuclear age, the popular and professional literature on contemporary international relations and international organization has been replete with exhortations that mankind should now move forward toward a higher form of international organization and coordination than that achieved to date. Typical references include Gerald Mangone (1951), Saul Mendlovitz (1962), Inis Claude (1962, 1971), Philip Jacob and Alexine Atherton (1965), William Olson and Fred Sondermann (1966), Stephen Goodspeed (1967), Milton Rakove (1972), David S. Sullivan and Martin J. Sattler (1972), Richard Falk (1975), James Dilloway (1986). While the rhetoric employed by some of these writers might suggest that radical transformations are necessary or at least advisable, close analysis of specific, practical recommendations normally reveals them to be extremely marginal adjustments of the existing status quo. In actual fact, the proposal put forward in this book toward a Federal Union of Democratic Nations would indeed realize the conventional rhetoric much more effectively than the conventional recommendations. However, it might not be easy to induce many of the authors in this field to recognize the fact.

2. That the aspiration toward democratic governance is justified will not be argued herein. For the moment, the human race seems to have achieved a sufficient consensus that—at least as a general rule—democracy is a beneficial political institution, as to render any attempt at justification unnecessary. Some illustrative references on democracy include F. Ernest Johnson (1947), Zevedei Barbu (1956), Norman L. Stamps (1957), Sidney Hook (1959), Herbert B. Mayo (1960), Giovanni Sartori (1962), M. Rejai (1967), Jack Lively (1975), William N. Nelson (1980), Banjamin Barber and Patrick Watson (1988).

3. The official consensus has been summarized by Edwin P. Reubens (1983, p. 179): "Internationalist doctrine envisages virtually unlimited, universal admission of all applicants, in whatever types and numbers. It rejects or ignores the national migration restrictions that everybody else takes for granted... In the real world, however, with vast economic disparities between the more and less developed nations (MDCs and LDCs), the intended unlimited flows would indeed make a drastic jump to worldwide equalization. It would probably be a zero sum, or even a negative

sum transaction, as employment and consumption levels in the MDCs tumbled violently, to make a small individual accommodation for the millions of poor migrants from the LDCs. Long before this came about, the MDC citizens would react to slam shut that open door."

4. The commonplace notion that the only plausible path to world government would be through the crucible of a devastating nuclear war is illustrated by the following representative quotes:

Richard Falk (1975, p. 245): "At the present stage of international relations, however, a world government solution does not seem attainable except in the course of reconstruction subsequent to a doomsday situation; the more likely world order system in this setting of catastrophic breakdown is a dysutopia of the doomsday-tyrannical sort..."

Roger Hilsman (1975, pp. 575): "Even though a world state would be a promising means of eliminating war in the long run, the attempt to establish it might have just the opposite effect in the short run... The point is that it might well take one or more wars of frightening proportions to establish a world state, and once established, mankind might well be destined to go through a series of violent civil wars as well."

Carl Friedrich von Weizsacker (1978, pp. 110-111): "The world-wide analogue to that development, however, would be the establishment of an absolutist world state through war, and its subsequent liberalization. Such an event may be our fate but it cannot be our goal."

5. It is widely assumed—in all probability correctly—that the development of nuclear weapons, by enormously increasing the costs of unrestrained war should it break out, has appreciably decreased the probability of such a war breaking out over any given period of time. However, it could be that the magnitude of the decrease is generally overestimated. This is because the increase in the costliness of war may induce nations to engage in somewhat more provocative behavior than they would be likely to if they were not able to rely upon the costliness of war restraining their opponents from retaliation. See the author's analysis of this possibility in *Conflict Management and Peace Science* (1989). The article demonstrates that owing to this factor, it cannot be theoretically proven that the development of nuclear weapons has in fact decreased the probability of unrestrained warfare. In this case, of course, one hopes that a proposition which is not theoretically provable is nevertheless empirically true.

6. The possibility that post-apocalytic human psychology might well be uncongenial to the idea of a world state is suggested by the following comment by Hedley Bull (1977, pp. 261-262): "The idea that world government may come about as a result of some catastrophe such as a global nuclear war or a world economic or ecological breakdown—Kant's idea

that states will be led by adversity to the course that they would have adopted in the first place, had they been willing to act rationally—presumes that in such a post-catastrophic situation international behavior will be more 'rational', but we have no means of knowing whether it would be more so or less."

7. See the author's 1992 article in *Coexistence* ("New Prospects for East-West Ideological Convergence: A Market Socialist Viewpoint") for a detailed discussion of the two alternative scenarios: ideological capitulation versus ideological convergence.

3

PROSPECTS FOR
IDEOLOGICAL HARMONIZATION

A. THE PROBLEM OF IDEOLOGY

Ideological conflict may be generally defined as a difference of opinion over proper individual behavior and/or social organization, in which the differing opinions are derived from relatively comprehensive and integrated systems of ideas. Of its nature, any ideological judgment or opinion is opposed by a different ideological judgment or opinion. If almost every person in the world agreed on a certain proposition regarding proper individual behavior or social organization, that proposition would no longer be described as an "ideological judgment or opinion" but as a "truth." By the same token, an ideological judgment cannot be established or proven by means of appeal to logical deduction, mathematical derivation, or universally acknowledged empirical reality. Once again, if a certain proposition regarding proper individual behavior or social organization could be so established or proven, then it would no longer be described as an "ideological judgment or opinion" but as a "truth," since almost every person in the world would accede to it.

Now of course the parties to an ideological conflict are naturally reluctant to admit, either to themselves or anyone else, that their own belief on a certain matter is merely a judgment or an opinion. There is inevitably a strong temptation to attribute either mental incompetence, hypocrisy, or a combination of the two, to the other side. Even if it were granted by an adherent to a certain ideological judgment that the proposition involved is not provable, on the basis of the available evidence, to the same level of certainty as a mathematical theorem, he or she will certainly deem the available evidence to be far more supportive of this proposition than of an opposed proposition. The question then arises of why another person believes in the opposed proposition. One possibility is mental incompetence: whether the result of ignorance of the available evidence, or simply of inability to understand and appreciate the available evidence (i.e., stupidity). A second possibility is hypocrisy: the other person does not actually believe in the opposed proposition, but simply uses it as a rationale for illicit and immoral personal aggrandizement at the expense of others.

"Ideological conflict," as the term is normally understood today, is associated with the modern historical era. Perhaps the first "ideologists," in the usual modern sense of the term, were the French Enlightenment figures, such as Voltaire, Diderot, and Rousseau, who espoused the principles of representative democracy against those of hereditary monarchy. But long before the Enlightenment period, mankind had had much experience with the disruptive effects of ideological conflict—in the guise of religious conflict. Although the greater emphasis in modern ideologies is on social organization while the greater emphasis in religious doctrine is on individual behavior, both modern ideology and religious doctrine encompass both individual and social prescriptions. Therefore it is reasonable to categorize religious doctrinal conflict as a form of ideological conflict. There are some dramatic examples of the powerful impact of religious conflict in human history: the Islamic wars of expansion, the Christian response in the Crusades, the numerous wars associated with the Protestant Reformation. Even after hundreds of years, some of these conflicts are not entirely extinct: there are distant echoes from the Crusades in the fighting among Christians and Muslims in Lebanon; and there are distant echoes from the wars of the Reformation in the periodic violence involving Catholics and Protestants in Northern Ireland.

In the modern era, ideological conflict more often involves social doctrines rather than religious doctrines. But social doctrines obviously share with religious doctrines a capacity to stir up trouble and contribute heavily to the intensity of human conflicts. The bloodiest wars of the nineteenth century were those of the Napoleonic period, during which the French armies were inspired by ideological visions of defending the "rights of man" at home, and of extending these same rights to other nations. At the same time, an important factor in the gradual formation of an overpowering European coalition against Napoleon was an ideological opposition to France's effort to export what were widely perceived as "excesses of the French Revolution." The final defeat of Napoleonic France at Waterloo in 1815 ushered in a century-long era of peace, prosperity, and growth, during which the nations of Western Europe were spared prolonged and devastating wars. But when balance of power politics eventually broke down in 1914 and produced the prolonged and devastating World War I, ideological overtones were again involved, in the form of the mutual disdain between the "modern democracies" of France and Great Britain and the "outmoded monarchies" of Imperial Germany and the Austro-Hungarian Empire. Once again in World War II, the Western enemies of the Axis coalition inspired themselves with an ideological vision of defending "freedom and democracy" against the menace of "totalitarian fascist dictatorship."

The most systematic and deep-rooted ideological conflict of the modern era—namely that between communism and noncommunism—has long threatened to instigate the dreaded World War III.[1] Ironically, during World War II communist and noncommunist nations cooperated closely against the Axis coalition, and at the time it was hoped by many that the spirit of wartime cooperation would carry over into the postwar world. Unfortunately, that hope was disappointed, and after World War II the major communist and noncommunist nations maintained a continuously antagonistic attitude toward one another, and accumulated massive arsenals of nuclear and conventional weapons with which to threaten one another. Important progress has been made on arms reduction in the recent past, but as of the moment of writing these arsenals are still extremely formidable and dangerous. Should these arsenals ever be employed in a major war, the ensuing monumental death, injury, and destruction would in all probability dwarf that brought about by any of the past wars in human history. Although hopes for the definitive end of the Cold War have intensified in recent years owing to encouraging developments in the Soviet Union and elsewhere, to this date the actual substantive progress achieved in terms of arms reduction has been relatively limited.

While ideological conflict may be a contributory factor in the genesis of wars, clearly it would be absurd to impute to it decisive importance in the case of each and every one of the thousands of wars which have occurred throughout human history. The one thing which all wars surely have in common is that those who instigate them do so in the hope of personally benefiting from them. To some extent the envisioned personal benefits have been purely material: the victor would eat better food, live in a bigger palace, possess more concubines and mistresses. But at least as far as the period of recorded history is concerned, a period during which polities have been relatively large and well-established, the personal benefits envisioned by high-level war-makers have probably been more of a psychological nature than a purely material nature. In other words, a successful war would enhance the war-maker's personal security: the objective would be not so much to increase his standard of living, as to ensure that his accustomed standard of living would be maintained indefinitely.

War-makers are no less human beings than anyone else, and as such they are not immune from moral sentiments and motivations. As children they underwent a process of socialization which instilled in them some respect for the notions of ethically correct behavior and mutual respect and cooperation. Even the most egotistical and brutal dictator imaginable must respect these principles at least within a narrow circle, otherwise he would be quickly struck down by a stab in the back from one of his entourage. The really successful rulers, whether they be monarchial, dictatorial, or democratically elected, are those who can convince as broad a circle as possible that they are persons of integrity, wisdom, and good will, and that their decisions and actions are widely beneficial. In *The Wealth of Nations* (1776), Adam Smith maintained that in the ordinary business of earning a living, a person will best pursue his own interest by pursuing the interests of others. Much the same may be said of political leaders— even when these leaders become war-makers. Thus when a war-maker initiates a war, he normally envisions his own interests in the matter as being highly complementary to the interests of many others. He may well imagine that the war will serve not only the interests of his own people, but also the interests of many if not most of those in the enemy camp as well. He may imagine this to be the case even when the war is blatantly aggressive.

This would appear to have been the case, for example, with respect to the most awesome military campaign in the history of mankind: the German invasion of Russia in World War II. Some have referred to this campaign as a gigantic plundering and murdering expedition akin to those of the Mongol hordes in the Middle Ages. More accurately, it is describable as a "campaign of imperial expansion" equivalent to those of the Islamic and Roman eras—although accompanied by a level of cruelty and destructiveness worthy of the Mongols. It is well-known that the savage brutality of this particular invasion defies belief: in addition to the normal carnage of battle, there were summary executions of both military and civilian prisoners by the hundreds of thousands, and compulsory deportations by the millions.

But despite all of this, there is little reason to doubt that Adolf Hitler, the primary instigator of the aggression, was comfortable in his own mind that this inconceivable violence was serving a beneficial larger social purpose. He imagined that after it was all over and the dust had settled, Russia would support a large population of well-fed, neatly-dressed, well-satisfied, cheerfully happy Slavs, presided over by a host of intellectually and morally superior Teutonic managers and administrators. He imagined that the German invasion of Russia represented a "liberation" of the long-suffering Russian people from the evil clutches of their Jewish and Bolshevik tormentors and despoilers. There was not a total absence of evidence to support this view: the Soviet purge trials of the 1930s manifested substantial domestic discontent with the Stalinist policies of agricultural collectivization and forced-pace industrialization. In addition to the trials, there were many reports from Russia of mass deportations and liquidations, and of a huge system of forced labor concentration camps. As it turned out, the German methods of conquest and colonization were so monstrously callous that the Russian people soon reached the conclusion that foreign Nazi oppressors were even worse than home-grown Bolshevik oppressors. Thereupon they fought the Great Patriotic War which, along with substantial help from the West, eventually smashed Hitler's regime.

The case of the 1941 German invasion of Russia raises the question of the relative importance of ideological conflict versus traditional nationalistic aggrandizement in the advent and development of World War II. Did Hitler determine to invade Russia because of his ideological judgment that Bolshevism represented an inferior form of social organization? Or did Hitler determine to invade Russia because the direct exploitation by Germany of Russian resources, both human and natural, would raise German living standards and augment German national power? One possible appraisal is that both factors were critical to the determination: that it was the conjunction of perceived national aggrandizement in the potential exploitation of Russian resources with perceived superior ideological purpose in the potential liberation of the Russian people from the shackles of Bolshevism, which resulted in the determination to invade. Neither factor in isolation would have been sufficient to motivate the invasion. As for which of the two factors was more fundamental, it might be argued that the lure of economic gain was "always there," and that it was the Bolshevization of Russia in 1917 which thereafter provided Hitler, and the rest of the German people, with a pretext for pursuing this economic gain. But there is another possibility, according to which the ideological factor might be deemed the prior and decisive factor: that it was the ideological repugnance which most Germans felt toward Bolshevism which "brought to their minds" or "created in them the recognition" that a military conquest of Russia would be to their economic benefit.

The Soviet government, from its establishment in 1917 down to the very recent past, has continuously proclaimed itself inspired, motivated, and guided by the ideological system of Karl Marx. The essence of Marxist ideology is an intense loathing directed against the capitalist economic system. According to Marx, capitalism is characterized not only by the morally repugnant exploitation of labor via the surplus value mechanism, but also by an inherent propensity toward business crises and depressions, which have a long-term immiserating effect on the populations of the capitalist nations, and which will lead ultimately to the abolition of capitalism. Most of Marx's own writing suggests the abolition of capitalism by means of violent revolution; but most contemporary Marxists, both inside and outside the communist nations, now allow for the possibility of a peaceful transition. In any event, so long as it exists, the capitalist economic system is held by Marxist ideology to impose heavy and needless burdens on the general population—excepting only the tiny handful of wealthy capitalists who profit from the system. The glasnost era has witnessed, for the first time since the consolidation of Communist Party power in the Soviet Union, publicly expressed skepticism toward the Marxist proposition of the inevitable evil and perversity of the capitalist economic system. But it is too soon to conclude that these expressions do in fact manifest a fundamental, permanent shift in the consensus of both the people and their leadership.

According to the view propounded by the Soviet government and other communist governments throughout much of the twentieth century, wealthy capitalists in the various capitalist nations are acutely conscious of the threat to their privileges represented by the existence of communist nations. Even aside from the support which the communist nations have been morally obligated to extend to socialist movements in capitalist countries (continuing according to the traditional Soviet view), there is also the fact that the existence of the socialist economies in the communist nations provides daily evidence of the superfluity and obsolescence of capitalists. Thus the capitalists would love nothing more than to see the collapse and disappearance of communist national governments. In the 1920s and 1930s, German capitalists supported Hitler in his plans for the conquest of Russia because of their personal interest in the preservation of capitalism. After the collapse of the German threat, capitalists in the United States and the other leading capitalist nations continuously abetted a systematic program of hostility, obstruction, vilification, and insinuation designed to keep the communist nations permanently in a weakened and defensive condition. Given the slightest opportunity, they would have quickly renewed the course of military conquest pursued by Adolf Hitler in June, 1941—the date of the Nazi invasion of Russia. It has therefore been imperative for the Soviet Union, and the other communist nations, to be ever on their guard against this ominous threat.

Ostensibly at least, the communist nations have been very ideologically oriented. But some Western historians and other social analysts have declined to take this ideological orientation at full face value. They have argued that communist governments have acted much more from motives of national interest than from motives of ideological conviction. The implication of this position is that it would have little if any favorable impact on relations between communist bloc nations and noncommunist bloc nations if certain institutional developments were to occur which would reduce the ideological distance between the two social systems. It is argued here, to the contrary, that the pursuit (for example) of Russian national interest by the Soviet government—without reference to Marxist ideology— provides a very unsatisfactory explanation for the precarious situation in international affairs throughout most of the post-World War II period, and that in fact the enthusiasm for Marxist ideology installed in the Soviet government by the Bolshevik Revolution of 1917 has indeed been the dominant determinant both of Soviet history generally and of the precarious situation in international affairs in particular. Although much progress has recently been made, the problem is by no means completely under control at the present time. If—despite our present optimism—World War III is indeed fought within the next 50 to 100 years, the principal precipitating factor will very possibly have been ideological conflict. Therefore the potential substantial amelioration of ideological conflict through either the capitalization of the communist nations or the socialization of the noncommunist nations would indeed be an extremely important contribution toward the cause of peace.

The primary difficulty with the Russian national interest hypothesis of Soviet behavior is that it sets up a false dichotomy and conflict between ideological motivations and nationalistic motivations. It implies that the Soviet government confronted a tradeoff between the pursuit of ideological goals and nationalistic goals: to the extent it pursued nationalistic goals it did not pursue ideological goals, and vice versa. But as discussed above, quite likely Adolf Hitler was simultaneously pursuing nationalistic and ideological goals in the Nazi invasion of Russia in 1941. Similarly, it might be proposed that the Soviet leadership simultaneously pursued nationalistic and ideological goals in its efforts to foster socialist transformations in other nations. Since its inception in 1917, the Soviet government always identified the cause of socialism with that of the Russian national interest, and considered that whatever enhanced Russian national power also assisted the long-term ideological goal of world-wide socialization. Nor was there anything preposterous about this identification. For almost 30 years after the Bolshevik revolution, the only socialist economy in the world was that of the Soviet Union, and had the Soviet government been overthrown that single enclave of socialism in a wide capitalist world would have been eliminated. From its inception the Soviet government did everything of which it was capable to aid socialist—or preferably communist—movements in other nations. It only demonstrated restraint in the pursuit of its ideological goal of world-wide socialization under dire and immediate threat of attack by capitalist nations. Such restraint could be plausibly interpreted as merely a tactical retreat, and not necessarily as a weakening of its long-term resolution to pursue the goal of world-wide socialization.

It might be argued that Russia desired the socialization of the world as a means of securing her national interest, since world-wide socialization would have eliminated the threat of invasions instigated by hostile foreign capitalists. Thus it was not ideology but national interest which motivated her behavior. But the Soviet government voluntarily brought upon itself the threat of invasions instigated by hostile foreign capitalists when in 1917 it proclaimed its allegiance to Marxist ideology and implemented a socialist economy in Russia. The socialization of Russia was an ideological decision based upon an ideological judgment. As far as Russian national interests are concerned, one can hardly escape the impression that the consequences of that ideological decision were veritably disastrous for both the Russian people and their leaders. The socialization of the Russian economy made Russia a virtual outlaw and outcast from the family of capitalist nations. The early hopes of the first Soviet leaders that the Bolshevik revolution in Russia would spark a chain reaction of socialist revolutions elsewhere in the world were quickly disappointed, and ever thereafter the Russian people and their leaders lived in perpetual fear of armed conflict with a hostile capitalist outside world.

Nor were these eternal fears of war purely paranoiac delusions. Sure enough, the apprehensions of Stalin were vindicated in 1941 when Nazi Germany did indeed invade Russia. The Soviet government was only preserved because at the time he invaded Russia, Hitler had already become involved in warfare with Great Britain and France, and shortly thereafter became involved in warfare with the United States. After World War II, the Russian people lived in perpetual fear—along with the rest of the world's population—of nuclear devastation. It would appear that the Soviet government's ideologically motivated imposition of socialism on Russia in 1917, and its ideologically motivated support thereafter for socialist and communist movements in other nations, has put the Russian national interest, whether interpreted in terms of the physical and mental welfare of the Russian people or of the Russian leadership, in severe peril from the very beginning. It would appear that had the Soviet government wanted to pursue the true Russian national interest, according to any sensible interpretation of the term, it would have very early in its history completely renounced socialism.

Whenever one closely examines the specific cases cited to support the proposition that the Soviet government put Russian national interests ahead of its explicit and acknowledged ideological commitments, one perceives that there was no actual sacrifice of long-term ideological goals implicit in the specific decisions or actions involved. Consider, for example, the Nazi-Soviet Non-Aggression Pact of August, 1939. Some analysts maintain that this treaty between the "sworn ideological enemies" of Nazi Germany and Soviet Russia demonstrates how quickly the Soviet government sacrificed its ideological ideals to the imperatives of national power as soon as the two came into conflict. There is no doubt that the Nazi-Soviet Pact was a spectacular about-face in the annals of diplomatic history, and that it thoroughly alienated a great many opponents of fascism who had previously been inclined to be sympathetic toward the Soviet Union.

But even so, it by no means implied that Stalin, and the Soviet government generally, had abandoned its ideological goal of world-wide socialization. Stalin perceived in the rise of Adolf Hitler and the rearmament of Germany both a serious threat and a golden opportunity. The threat emanated from Hitler's firm intention, clearly stated in *Mein Kampf* and other documents, to invade Russia, overthrow the Soviet government, and transform Russia into a vast German dependency. This would surely represent the "capitalist counterthrust" so dreaded by Soviet leaders since the days of Lenin. But there was also an opportunity resident in Hitler's imperialistic dream: because Great Britain, France, and other Western nations were fearful that a successful German invasion and colonization of Russia would completely upset the balance of power and pave the way toward world-wide hegemony by a totalitarian fascist regime. Thus the possibility existed of a devastating Second World War, fought out mostly by the capitalist nations among themselves, that would further the prospects for world-wide socialist revolution. Just as the First World War had made a socialist revolution possible in Russia, so too a Second World War might make socialist revolutions possible in Germany, France, Great Britain, and elsewhere.

But for sound reasons given the information available to him at the time, Stalin was far more concerned about the threat of Nazi invasion than he was hopeful of an internecine war among the capitalist nations. His first priority, once the Nazi threat started to emerge unmistakably in the mid-1930s, was to try to form a coalition against Nazi Germany with France, Great Britain, and other Western powers. A determined coalition, backed by a strong treaty, might have deterred Nazi expansionism. But the Western powers were reluctant to confront Hitler prematurely, and they attempted conciliation up through the Munich agreement of September, 1938. Naturally enough, during the conciliatory period, Stalin became increasingly apprehensive that the Western powers intended to sit by comfortably while the Nazi and Soviet dictatorships fought out a devastating war of attrition among themselves.

But he need not have worried about this, because the Western powers were operating under the assumption that Nazi Germany would, if allowed to proceed unmolested, quickly and easily topple over the "socialist house of cards" represented by the Soviet Union, and thereupon turn Russia, with all its rich resources and large population, into a German colony, thus setting the stage for a German world empire. This the Western powers could not allow to happen, and they finally proposed to draw the line against Hitler at Poland, which in 1939 was the last remaining territorial barrier between Nazi Germany and the vast resources of the Russian land-mass. As soon as it became apparent that after all, Great Britain and France were prepared to fight if Germany invaded Poland, Stalin clearly perceived the opportunities for Soviet gain inherent in the situation. Hitler, following a sensible policy of "one enemy at a time if possible," was delighted to receive Stalin's application for a pact which would spare him (Hitler), for a time at least, from a two-front war of the sort that had defeated Germany in World War I. The pact was duly signed, and World War II was duly commenced in September of 1939 with the Nazi invasion of Poland.

At the time, Stalin was very hopeful that matters would work out well for both the Soviet Union and the world socialist movement. If all went well, the Allied and the Axis powers would all bleed themselves white in a prolonged and devastating war of attrition similar to World War I, while the Soviet Union sat quietly on the sideline, biding its time. When the time was ripe, possibly in the midst of postwar chaos, domestic socialist movements—perhaps assisted by Russian military forces—would sweep into power in the major Allied and Axis nations, thus achieving the Soviet government's ideological aspiration of world socialist revolution, and simultaneously rendering the Russian nation immune from future invasions instigated by hostile foreign capitalists.

Therefore the Nazi-Soviet Non-Aggression Pact of 1939 by no means represented a betrayal of the Soviet government's long-term ideological goal of world-wide socialization in the interest of crass Russian national self-interest. The Pact was in fact perfectly consistent with that long-term goal. Of course, in the event, Stalin's fondest hopes were not realized. The European war of 1939-41 did not exhaust the capitalist powers. The French caved in almost immediately, and the British retreated to their island to await developments. Confident that he had secured his rear, Hitler turned back to his original objective of eastward expansion in the June, 1941, invasion of Russia. Therefore the worst of World War II did not involve Britain and France versus Nazi Germany, but rather Nazi Germany versus Soviet Russia. Nevertheless, the Soviet government, and the cause of world socialist revolution, came out ahead in the end, as a bevy of small Eastern European nations, plus China and North Korea, were added to the Communist camp from 1945-49.

The Nazi-Soviet Non-Aggression Pact of August, 1939, is merely one out of a number of historical episodes which some analysts declare as evidence of the primacy of nationalism over ideology in the determination of the decisions and behavior of the various communist governments in the world. One implication of this putative primacy is that the alleged ideological motivation of assisting world socialist revolution has been merely a hypocritical effort to disguise and conceal base and unworthy motivations of imperialistic aggrandizement. Another implication, of course, is that any attempt to seek fundamental ideological harmonization (by means, for example, of the inauguration of pragmatic market socialism in the Western nations) would have a negligible impact on the international confrontation between the communist and noncommunist blocs of nations. Quite obviously it would be impractical to try to deal with all of this alleged evidence, but any fair-minded historian or political scientist could analyze any one of these proposed episodes, and find that it involved no fundamental lapse in long-term ideological commitment.

As a matter of fact, very few Western historians or political scientists would go to the extreme of asserting that ideology has been a "trivial" or "negligible" factor in the history of the communist nations and their relationships with noncommunist nations. The general consensus among reputable analysts is that ideology certainly plays "some" role, and the only real question concerns how much of a role.[2] A considerable number of Western historians and political scientists would characterize the role of Marxist ideology in the historical development and present condition of Russia in such terms as "highly significant," "critical," and "decisive." Metaphorically speaking, Russia—both her people and her leaders—succumbed to an "ideological fever" as a result of the Bolshevik Revolution, and that fever initiated a long-term bout of "national insanity." A sane conception of national interest involves a reasonable concern for territorial integrity, and for the welfare of the population currently resident in that territory. It does not involve an intense desire for radical social transformations in the rest of the world. As a result of its communist ideological infection, Soviet Russia became an extremely disruptive and dangerous force in the modern world. It became excessively self-righteous, belligerent and paranoiac. This ideological infection has been slowly and gradually ebbing over the course of the years and the decades since the Bolshevik Revolution of 1917, but it has proved remarkably resistant to complete eradication. Some three decades after the Bolshevik Revolution, ideological conflict contributed heavily to the Cold War which followed close upon the heels of World War II. The Cold War was well established by 1950, but the alleged "thaw" in the Cold War officially commenced as early as 1953, upon the death of Stalin. Notwithstanding several decades of thawing since 1953, the threat of a nuclear armageddon is still with us.

The conventional attitude in the leading noncommunist nations has been that the arms competition would continue on until such time as weakening ideological resolution in the communist world, together with growing awareness of the catastrophic costs which a nuclear war would impose on humanity, will enable a serious and sincere move toward disarmament. Until such time arrives, it remains incumbent upon the leading nations of the noncommunist world to maintain both an arms parity, and a general power parity, with the communist world, as the only reliable safeguard against the compulsory communization of the noncommunist world.

While one cannot deny the possibility of permanent coexistence and significant arms reduction in the absence of any tangible movement toward ideological harmonization (such as would be involved in the establishment of capitalism in the leading communist nations, or of pragmatic market socialism in the leading noncommunist nations), we should perhaps not be overly confident about such an outcome. As for weakening ideological resolution, it has to be recognized that Marxist ideology is remarkably resilient and adaptable to changing evidence. For at least a hundred years, apologists for capitalism have been arguing that the rise in working class living standards in the industrialized capitalist nations refutes the Marxist prediction of immiseration, and with it the entire Marxist ideological system. In spite of this evidence, the last hundred years have seen the rise of Marxist ideology from a purely abstract and academic concept to the avowed policy guide of several populous and powerful nation-states in the contemporary world, most notably the Soviet Union and the People's Republic of China. It is suggested below that a possible reason for the durability of Marxist ideology is that, notwithstanding the ideology's excessively harsh verdict on capitalism, the ideology is essentially correct on the point that some form of socialism would be preferable to contemporary capitalism.

As for the fear of nuclear war, Soviet Russia has been perfectly willing to assume the risk of nuclear war, in pursuit of its ideological convictions, for nearly half a century. It would seem that if anything, with the gradual passing of the older generation of Russians who personally experienced the perils, hardships, and suffering of war during World War II, awareness and appreciation of the threat of war in Russia may have gradually been ebbing. As for the United States, none of its living citizens have any personal experience of a war fought within the boundaries of the nation. In any event, the fear of war and of premature death is probably not as potent a factor in human mentality as it might at first seem. All of humanity is mortal in the end, and no matter what any human individual does, he or she cannot evade death for more than a few short decades. That the human race is not overly intimidated by the possibility of premature death is perhaps suggested by the enthusiasm for war which it has displayed throughout history. It would appear that mankind has thrown itself into warfare at the slightest provocation, whether the nebulous incentive consisted of material benefit, psychological satisfaction, moral conviction, or a combination of all three. At the present time, U.S. citizens are almost universally prepared to fight and die in defense of the American way of life. Meanwhile, the Russian citizenry has been (at least until very recently) equally determined to defend the Soviet way of life. The weapons have been—and continue to be—poised and ready, and all it would take is a single spark to ignite an all-consuming conflagration.

But while the danger is apparent to all reasonable persons, we should try to address the question of exactly and specifically how it is expected that ideological harmonization might tip the scales in favor of disarmament, in the face of continuing concerns for national security. To begin with, it should be recalled that the principle of the desirability of disarmament has long been officially accepted by all the major national powers. Both the United States and Soviet governments have continually proclaimed their constant readiness to engage in good faith disarmament at any time the other party demonstrates a similar readiness. "Good faith disarmament" refers to a plan of arms reduction that would maintain the balance of armed power that currently exists: both sides would reduce the absolute levels of their armed power in such a way that the ratio of the two sides' armed power remains constant.

But what is simple enough in principle has been very difficult to achieve in practice. Arms control negotiations have gone on intermittently between the United States and the Soviet Union ever since the 1950s.[3] There have been some agreements reached during that period, most notably the Strategic Arms Limitation Treaty (SALT) of 1972, which placed a temporary freeze on numbers of strategic missiles, and the Strategic Arms Reduction Treaty (START) of 1991, which if carried through will result in a 20-30 percent reduction in strategic nuclear capability on both sides. The SALT agreement and the START agreement have been very encouraging, but it must be acknowledged that there is still a very long path to travel before the threat of nuclear war will be describable as a negligible consideration in human affairs. Nuclear arms competition remained intense throughout most of the post-World War II period—the better part of half a century—despite the fact that virtually every rational and reasonable individual who has ever looked at the evidence has concluded that a nuclear war, using existing stockpiles of weapons, would quite possibly have a permanently crippling effect on human civilization.

Anyone with even a passing familiarity with the arms control literature recognizes the extreme difficulty of determining what constitutes the "parity in armed power" which the major powers insist that any arms reduction agreement must maintain. A host of uncertain variables and sheer imponderables are involved, and the matter is therefore highly subjective, even for the technicians. Whenever one side proposed some arms reduction formula, which it claimed would maintain parity in armed power, the other side normally rejected it, on grounds that the formula would not maintain armed power parity, but would rather shift the balance toward armed power superiority of the side proposing the formula. This pattern was repeated endlessly throughout several decades of arms control negotiations.

The possibility of comprehensive agreement always foundered on the shoals of suspicion and distrust. Neither side had any degree of trust in the other side, any degree of confidence that the other side had a genuine desire for permanent peaceful coexistence. Thus the inability to arrive at major agreements. It would seem that after several decades of fruitless negotiation, it should be obvious that the problem is not a straightforward technical problem with a straightforward technical solution which will eventually be found. It would be extremely naive to believe that someday some brilliant and ingenious arms expert will come up with some complex formula for arms reduction which both sides would be compelled to admit maintains a mutually satisfactory parity of armed power. The arms experts have been trying to find just such a formula for several decades. But the profound complexities and numerous uncertainties involved in the problem have defied every attempt to arrive at a technical solution in the past, and almost certainly the same will hold true in the future.

It seems unavoidable that any feasible arms reduction plan will affect the balance of armed power, at least to some slight extent, in an unpredictable direction. Even though both sides would reduce the absolute level of their armed power, the ratio of the armed power of the two sides will change, at least slightly. One side or the other would be "benefited." Thus for an agreement to be undertaken, both sides have to have a reasonable amount of faith, trust, and confidence in the other side. Both sides must believe that there is relatively little likelihood that the other side would attempt to exploit any advantages that the arms reduction process would happen to give it. Both sides must believe that the other side really has, as its primary motivation for the disarmament agreement, a genuine and sincere resolution toward permanent peaceful coexistence.

Unfortunately, the ideological conflict between communism and noncommunism constitutes a serious impediment to the development of faith, trust, and confidence. People in the noncommunist world believe, on the basis of considerable documentary and historical evidence, that the communist governments want nothing so much as the destruction of capitalism in all nations of the world. The perceived noxiousness of this goal of the communist governments is greatly aggravated by the invalid, but nevertheless very strong, tendency in the West to identify capitalism with political democracy and market allocation. Meanwhile, people in the communist world have believed that the noncommunist governments, controlled as they supposedly are by scheming, malevolent capitalists, want nothing so much as the destruction of socialism in all nations of the world and the reestablishment of the horrors of capitalistic exploitation. Under this view of the motivations and intentions of the other side, each side expects that were the process of disarmament to place unforeseeable advantages at the disposal of the other side, the other side would immediately seek to exploit these advantages. So long as communist ideology continues to harp on the alleged gross evil, degradation, and corruption of capitalism, and so long as noncommunist ideology continues to assail the alleged "totalitarian dictatorship" represented by the communist social system, the achievement of a sufficient degree of faith, trust, and confidence to enable an important disarmament program would be very difficult indeed.

There has indeed been a considerable amount of ideological harmonization relative to the situation circa 1950, at the commencement of the Cold War. Even before the Gorbachev era in the Soviet Union, the level of rhetorical vituperation, scorn, contempt, and hostility against the other side in the literature of ideological confrontation had become appreciably less than it was then. The West conceded that Soviet society had become far more open, humane, and tolerant than it was during the Stalinist purgatory of the 1930s. For their part, communist ideologues generally credited U.S. society with substantial progress, relative to the severe economic depression, breadlines, racial lynchings, and riotous strikes of the 1930s. Nevertheless, at most there had been a reduction in the intensity of the negative verdict on the social system of the other side. But the qualitative fact of a negative verdict on the social system of the other side was not fundamentally altered.

Ideological harmonization between the United States and the U.S.S.R. accelerated rapidly during the latter 1980s and early 1990s. Dramatic transformations have occurred: the U.S.S.R. has been dissolved and replaced by a loose confederation of constituent republics, the Communist Party of the U.S.S.R. has been formally deprived of its political authority, free elections have been held. Mikhail Gorbachev, the man who more than anyone else was the initiator of perestroika and glasnost, was unable to keep pace with events and fell from power. Economic reform has quickly evolved from relatively limited proposals to plans for the wholesale marketization and privatization of the economy. Many authorities in the West anticipate that within a very few years the various republics of the ex-U.S.S.R., including Russia herself, will be reasonable approximations to democratic market capitalist nations. The processes being observed in the ex-Soviet Union are even further advanced in the Eastern European nations which only a short while ago were important components of the communist bloc of nations. Presumably if both the Soviet Union and Eastern Europe abandon communism, the same abandonment will sooner or later occur in the People's Republic of China and the rest of the communist nations of the world. Should these expectations be realized, the ideological gap will no longer hamper the achievement of further progress on disarmament among the superpowers.

Clearly this outcome would be marvelously beneficial, and would bode well for the future of human civilization throughout the world. But it would be unwise and excessively complacent to merely assume that all of the communist nations will indeed abandon every aspect of communism within a short period of time. Ideological belief systems have proven themselves extremely resistant to change, especially where fundamental principles are concerned. The dramatic dissolution of the U.S.S.R. does not necessarily mean that the ideological system of communism is finished. To begin with, Russia was always the largest and most important republic in the U.S.S.R., and even on its own—without a belt of Eastern European satellite states and without a buffer zone of peripheral republics—it remains a very formidable national entity. Successful arms reduction still requires Russia's cooperation, and ideology might still constitute an impediment to achieving the level of mutual trust and goodwill necessary to guarantee Russian cooperation.

The core of the communist ideological system has always been socialism in and of itself—public ownership of capital as a means of overcoming surplus labor exploitation. This core might easily be retained even if Russia becomes a genuine, multi-party democracy with a free market economy. It is a fallacy to suppose that socialism is not compatible with either democracy or the free market—the pragmatic market socialist alternative stands as testimony to this. What has been witnessed in the ex-Soviet Union is a revolt against Russian domination by the peripheral republics, and a revolt against Communist Party domination throughout the nation. It is still too early to predict whether these revolts will be ultimately successful and will lead to substantive alteration of the fundamental socioeconomic system. The situation within the ex-U.S.S.R. is extremely troubled and fluid at the present time. Severe material hardship has been imposed on the population because of the chaotic disorganization caused by the initiation of drastic change prior to the achievement of a reasonable degree of consensus among either the population or the leadership as to exactly what the change should consist of. Conditions are obviously ripe for a conservative reaction of some sort. This is not to predict that a conservative reaction will indeed occur—but is only to point out that one is certainly possible.

Even if a conservative reaction does not occur, and the reform process pushes ahead in the ex-U.S.S.R. and elsewhere in the communist world, it will probably be many years before capitalism as it is known in the West is fully established in the East. In the meantime, ideological harmonization could be furthered through East-West convergence on a common pattern of democratic market socialism, and thereby the difficulties and uncertainties that would be involved in the capitalization of the communist East would be avoided. It would constitute a fundamental qualitative breakthrough in ideological harmonization if the major noncommunist nations were, as suggested herein, to abolish capitalism and inaugurate pragmatic market socialist economies. Such an historic transition would have a major impact on the minds and emotions of everyone with even the least awareness of the traditional ideological conflict between communism and noncommunism. Undoubtedly it would require some length of time for the full implications of the transition to be entirely absorbed. Undoubtedly the most unrepentant, hard-line, traditionalist communist ideologues remaining in the communist world would be dubious about certain aspects of pragmatic market socialism. But in the end, even the most conservative communist ideologues would not be able to evade the fact that pragmatic market socialism is an authentic variety of socialism, and that its implementation constitutes a genuine abolition of capitalism.

With the source of their traditional paranoiac obsessions removed, it seems likely that the Russian and other communist leaders would become significantly more friendly, tolerant, cooperative, and progressive in their dealings with the outside world. The existing reform movement toward market allocation and political democracy in the communist nations would be greatly strengthened. The chances for important progress in disarmament negotiations would also be significantly augmented. We have already seen, with the advent of the forward-looking Mikhail Gorbachev in the Soviet Union, a significant reduction in tension and a resurgence of optimism concerning major arms reduction. This occurred even before any major institutional transitions in the Soviet Union—merely on the basis of freer discussion of possible reforms. If this much progress was made simply on the basis of *talk* about ideological harmonization, one can well imagine the impact of actual, substantive, ideological harmonization.

B. SOCIALISM IN THE WEST

According to the epochal codification of socialist thought by Karl Marx in the nineteenth century, the capitalist economic system is both morally perverse and economically inefficient.[4] Moral perversity resides in surplus labor exploitation: the capitalist class utilizes its property rights in capital to illegitimately deprive the working population of a substantial proportion of the value which it has created through its labor. Economic inefficiency resides in the dynamic instability of capitalism: in its inherent propensity toward ever-worsening business depressions. Such depressions emerge naturally from the surplus labor exploitation mechanism. Exploitation simultaneously constrains the purchasing power of the working population while it inflates the disposable income of the tiny minority of wealthy capitalists. The capitalists endeavor to reinvest most of their ill-gotten gains, leading to overinvestment, decline of the profit rate, and ultimate panic, collapse, and depression. Depressions lead to further concentration of capital property ownership, which intensifies the cyclical process. Eventually depressions will become so severe, and the material and/or psychological immiseration of the working population will become so aggravated, as to precipitate a socialist revolution. It is extremely significant that while Marx believed that the perversity of surplus labor exploitation justified the abolition of capitalism on moral grounds, the actual mechanism of abolition was to be business depressions. This suggests that if a capitalist economy can achieve sufficient anticyclical control, then the Marxist prediction of socialist revolution is falsified, regardless of the moral issue.

During the nineteenth century, orthodox economists more or less complacently dismissed Marx's dynamic theory of capitalism. Among other things, they had "Say's Law" to buttress their confidence that business depressions were relatively mild and ephemeral occurrences. The available statistical evidence was relatively crude, and was certainly not adequate for a firm judgment on the Marxist proposition of the increasing severity of business depressions. Moreover, in the absence of a real-world socialist economy, it was relatively easy to conjecture that socialism is inherently unviable, and therefore does not provide a potential cure for any problem, whether it be exploitation, depression, or anything else. A great watershed in modern intellectual history was encountered during the 1930s. The persistence of the Soviet Union throughout the 1920s and its impressive effort at self-sufficient industrialization in the early 1930s established a basic degree of viability for the socialist alternative to capitalism. Perhaps even more seriously, the unprecedented scope and severity of the Great Depression of the 1930s cast severe doubt on the conventional nineteenth century viewpoint that laissez faire was the best possible response to the problem of business depressions. The economic success of Soviet socialism and the rigors of the Great Depression inspired Western capitalism to reform itself. Keynesian anticyclical policy was promulgated, and after World War II most national governments accepted responsibility for the maintenance of a reasonable degree of cyclical stability. Several decades have passed without a recurrence of the disastrous Great Depression of the 1930s. Clearly Western capitalism remains prey to various economic vicissitudes (unemployment, inflation, etc.), but on the whole its long-term economic performance seems clearly superior to that of Eastern socialism as practiced in the communist nations. At least this seems true for the advanced economies such as those of the United States and Russia. In the case of less advanced economies (e.g., India versus China), the indications may not be as clear.

Toward the end of the nineteenth century, orthodox economists perceived little merit in Marx's critique of the dynamic performance of capitalism. Toward the end of the twentieth century, orthodox economists now concede that their nineteenth century counterparts may have been somewhat overconfident, but they also hold that whatever validity may once have existed in Marx's critique has been thoroughly abrogated by the development and implementation of Keynesian anticyclical policy. One might well agree with the viewpoint that business depressions will almost certainly never become so severe as to precipitate a socialist revolution. One might well also agree that the business depression problem is not even sufficiently severe to indicate the *desirability* (as opposed to the *inevitability*) of socialism. This still leaves unanswered Marx's accusation of the moral perversity of surplus labor exploitation. The term "exploitation" is perhaps too harsh. What is really at issue here is whether various forms of capital property income, including dividends, interest, capital gains, and certain forms of rent, are "earned" or "unearned." While it may seem rhetorically excessive to describe these types of income as the result of "exploitation," it does not seem so implausible and intemperate to describe them as "unearned." It could be that the modern capitalist is not so much an active exploiter as he is a passive rentier. But even if we were to accept the latter designation as more accurately descriptive than the former, the essence of the Marxist accusation of the moral perversity of capitalism would remain. This is so because of the highly unequal distribution of capital property income under contemporary capitalism. Highly unequal distribution of unearned income is clearly inequitable.

Capitalist apologetics, starting with the work of Eugen von Böhm-

Bawerk in the latter nineteenth century and continuing down to the present day, has indeed offered a number of potential responses to this accusation. But these responses are not entirely satisfactory.[5] It is alleged that capital property return recompenses the supervisory activities of capitalists in the conduct of business enterprise. But such supervisory activities seem mostly performed by salaried executives of business corporations, and the ownership interest in most large, modern corporations is mostly held by passive and inactive stockholders and bondholders. It is alleged that capital property return recompenses entrepreneurs and other investors for their efforts in the rational allocation of financial capital. But in the modern economy we see apparently competent investment analysis being performed for relatively modest salaries and bonuses by the loan officers and investment analysts of commercial banks, investment banks, insurance companies, pension funds, and other types of financial intermediaries. We also see that most research, investment, product and process innovation, and so on, is undertaken by large, established, nonentrepreneurial corporations, and that only a relatively small part of the overall flow of capital property income is received by individuals with personal experience of genuine entrepreneurship. It is alleged that capital property income recompenses the sacrifices of saving (i.e., the psychological stress of postponing consumption). But in reality there are numerous incentives to saving other than "to take advantage of the interest rate"—such as provision for old age, for the education of children, and for the enhancement of one's security in the face of an unpredictable future. Not only is it uncertain that the private saving rate would decrease in the absence of interest income, any loss in private saving could easily be compensated by an increase in public saving. The above are the most fundamental arguments for the capitalist status quo, because they directly address the moral issue raised by Marx by means of asserting that capital property income is indeed earned in an economically and morally legitimate sense.

Other arguments for capitalism are indirect because they do not address the accusation that capital property income is unearned: these include what might be termed the "people's capitalism" thesis, and the political argument for capitalism that it separates economic from political power and hence fosters the preservation of freedom and democracy. These indirect arguments are also seriously flawed. The people's capitalism thesis is more or less definitively refuted by available statistical evidence. This evidence manifests extreme inequality in the distribution of the capital property wealth (stocks, bonds, etc.) which produces capital property income (dividends, interest, etc.). The available evidence also suggests the strong role of inheritance and chance—as opposed to entrepreneurship and other productive contributions—in the accumulation of large-scale capital fortunes. The association of the economic institution of socialism with political oligarchy in the communist nations is more plausibly attributed to historical circumstances than to the inherent properties of public ownership of capital. Moreover, the extreme inequality of capital wealth ownership under contemporary capitalism to some significant extent reduces the purity of democratic decision-making in the West.

Finally, we come to the extremely important argument from capitalist apologetics that whatever the imperfections of the capitalist status quo, there is no viable socialist alternative to this status quo which promises significantly better economic performance. This argument is empirically founded upon the inferior economic performance of the leading communist nations versus that of the leading capitalist nations. To the extent that we define "socialism" in its original and pure sense (a sense still maintained in the typical dictionary definition of socialism) as necessarily involving public ownership of the preponderance of nonhuman factors of production (i.e., capital and natural resources), then only the communist nations can correctly be defined as socialist. In the latter nineteenth century, the socialist movement diverged into two major channels. The "classical socialist" channel, maintaining close adherence to the original Marxist prescriptions (the need for violent revolution, preponderantly public ownership of land and capital, etc.), went on to the 1917 Bolshevik Revolution in Russia and communism as we know it today.[6] The revisionist or "social democratic socialist" channel, abandoning many of the original Marxist prescriptions (in particular, the need for violent revolution and preponderantly public ownership of land and capital), went on to numerous electoral successes in various Western European and other nations during the twentieth century.[7] Social democrats following in the revisionist tradition tend to label themselves "socialists," which creates a certain amount of semantic confusion. However, the critical distinction between social democratic socialism and "genuine" socialism, as practiced in the communist nations, is well appreciated, both by most capitalists and by most serious students of social organization. Throughout this book, the term "socialism" will be taken in its "classical" sense: public ownership of the preponderance of the nonhuman factors of production: capital and natural resources. In this sense, only the communist nations are socialist nations.

Owing to their central role in the international confrontation between communism and noncommunism, the economic performance of the United States and the Soviet Union have often been compared. As the twentieth century draws to a close, it seems clear that the United States has won this economic competition. Assuming that this perception is correct, the question is why. The conventional consensus throughout the West is that market capitalism as embodied in the United States economy is superior to planned socialism as embodied in the Soviet economy. To many minds, there are very strong interrelationships between "market allocation" and "capitalism" on the one hand, and "central planning" and "socialism" on the other. To some, indeed, the respective terms are virtually synonymous: capitalism *is* market allocation, and socialism *is* central planning. It will be argued here that this is a very serious misperception of reality, and that in fact the range of alternatives to market capitalism is not confined to *planned* socialism, but it also embraces several *market* socialist possibilities.[8] It will be further argued that a specific variety of market socialism, descriptively designated "pragmatic market socialism," provides a very serious, sensible, and attractive alternative to the capitalistic status quo.

As is well known, Karl Marx had very little to say about the socialist economy which would succeed the capitalist economy. He deemed his critique of capitalism sufficient to show that capitalism is perverse and doomed, and he declined to "provide recipes for the social cooks of the future." When the Bolsheviks gained power in Russia in 1917, they quickly implemented the basic Marxist prescription by nationalizing almost all land and capital. Once this had been done, they confronted a question on which no consensus had yet been reached by the Party's intellectuals: how exactly should this publicly owned land and capital be applied in production? The early Bolshevik leaders were sufficiently sensible to realize that the basic economic problems (what to produce, how to produce it, etc.) were the same under both capitalism and socialism, and that many if not most of the established economic mechanisms under capitalism must be preserved under socialism. No serious consideration was therefore given to various radical proposals to abolish monetary exchange, to eliminate standard accounting categories such as profit and interest, and to implement a totally centralized system of planned physical production and distribution.

In fact, under the New Economic Plan (NEP) of the 1920s, the Soviet economy operated very much as it had before the socialist revolution. Farmers were given long-term leases on the land they farmed, and the fact that the land was theoretically public property did not have much of an impact on its usage in practice. Managers of industrial enterprises were told to operate these enterprises on a commercial basis, and the fact that the profits and interest produced by these enterprises went to the state rather than to private capitalists did not have much of an impact on their practical operations of production and marketing. Under the New Economic Plan, the Soviet Union prospered, and it made rapid progress toward the restoration of economic conditions prior to the ravages of World War I, the Bolshevik Revolution, and the Civil War. The Soviet Union's experience under the New Economic Plan was probably the closest approach to an implementation of current concepts of market socialism as ever occurred in the real world.

A large number of Soviet economists believed that the Soviet Union should stay with the basic concepts of the NEP for an indefinite period. But another body of opinion in the Soviet Union believed that the industrialization and modernization of Russia could and should be speeded up. According to this body of opinion, economic progress *could* be accelerated because of the systematic coordination and planning made possible by public ownership of the means of production. Furthermore, economic progress *should* be accelerated because of the ominous possibility that the Soviet Union might someday be invaded by hostile capitalist nations. This latter possibility was considerably enhanced by the fact that although the Soviet Union moderated its support for communist movements in other nations during the 1920s, its ideological commitment precluded its full and explicit renunciation of the goal of world-wide socialization. History records that the latter body of opinion, under the leadership of Josef Stalin, won out in the Soviet Union.

Thus was commenced in the late 1920s and early 1930s a tremendous effort toward the rapid modernization of the Soviet Union.[9] The effort comprised two principal aspects: (1) the collectivization of agriculture; (2) central planning of industrial production. It was thought that collectivization of agriculture would permit the application of "factory methods" and the realization of important economies of scale, so that agricultural production would soar, making available a large surplus with which to support a growing urban population employed in the industrial sector. Meanwhile, there would be massive investments made in social infrastructure (dams, roads, public buildings, etc.) and in industrial plant and machinery. That the planned modernization effort achieved its basic objective of significantly enhancing the military power of the Soviet state within a very brief period of time was proved beyond a shadow of a doubt by the impressive resistance put up by Russia from 1941 through 1945 against the Nazi military machine, a machine constructed by one of the most modern and industrialized nations in the world. But at the same time, the effort placed enormous physical and mental stress on the Soviet people. The weakest link in the plan turned out to be agriculture. The Communist Party leadership overestimated the benefits of applying "factory methods" in agriculture, and underestimated the resistance among the agricultural population to the excessively communalistic way of life imposed by the collective farm system. Stalin reacted to growing dissent by carrying out massive deportations, by establishing a huge system of forced-labor camps, and by orchestrating a comprehensive campaign of Party purges. What was once perceived by idealistic socialists throughout the world as a potential workers' paradise quickly evolved into a totalitarian nightmare.

But the fact remains that it was not socialism per se, the public ownership of land and capital, which precipitated this totalitarian nightmare. It was rather the forced-pace modernization campaign: the collectivization of agriculture, the central planning of industry, and the allocation of an extremely high proportion of current output to capital investment. Throughout most of the 1920s, during which the New Economic Plan was in operation, the Soviet Union had had a socialist economy—but without collectivization of agriculture, central planning of industry, and extremely high rates of capital investment. The NEP system of market socialism worked well, and it is arguable that had that system been maintained within the context of a more subtle and leisurely modernization campaign, the long-term rate of progress in the Soviet Union would probably have been higher, and even its military capacity during World War II might conceivably have been greater.

This is not to say that the Soviet model of centrally planned socialism represented a clear break with the consensus socialist blueprint prior to the 1930s. There *was no* consensus socialist blueprint prior to the 1930s. All adherents to socialism agreed that the pure laissez faire prescription of "bourgeois economics" (the state as simply a "policeman" presiding over the "anarchy of the market") was inappropriate and had to go, because this prescription served as a rationalization both for the exploitation of labor and for the persistence of business depressions. Traditional socialists believed that public ownership of capital was necessary to abrogate these problems, while social democratic socialists felt that they could be abrogated by various forms of state intervention in the economy short of public ownership of capital: forms such as regulation of business enterprise, progressive taxation, social insurance, welfare programs, and (from the 1930s onward) active anticyclical policy along Keynesian lines. But neither the traditional socialists nor the social democratic socialists had achieved any appreciable consensus prior to the 1930s on the precise institutions and policies that would best eliminate the perceived capitalistic problems of exploitation and depression, and at the same time maintain a high level of short-run and long-run efficiency. The Soviet model of centrally planned socialism adopted in the 1930s was indeed basically consistent with the nebulous policy prescriptions of the earlier socialist literature. But so also are several potential models of market socialism.

The term "market socialism" became established in orthodox Western economics owing largely to the work of Oskar Lange (1904-1965), a Polish economist with socialist leanings who spent his most productive years as a faculty member at several leading British and American universities.[10] Prior to Lange, it was widely assumed, both by orthodox economists and orthodox socialists, that there was a direct and necessary opposition between mainstream economics and the socialist prescription of public ownership of capital. Specifically, it was widely believed by orthodox economists that the theory of marginal productivity pricing of factors of production, applied to the nonhuman factors land and capital, simultaneously refutes the labor theory of value and indicates the economic inefficiency of public ownership of land and capital. For their part, socialists were mostly inclined to dismiss this theory contemptuously as pseudoscientific obfuscation and obscurantism designed solely to provide a specious justification for capitalism. Oskar Lange had been thoroughly educated in both the logic and the mathematical tools of mainstream economics, and he did not share the usual skepticism and distrust among socialists for this body of thought. He arrived at the conclusion that the marginal productivity theory of factor pricing indicates only that business enterprises should pay interest and other forms of property return for the use of land and capital—not that these factors need to be privately owned. If these nonhuman factors were publicly owned, profits and interest would be paid to the appropriate government agencies and not to private capitalists. The nonhuman factors of production would thereby be appropriately priced and would be utilized efficiently in the productive processes of the economy, but without the inequity embodied in the extremely unequal distribution of capital property income under contemporary capitalism.

Lange developed this idea in a work entitled "On the Economic Theory of Socialism," first published in the mid-1930s, which has since become what might be described as a "cult classic" within the discipline of economics. By the mid-1930s, the modernization campaign in the Soviet Union was in full swing, and there was an increasing tendency, both in popular and professional thinking, to identify "socialism" as the centrally planned economic system of that nation. At the same time, for all of the notable achievements of the Soviet modernization campaign, the general consensus in the West was that this campaign was basically vindicating the traditional objection to socialism that it would necessarily lead to the economy being engulfed in an enormous, strangling, bureaucratic apparatus. Lange tried to demonstrate that there were socialist possibilities available (now referred to as plans of "market socialism") which would not be over-burdened by bureaucracy and excessively central- ized planning. His essay "On the Economic Theory of Socialism" was taken very seriously by the profession, not least of all because through numerous "conventional" contributions to economic theory and econometrics, Lange demonstrated a high level of understanding and mastery of mainstream economics and methodology. "On the Economic Theory of Socialism" originally appeared in an important theoretical journal, was later published in book form by a university press, and by the 1960s was regularly discussed in textbooks on comparative economic systems under the designation "market socialism."

There are two central elements of Lange's specific market socialist proposal: (1) administrative guidance of prices on the basis of inven- tory changes; (2) guidance of production by the marginal cost pricing principle. According to the first, the government price-setting agency would raise prices of commodities displaying decreasing inventories and lower prices of commodities displaying increasing inventories. According to the second, each business enterprise would set the output of each commodity at the level which equates the marginal cost of production to the externally set price of the commodity. The plan represents an effort to implement as specific administrative policy the theoretical model of market pricing and profit maximiza- tion under perfect competition enunciated in the nineteenth century by such mainstream economic luminaries as Leon Walras and Alfred Marshall. According to economic welfare theory, this model posses- ses highly desirable efficiency properties. During the 1930s, the "Keynesian revolution" in orthodox macroeconomics was comple- mented by what might be termed a "Robinsonian revolution" in orthodox microeconomics. A very comprehensive theory of imperfect competition was developed by Joan Robinson and others. The imperfect competition theory seemed to fit the real-world facts rather better than the perfect competition theory, and very significantly, it was shown that under conditions of imperfect competition, profit maximization by business enterprises does not possess the desirable efficiency properties which it possesses under conditions of perfect competition. Since profit maximization by business enterprises has always been deemed a natural and inescapable consequence of capitalism, Lange was utilizing the very latest and most potent economic theory available to argue for the greater economic efficiency of socialism relative to capitalism.

The verdict of the economics profession on the Langian market socialist proposal was soon reached: interesting in theory, but unpromising in practice.[11] This verdict perhaps manifests the doubts which economists themselves harbor regarding the realism and relevance of the elaborate theoretical constructions for which they are renowned. When theoretical prescriptions, no matter how impressively grounded in formal mathematical models, come into direct conflict with commonsensical intuitions, no matter how informal and nebulous they may be, it is usually the former which give way and not the latter. Two primary reasons have been emphasized for the probable inefficacy of the Langian market socialist proposal: the administered pricing system would be unwieldy; in the absence of an observable success criterion (such as profits), there would be high administrative costs of enforcing the marginal cost production principle on business firms. The speculations of "unwieldy pricing" and "high enforcement costs" are unsupported by any rigorously developed model specifications and analyses. But in the absence of any appreciable political movement toward the establishment of Langian market socialism, such relatively extemporaneous quibbles as these are apparently all that is required to relegate the proposal to impotence and irrelevance, despite the fact that it was based upon a very sophisticated and up-to-date appreciation of contemporary economic theory.

Oskar Lange was deeply immersed in advanced economic theory at the time he wrote "On the Economic Theory of Socialism," and perhaps his specific plan of market socialism is indeed too abstract and inflexible for the real world. But even if we were to conclude that the specific Langian plan of market socialism is indeed unpromising, there are other concepts of market socialism which may be deserving of consideration. Three well-defined concepts of market socialism to be found in the comparative economic systems literature, aside from the Langian concept, are as follows: (1) service market socialism; (2) cooperative market socialism; (3) pragmatic market socialism.[12] Of the three, the pragmatic market socialist proposal envisions an economy that would be the most similar to the market capitalist economy as it presently exists in the United States, the Western European nations, and in similar nations. After brief comments on service market socialism and cooperative market socialism, we shall proceed on to a more elaborate description and analysis of pragmatic market socialism.

Service market socialism envisions publicly owned business enterprises operating as nonprofit enterprises: the typical real-world analogue would be the nationalized public enterprise as it is known in Great Britain and elsewhere. In principle, the operations of a conventional public enterprise are guided by a social welfare maximization objective. The practical problem is that social welfare, unlike profit, is not directly and objectively observable: this makes it very difficult to evaluate the success being achieved by the enterprise in pursuing its goal. In practice, objectively quantifiable measures such as physical output, financial revenues, average cost, employment, and so on, are used as partial proxies for social welfare, but doubts remain as to how well any particular weighted average of such measures correlates with the overall social welfare criterion. Over the last 20 years there has been a world-wide trend toward privatization of public enterprises, and on reorienting the remaining public enterprises more toward standard commercial motivation, i.e., the pursuit of profit. This apparently reflects a general trend toward restored confidence in the desirable properties of profit maximization, notwithstanding the imperfect competition theory developed by Joan Robinson, and other important caveats about profit maximization raised by economic theory, such as external effects. In any event, a great many individuals at the present time, intellectuals and otherwise, seem ready to assume a very strong propensity in traditional, nonprofit public enterprise toward inefficiency and ineffectiveness. Such a propensity might effectively counteract any theoretical advantages which nonprofit enterprise possesses in regard to the direct pursuit of social welfare.

Cooperative market socialism envisions the direct ownership and control of business enterprises by their current employees. The idea of labor-management or self-management has been important in socialist thinking from even before the work of Karl Marx, and there have been a number of efforts to put the idea into practice in the real world, ranging from the Soviet collective farm to a number of wood processing firms in the U.S. Pacific Northwest. No doubt the most ambitious attempt to put the cooperative production principle into practice has been the Yugoslavian economy. Although mainstream economics has never been particularly sympathetic toward cooperative business enterprise, since the 1950s there has been a proliferation of theoretical work on the subject.[13] This theoretical work is extremely heterogeneous, but it is probably safe to say that much if not most of it seems motivated by a desire to put into terms of formal theory the traditional skepticism of economists toward cooperative production. The traditional skepticism seems grounded fundamentally on a suspicion that a business enterprise governed by its own employees and not subject to an outside ownership interest would lack an adequate degree of internal discipline and cohesion to constitute an effective competitor in the economic marketplace. The proponents of cooperation emphasize alleged favorable incentive effects of the employees working for themselves rather than for outside owners, and they attribute the poor record of success of cooperative firms relative to conventional firms to prejudice and discrimination against the former by banks and other financial intermediaries.

The service and cooperative concepts of market socialism are far less rigidly theoretical than the original Langian proposal. They are more general and no doubt a large part of their potential effectiveness in practice would depend on the specific institutional forms through which they might be realized. However, both plans of market socialism would necessarily involve rather radical departures from the economic status quo under capitalism. Under contemporary capitalism, most business enterprises are guided by a relatively straightforward and uncomplicated profit maximization incentive. Most of them are also subject to an outside ownership interest, in that the vast majority of ownership instruments issued by the corporation (stocks, bonds, and so on) are held by individuals who are not employees of the corporation. Whatever the potential liabilities of profit maximization as a guide to business enterprise, and whatever the psychological disadvantages inherent in the fact that the employees "are working for outsiders rather than for themselves," the fact remains that the contemporary capitalist system—at least as it operates in the industrialized and economically advanced nations of the West—has achieved an historically unprecedented level of economic efficiency and effectiveness. In light of the high level of economic success, a very cautious and conservative approach toward socialism would seem to be indicated.

Of course, the most cautious and conservative approach of all would be to leave the capitalistic status quo entirely untouched on the basis of the adage: "If it isn't broken, don't fix it." But for all of its marvelous successes, the contemporary capitalist system does suffer from the moral liability of extremely unequal distribution of a substantial flow of capital property income that strongly appears to be unearned. Apologists for capitalism have proposed a plethora of justifications for capital property income: corporate supervision, investment analysis, enterprise, entrepreneurship, risk-taking, and so on and so forth. But the very multiplicity of these justifications may suggest that no one of them is legitimate. The fact is that when subjected to careful and critical scrutiny, none of these putative justifications ring true. Admittedly, at the present moment in the Western capitalist nations, very few individuals are subjecting these justifications to careful and critical scrutiny. This is unfortunate, but the situation may change as the future unfolds.

Pragmatic market socialism represents an effort to achieve a reasonable and attractive compromise between the objectives of maintaining economic efficiency and of substantially equalizing the distribution of capital property return.[14] It proposes that publicly owned business enterprises be operated according to the same simple and straightforward profit maximization incentive presently operative under the market capitalist system. The profit maximization incentive would be enforced upon the executives responsible for day-to-day administration of these corporations by essentially the same mechanisms operative under capitalism. There are three major mechanisms involved: (1) direct competition among firms for markets and profits; (2) competition among firms for investment capital in the financial markets; (3) disciplinary pressure from outside owners with an interest in profits. With respect to the first mechanism, although most firms operating in any given industry would be publicly owned, they would be separately and independently evaluated in terms of their respective long-term rates of profitability. At stake would be the same generous managerial salaries, bonuses, and perquisites utilized under capitalism. With respect to the second mechanism, although there would be no private investors operating in financial capital markets under pragmatic market socialism, institutional investors such as banks, insurance companies, and so on, would provide investment capital to firms on the same competitive, profit-seeking basis which holds under capitalism. The third mechanism would be the discipline of the outside ownership interest. Whereas under capitalism the interests of outside private owners are represented by boards of directors elected by stockholders, under pragmatic market socialism the outside public ownership interest would be represented by an agent of the Bureau of Public Ownership (BPO). The BPO agent's authority would in key respects be analogous to the board of directors' authority: in particular, the BPO agent would exercise the right of dismissal over the high executives of a corporation displaying inadequate long-term profitability.

The net profits and interest generated by publicly owned corporations would be paid over to the Bureau of Public Ownership. The Bureau would retain a small fraction of this capital property return, not to exceed five percent, to cover its administrative expenses and the incentive bonuses of its agents, and the balance would be distributed to the general population as a social dividend supplement paid out proportionately to wage and salary income. That is, each working person's entitlement to social dividend income would be proportional to his or her earned labor income. Dividends, interest, and other forms of capital property income could not be paid to private individuals under pragmatic market socialism (aside from certain limited exceptions), but the loss of capital property income to the individual household would be compensated by the gain of social dividend income. Owing to the extreme inequality of capital property ownership under contemporary capitalism, in all probability well over 90 percent of the population in an advanced capitalist nation would receive more social dividend income on an annual basis under pragmatic market socialism than they currently receive capital property income under capitalism.

There would be certain exceptions to the general principle of public ownership of business enterprise. Public ownership would apply to *large, established* corporations. Private ownership would be maintained in the case of small businesses such as family farms, retail outlets, and professional proprietorships and partnerships. Private ownership would also be maintained in the case of entrepreneurial business firms, regardless of the scale which they achieve. An entrepreneurial firm is defined as a firm in which the founder-owner remains active as the chief executive officer. One of the most effective allegations of capitalist apologetics is that capital property income is a reward to the productive contribution of entrepreneurship. There is only a very small kernel of truth in this allegation. The vast majority of product and process innovation, physical capital investment, development of new markets, and so on and so forth, is carried on by large, established corporations whose founders departed management many decades in the past. Similarly, the vast majority of capital property income is received by capitalists whose capital property wealth was gained through inheritance and financial speculation, as opposed to productive entrepreneurship. Nevertheless, very often entrepreneurship plays an important catalytic role in the modern economy, and pragmatic market socialism would maintain essentially the same strong financial incentives to individual entrepreneurs as exist under capitalism.

One popular contention of capitalist apologetics is that while conceivably socialism might display a certain amount of static efficiency, its dynamic performance would be abysmal, owing to inadequate incentives to investment, innovation, entrepreneurship, and so on and so forth. This contention is largely falsified simply by objective observation of the real-world economy. The overwhelming majority of investment and innovation is carried out by established corporations in their continuing quest for profits: these corporations also account for a substantial proportion of entrepreneurial activity by establishing subsidiary firms in new markets. In addition to activity by established nonfinancial corporations, there is also a great deal of dynamic activity by established financial intermediary corporations. All this would remain the same under pragmatic market socialism, as would private entrepreneurial activity owing to the exclusion of genuinely entrepreneurial firms from the usual public ownership provision. Finally, investment and entrepreneurship under pragmatic market socialism would be given further institutional support through the establishment of two new national government agencies: the National Investment Banking System (NIBS) and the National Entrepreneurial Investment System (NEIB). Both of these agencies would be largely financed from public revenue, and they would allocate their appropriations to the publicly owned business enterprise sector on essentially the same profit-seeking guidelines used by the conventional financial intermediaries (banks, insurance companies, etc.) which are already active under capitalism and which would remain active under pragmatic market socialism. Owing to the additional institutional support provided to investment and entrepreneurship under pragmatic market socialism, it is altogether possible that this economic system would actually allocate a larger proportion of raw saving resources to business physical capital investment in new and existing firms than does the capitalist economic system today. Therefore allegations of dynamic inefficiency are no more convincing, when applied to pragmatic market socialism, than are allegations of static inefficiency.

The central purpose of pragmatic market socialism is to achieve a greater degree of equality in the distribution of the capital property return produced by business firms in the profit-maximizing economic processes required for efficient allocation and utilization of the nonhuman factors of production. There is not a primary emphasis in the proposal, as there is in other socialist proposals, on the potential enhancement of the static or dynamic efficiency of the economy. Of course, the drawback to these other socialist proposals is that in the pursuit of a higher level of efficiency, they specify very substantial departures from the economic status quo under capitalism, a status quo which is recognized as being highly efficient, at least in some nations. As has been emphasized, there are no radical departures from the economic status quo in the pragmatic market socialist proposal. Nevertheless, there are at least two important reasons why the pragmatic market socialist economy might display a higher level of economic efficiency than the contemporary capitalist economy.

The first possibility is that the conversion of a flow of unearned capital property income into a flow of social dividend income proportional to earned labor income might provide an effective incentive to additional labor and higher production. According to conventional economic theory, unearned income flows are a deterrent to labor, and there is every indication that capital property income is indeed largely unearned. Also according to conventional economic thinking, the supply curve of labor is upward-sloping: people will generally provide more labor if their rate of remuneration, in the form of wages and salaries, is higher. The social dividend income supplement under pragmatic market socialism implies an increase in the effective wage and salary rate applicable to every household. Thus according to conventional economic thinking, this should augment the supply of labor and the level of production.

The second possibility is that of stronger discipline among the corps of high corporation executives responsible for the daily administration of business enterprise. Under modern capitalism, there has developed a very pronounced separation of ownership and control. In the typical large contemporary corporation, the outside ownership interest is sub-divided over hundreds and sometimes thousands of stockholders. The dispersion of the outside ownership interest over a host of unorganized individuals has reduced the effectiveness of this interest among high corporation executives. In the current period, high corporation executives do not stand in awe of boards of directors representing the stockholders, rather these boards are mostly managed and manipulated as mere adjuncts to the administrative function. What this means in practice is that the corporation's performance must normally sink to abysmal levels before the board of directors becomes a serious threat to the incumbent managers. Under pragmatic market socialism, the outside public ownership interest would be highly concentrated in the hands of the single Bureau of Public Ownership (BPO) agent assigned to any particular corporation. The possibility of dismissal of high corporation executives for inadequate profitability would be considerably higher than it is today under capitalism, and there is a good likelihood that this would lead to a more effective and professional prosecution of the vital function of business enterprise management. Owing to the pervasive role of large-scale corporate business enterprise in the modern economy, a higher level of individual performance in the various executive suites would foster a higher level of overall economic performance.

None of this is to deny that the capitalist economic system has been a powerful engine of economic progress throughout the modern historical period. The high living standards of the advanced nations are directly attributable to the application of sophisticated technology to large-scale production under the corporate form of business organization. But the same evolutionary processes which brought about the modern mode of production have at the same time rendered the function of capital ownership, in and of itself, vestigial and superfluous. The essential Marxian insight, dating back more than 150 years, is that production has become social rather than individual, and that individual ownership of capital is no longer fully consistent with the social application and utilization of capital in the production process. The various apologetic arguments for capital property income, which may have possessed some credibility when handicraft production was the rule and not the exception, are no longer even remotely applicable at the threshold of the twenty-first century. The further development of the capitalist economy over the last 150 years has confirmed this fundamental Marxian insight. In the contemporary era, the owning capitalist, as such, has become no more than a parasitical rentier. It is time to move beyond capitalism to some appropriate form of socialism. Pragmatic market socialism represents a cautious evolutionary step beyond contemporary capitalism.

An impressive case may be made for pragmatic market socialism simply on the basis of the enhanced current welfare of the populations of the capitalist nations. Owing to the substantial overlap between the practical operations of pragmatic market socialism and contemporary capitalism, there is little likelihood of an appreciable loss in efficiency. Indeed, as we have seen, possibilities exist for a somewhat higher level of efficiency under pragmatic market socialism. At the same time, social dividend distribution of capital property return would eliminate the inequity of highly unequal distribution of this unearned income flow under capitalism, and thereby eliminate the unseemly parasitical element which is inherent in contemporary capitalism. All this might be termed the "internal" case for pragmatic market socialism—the case which would be relevant even in the absence of ideological conflict between the communist and noncommunist nations. However, given that this conflict exists, we perceive an important "external" addendum to this case: the possibility that the inauguration of pragmatic market socialism in the Western capitalist nations might significantly ameliorate the ideological conflict situation, and thereby significantly increase the probability of permanent peaceful coexistence, important arms reduction, and the foundation of the Federal Union of Democratic Nations.[15]

From the Bolshevik Revolution of 1917 down to the recent past, the Soviet state and the various other more recently established communist states have promulgated an extremely negative view of the capitalist economic system, and indeed, of the overall social superstructure founded upon this economic system. Not only is capitalism allegedly responsible for the fundamental economic problems of exploitation and depression, these fundamental economic problems are held to generate a host of higher-order social problems, including crime, drug abuse, alienation, racism, sexism, militarism, imperialism, and so on and so forth. While there has been considerable progress made toward the amelioration of the intensity of this critique of the Western social system, the generally negative appraisal is still basically intact. Most citizens of the advanced capitalist nations reject the traditional communist appraisal of the capitalist economic and social system as logically muddled, empirically false, and rhetorically overblown. Nevertheless, it seems inescapable that this appraisal has been regarded as at least "basically" true by hundreds of millions of adherents to communism throughout the twentieth century. As soon as it is recognized that most if not all of these people have sincerely believed in this highly negative judgment on capitalism, it becomes obvious that to the extent they have regarded themselves as decent, ethical, and responsible human beings, they would have considered it their moral duty to assist those in the capitalist nations seeking to bring about socialist transformations. It would appear that the populations of the communist nations have sincerely believed that they were doing the great majority of the populations of the noncommunist nations a very large favor by trying to undermine capitalism and establish socialism in these nations.

Unfortunately for the cause of world peace, the great majority of those living in the noncommunist nations, particularly in the industrially advanced capitalist nations, at the present time perceive only minor flaws in the operation of the contemporary capitalist system, and at the same time they judge the potential flaws of socialism to be much more serious. Therefore they interpret the aspirations of the communist ideological system toward world-wide socialization as completely erroneous, perverse, and hazardous. They find it very difficult to conceive that, given the currently available evidence, anyone could sincerely believe in the Marxist condemnation of capitalism. Such beliefs must therefore be the result of ignorance or stupidity, or alternatively they must be feigned and hypocritical. Ignorance may reasonably be attributed to the "masses" of communist adherents, but it is hardly reasonably attributed to their elite leadership. Similarly, it is not reasonable to attribute stupidity to the elite leadership.

That leaves only hypocrisy. Thus the speculation that the communist leaders fully recognize the economic and ethical defensibility and worthiness of the contemporary capitalist system, but continue to preach and support what they know to be a false vilification of it, so that they may retain and augment their own personal power and prestige. In an extreme form which is not accepted by many reputable authorities on the Soviet Union, the Soviet leaders have cynically exploited communist ideology as an instrumentality toward the establishment of a Russian world empire equivalent to the German world empire conceived by Hitler. But the "hypocrisy hypothesis" itself seems rather farfetched, at least on the basis of a commonsensical appreciation of human psychology. Sane and well-adjusted people simply cannot tolerate acting in a manner that they recognize to be grossly immoral, and surely it would be grossly immoral to espouse a perverse social philosophy for purposes of personal benefit. For their own psychological well-being, the Soviet and other communist leaders simply *must* have believed that capitalism has an adverse effect on the welfare of the people who live under it. But this observation seems to be bringing us back to ignorance or stupidity, which as just indicated have their own drawbacks as explanations of adherence to communist ideology, particularly when applied to the high leadership.

There is one possible answer to this riddle: that the communists have been *correct* regarding capitalism, and that indeed socialism (or at least some possible form of socialism) is in fact preferable to capitalism on overall social welfare grounds. The pragmatic market socialist system proposed here would quite likely enjoy a level of economic efficiency at least comparable to, and possibly superior to, that of contemporary capitalism. At the same time it would substantially equalize, and therefore render more fair and equitable, the distribution of unearned property income produced by the efficient market allocation of nonhuman factors of production. The difference between the view of capitalism implied by the pragmatic market socialist proposal, and that embodied in the official communist view of capitalism, is a difference in degree and not in essence. According to the official communist view, capitalism is "evil," and it has a "drastic" diminishing effect on social welfare. According to the view expressed herein, capitalism is merely "adverse," and it has only a "significant" diminishing effect on social welfare.

If we accept for purposes of argument (or possibly out of conviction) that contemporary capitalism is indeed inferior to a feasible socialist alternative such as pragmatic market socialism, are we not left with another riddle—the riddle of why it is that hundreds of millions of people in the noncommunist world do not presently recognize this to be the case? Does not this failure to recognize the superiority of socialism suggest that hundreds of millions of people in the noncommunist countries are either ignorant, stupid, or hypocritical? These are certainly valid questions. But they bring to light a fact which, however unpalatable and extraordinary it may be, seems to be inescapable: one way or the other, hundreds of millions of people in the modern world have been in serious error. Either capitalism is generally preferable to socialism, or socialism is generally preferable to capitalism, or neither capitalism nor socialism is generally preferable to the other. If the first is true, then hundreds of millions of proponents of socialism, comprising principally the great majority of the populations of the communist nations, have been in serious error. If the second is true, then hundreds of millions of proponents of capitalism, comprising principally the great majority of the populations of the noncommunist nations, have been in serious error. Finally, if the third is true, then all of them have been in serious error. There is no avoiding the conclusion of massive error. Once the certainty of massive error is acknowledged and absorbed, one can examine more calmly and objectively the question of where the error lies. In particular, it does not amount to a particularly strong argument for capitalism that hundreds of millions of people in the noncommunist nations believe in capitalism.

Quite possibly an important reason for the intractability of the contemporary ideological conflict between adherents to communism and opponents of communism is that both sides are partially correct. The conflict between communism and its opponents is based on not one but at least three major issues, which may be listed in probable order of importance as follows: (1) whether a socialist economic system or a capitalist economic system, all other things being equal, generates higher social welfare; (2) whether a centralized, one-party political system or a decentralized, multi-party political system, all other things being equal, generates higher social welfare; (3) whether a relatively centralized system of economic planning or a relatively decentralized system of market allocation, all other things being equal, generates higher social welfare.

It is the firm judgment of the present author that with respect to the first area of social choice, communist ideology has indeed been correct all along: a socialist economic system is preferable to a capitalist economic system. But this judgment is complemented by an equally firm judgment that with respect to the second and third areas of social choice, noncommunist ideology has been correct: the multi-party political system is preferable to the one-party political system, and the market system is preferable to the planning system.

This partial perception of truth on both sides could be responsible for the intransigence of the contemporary ideological conflict situation, and for its reluctance to yield to the ordinary processes and conclusions of human rationality. Communists have tended to focus intently upon the issue of socialism versus capitalism, because on that issue they happen to be correct. Noncommunists have tended to focus intently upon the issues of democracy versus oligarchy and market versus planning, because on those issues they happen to be correct. Because of the emotional intensity of the conflict, due mainly to the possibility of nuclear war erupting between the two sides, both sides have found it very difficult to disentangle the separate issues and examine each one in isolation. Rather everything tends to be lumped together: noncommunists have tended to view socialism as a threat to democracy and the market, communists have tended to decry "bourgeois democracy" and "the anarchy of the market" as contradictory to socialism.

It was asked above how it could be that hundreds of millions of human individuals could hold erroneous ideological beliefs. Three possibilities were suggested: ignorance, stupidity, or hypocrisy. Of the three possibilities, "ignorance" is no doubt the primary culprit. In particular, it is the widespread ignorance in the noncommunist world at the present time that a fully viable and satisfactory socialist alternative to contemporary capitalism does indeed exist: namely the pragmatic market socialist alternative. If simple awareness of this alternative could be sufficiently disseminated, and the appropriate social action taken, this would strike to the very heart of the contemporary ideological conflict situation which continues to seriously threaten world peace and human welfare, and which still stands as a major impediment to world government.

C. REFORM IN THE EAST

If indeed it is true that the ideological conflict between communism and noncommunism is based upon three separate issues and not one, the implementation of pragmatic market socialism in the Western nations would address only one of the three. It could be argued that the remaining two issues could prevent a sufficient amount of

ideological harmonization to allow important progress toward rapprochement. This is of course within the realm of possibility. However, a careful examination of traditional communist ideology
suggests strongly that its basic impetus derives from its complete
contempt for the capitalist economic system, and that its expressed
disdain for "bourgeois democracy" and "the anarchy of the market"
are relatively minor considerations of little independent significance.
In the traditional communist view of the world, political democracy
and the market system are not evil in themselves, but only derive their
negative aspects from the existence of capitalism. Let us consider in
turn political democracy and market allocation.

Political Democracy. Communist ideology has never taken a dis-
paraging stand toward democracy per se, defined in general terms as
government of, by, and for the people. Indeed, the Soviet government
and other communist governments have always asserted that communist social systems were fully democratic in this general sense.
Scorn and contempt has only been heaped upon "bourgeois
democracy," that is, Western-style, multi-party, open-election
democracy of the sort operative in such capitalist nations as the
United States, Britain, France, and so on. The reason for the scorn
and contempt is that the democratic trappings (multiple parties and
open elections) are alleged to serve the purpose only of concealing
the fact of social domination by the capitalist class, of creating in the
people the delusion that they are the masters of their own destiny.
According to the argument, the capitalist class not only biases public
opinion against socialism through its manipulation of the privately
owned media of communication, but it furthermore exercises direct
control over key public officials by financing the election campaigns
only of those individuals whose loyalty to the capitalist status quo is
fully demonstrable and unquestionable.[16]

While communist ideology undoubtedly exaggerates the direct
power and influence of capitalists in social decision-making, there
may well be some kernels of truth in the argument, so that the
abolition of capitalism in the West would achieve a somewhat more
equal distribution of political power, and consequently a somewhat
more authentic form of democracy. This judgment naturally
presumes the preservation under pragmatic market socialism of all

the democratic institutions and procedures to which the Western noncommunist nations are accustomed: freedom of speech and the press, rights of political organization and activity, and periodic open elections for important government offices. If one reads traditional communist critiques of "bourgeois democracy" carefully, one discovers that these critiques would be drastically deflated, even to the point of complete collapse, were the nations against which they are directed to be socialist rather than capitalist. These critiques only make sense if they are applied to capitalist nations.

It is certainly the case that other arguments may be advanced against Western-style democracy, aside from its alleged role in cloaking and dissimulating capitalistic exploitation and domination. Prior to the rise of the modern democracies, conservative apologists for aristocracy and monarchy warned that democracy would inevitably lead to the rise of base and uncultured demagogues, among whose senseless and erratic policies would surely be counted the abolition of meritorious distinction and the leveling of society. In the twentieth century, fascist ideologues added new arguments against democracy: that political debates needlessly divide the people, and that periodic open elections hamper the sort of bold and decisive leadership under which nations best flourish and progress.[17] Although there are many practical similarities between fascist oligarchy and communist oligarchy—and these similarities were particularly obvious and striking during the contemporaneous dominions of Hitler and Stalin—the difference is that unlike fascist ideology, communist ideology never denigrated the term "democracy," nor has it stridently proclaimed fascist-style arguments against democracy in its critique of Western democracy and its defense of the communist political system.

As for the absence of Western democratic institutions and procedures in the Soviet Union and the other communist nations, communist ideologues preferred to deal with this question by ignoring or evading it. On rare occasions when they did address it, they relied mainly on two arguments. The first is that these institutions and procedures are unnecessary under communism, because the abolition of capitalism abrogates the social divisiveness inherent in a class society, and absolves the various classes from forming separate political parties to represent their interests. This first argument, in itself, clearly suggests no positive problems arising from a multi-party system within a socialist (i.e., classless) society. In other words, it could not serve as a serious basis for ideological dispute between pragmatic market socialist nations and communist nations. The second argument is that the communist nations cannot afford the divisive party politics of the Western democratic nations because of the existence of a hostile capitalist outside world. This argument was used to justify the authoritarian Soviet regime since its beginning. The argument actually represents a muted echo of the fascist argument against democracy, although it differs from the latter in its implication that the suppression of political debate and free public choice is merely a temporary expedient and is required only so long as capitalism continues to pose a threat. Once again, this argument hardly constitutes a fundamental assault on the validity of Western-style democracy. As a matter of fact, it suggests that were pragmatic market socialism to come about in the West, and the threat from the "hostile capitalist outside world" to be thereby eliminated, more rapid progress might be made thereafter within the communist nations toward a more relaxed, tolerant, and open political system.

It suggests that in due course, conditions might be achieved by which the communist nations might be accepted as authentic democracies even by Western standards.[18] This might even be accomplished without benefit of formal departure from the principle of the one-party state. For example, formally organized and highly independent subgroups might be allowed to operate within the Communist Party, and these subgroups would compete in free elections for high Party positions. Alternatively, the Communist Party might authorize the formation of independent political parties which which would be allowed to compete openly with the Communist Party itself for elected state offices. Traditionally, these possibilities would have been seen as intolerable "factionalism" within the communist nations. But if we think ahead to a possible future in which ideological controversies and war-risk are subsiding at a rapid rate, they might ultimately be deemed a progressive reform and put into practice.

Already we have witnessed in the recent past very considerable progress in the ex-Soviet Union toward freer discussion of political issues and the elimination of Communist Party control over the state apparatus. But the gains which have been made to this point are still relatively limited, and even these limited gains appear decidedly tenous. Relatively few free elections have been held so far, and there is not yet a fully functioning multi-party system. Although the Communist Party apparatus has been formally deprived of its authority, no doubt there is a tremendous amount of behind-the-scenes activity by Party members and sympathizers. Economic difficulties are making it difficult for the elected leadership to gain the degree of public support and legitimacy necessary for stable democracy. Obviously there remains a long way to go before the ex-Soviet Union will be clearly recognizable as a solid, permanent, democratic polity. And, of course, at this point the communist nations of the Far East, in particular the People's Republic of China, have an even longer way to go.

Perhaps the implicit admission by the Western nations, through their adoption of pragmatic market socialism, that they were previously in error on the socialism-versus-capitalism issue, would inspire all the communist nations to admit openly that contested elections produce a superior form of democracy than do uncontested elections. Our everyday experience of conflict resolution suggests strongly that voluntary and unilateral admissions of error on one side frequently elicit similar admissions on the other side, and lead ultimately to a more or less definitive and permanent solution of the problem. This is not to suggest that the democratization of the communist nations should be sought as a quid pro quo for the socialization of the noncommunist nations. Rather this convergence should occur naturally: through the recognition by the noncommunist populations that their own best interests lie with socialism, and through the recognition by the communist populations that their own best interests lie with Western-style democratic institutions and procedures.

Market Allocation. Even the most conservative communist ideologues are by now reasonably well aware of the fact that socialism does not necessarily require or imply the establishment of Soviet-style central planning. The basic institutions and procedures of central planning were indeed not established in the U.S.S.R. until more than ten years after the Bolshevik Revolution of 1917 socialized the Russian economy. The purpose of central planning was to guarantee the rapid industrialization of the Russian economy as a means of averting the invasion and conquest of Russia by hostile capitalist nations. Quite a high level of industrialization has now been achieved, and there is consequently a diminished need for central planning. In fact, Soviet economists kept on talking about the need for major economic reforms, decentralization of decision-making, individual responsibility, and commercial motivation ever since the death of Stalin. Over the years some fairly dramatic proclamations were issued by the Soviet government in pursuit of these goals. With the advent of Gorbachev and the perestroika campaign, the rhetoric of reform reached what might be described as a fever pitch.

Despite all the talk and all the proclamations, in the judgment of most Western analysts very little tangible, substantive, meaningful progress was actually made toward dismantling the central planning system established during the Stalinist era. This remained the case no less under Mikhail Gorbachev than under his predecessors. Soviet-style central planning was established in all the other communist nations shortly after their communizations in the post-1945 era, and perhaps because of their shorter planning tradition, most of these nations made much more progress toward the economic decentralization goal than the Soviet Union itself. This was true of most of the Eastern European nations, and more recently of Red China. With the effective dissolution of the Warsaw Pact in the late 1980s and early 1990s, the Eastern European economies have departed even further from the traditional communist economic orthodoxy. Even so, Western authorities on the various other communist economies continue to perceive a great deal of government intervention with business decision-making, and continue to view them as substantially less market-oriented than the major noncommunist economies. An exception to this general rule, of course, is East Germany, which has been effectively reabsorbed into West Germany, and which therefore retains very little evidence of its historic encounter with Soviet-style socialism.

Those who study various past disputes within the communist bloc of nations will find a body of literature by Soviet ideologues in which they chided and chastised other communist nations, particularly those in Eastern Europe, for what they judged to be excessively enthusiastic experimentation with commercial motivation and market allocation. In fact, the term "market socialism" is encountered in some of these critiques, as a designation for the recommendations of certain Eastern European economists considered to be excessively radical in their espousal of market allocation. But while some of this criticism leaned in the direction of asserting an ideologically fundamental "betrayal of socialism," it did not usually go as far as an explicit statement of such a charge.[19] The general impression gained from this literature is that the authors believed that market socialism would be an unwise and badly performing variant of socialism—not that it would bring back the capitalist class and capitalist exploitation. Market socialism was criticized more on economic grounds of alleged inefficiency, rather than on ideological grounds that it constitutes "capitalism in disguise."

The erstwhile Soviet critique of market socialism in the Eastern European nations is in some ways rather reminiscent of the critique made by some conservative U.S. economists of the "runaway welfare state" in the Scandinavian nations. As convinced as these U.S. economists may be of the adverse effects of excessive egalitarianism and overgenerous welfare benefits, they will still usually concede that the welfare state is not, strictly speaking, "socialism," and they will certainly recognize the distinction between the welfare state and "communism." Thus the "runaway welfare state" in Scandinavia is not regarded by these economists as a fundamental and dangerous ideological enemy to the capitalistic status quo. Similarly orthodox communist ideologues in the Soviet Union did not regard market socialism as practiced in Eastern Europe as a fundamental and dangerous ideological enemy to the socialistic status quo. Until very recently, any actual effort to reestablish capitalism in the Eastern European orbit of Soviet power would have been immediately quashed by Soviet military forces. But "market socialism," even in a more extreme form than that actually attained, would not have brought about Soviet military intervention. There is an important line between what Soviet ideologues considered merely inefficient, and what they considered ideologically unacceptable.

Commmunist ideologues have traditionally deemed contemporary capitalism in the United States and elsewhere to be ideologically intolerable—let alone unacceptable. But if the United States and other capitalist countries were to abolish capitalism and establish pragmatic market socialist economies, even the most conservative communist ideologues would at most consider this to be merely an inferior and relatively inefficacious form of socialism relative to centrally planned socialism—but in no way either intolerable or even unacceptable. Of course, in the West the prevalent judgment has always been that it is central planning which is inefficient—not market allocation. In a post-capitalist world, with this judgment no longer being rendered suspect through its capitalistic associations, communist ideologues would be inclined to take it more seriously than they do now.

The possibility has already been raised that the socialization of the noncommunist world might indirectly inspire a democratization of communist political systems. It might also indirectly inspire the abandonment of Soviet-style central planning in communist nations and the implementation of more market-oriented institutions and motivations—institutions and motivations closely aligned to those of pragmatic market socialism. But whether these two additional convergences occur or not, the convergence achieved on the issue of social ownership of capital plant and machinery utilized by large-scale business enterprises would by itself deflate the contemporary ideological controversy between communist and noncommunist nations to a small fraction of its present magnitude.

Of the two possible areas for additional ideological harmonization—political democracy and market allocation—clearly the first is the more significant. The level of reliance on market allocation versus direct government intervention in economic processes is a relatively nebulous and unemotional issue in comparison with the issue of democracy. Although the Soviet Union was long renowned as the formulator of "centrally planned socialism," the fact is that even during the Stalinist period, as well as afterwards, the Soviet economy has always relied quite heavily on market allocation—at least relative to a theoretical ideal of central planning. First and foremost, the Soviet economy always remained a money economy, in which all physical exchanges are matched by financial exchanges. Under pure central planning, no purpose would be served by financial exchanges and they would not occur. Secondly, the accounting categories of profit and interest have been retained, and the success criteria applied to the managers of industrial enterprises have always involved profitability to at least some extent. In a more general sense, the Soviet economy has always relied heavily on material incentives to effort at every level. From the beginning, strict egalitarianism was eschewed on grounds of maintaining material motivations to effort. In sum, Soviet central planning has always been highly adulterated in many ways by market mechanisms.

At the same time, the free enterprise economy of the United States is subject to a tremendous amount of government intervention. The Federal Reserve Board and the Treasury Department engage in anticyclical policy, there are dozens of regulatory agencies overseeing business activity (the Food and Drug Administration, the Environmental Protection Agency, the Occupational Health and Safety Administration, etc.), individual households are subject to progressive federal income taxation and many other forms of taxation, there is a large welfare system (the Social Security Administration, state unemployment insurance, state and local subsidization of education, and so on and so forth). All this very much adulterates the reliance on market allocation displayed by the United States economy. And so in practice the United States and the ex-Soviet Union are not as far apart on the matter of market reliance as is often imagined.

The issue of democracy is much more potent than the issue of the free market. "Free enterprise" is an important component of the American way of life, which is to be defended at all costs against the menace of communism. But a far nobler and more important component of that way of life is the "freedom and democracy" embodied in the United States political system. One can easily imagine a genuinely democratic nation which has implemented so much government taxation and regulation of business enterprise, and of economic activity in general, that the term "free enterprise" would clearly constitute mere rhetorical hyperbole. Indeed, it is arguable that this is already the case in the United States. But the really important thing to the American people is and remains democratic governance—so that whatever government intervention in the economy takes place is duly authorized by a majority of the citizen body.

Of course, Soviet-style Gosplan central planning of physical output seems to be a form of state intervention in the economy that goes well beyond anything currently present in the U.S. economy. But if we imagine a genuinely democratic Russian polity in which the voters had approved by a clear majority the continuation of the Gosplan central planning system, it is difficult to imagine the U.S. population being very disturbed about it. In the West the central planning system is thought of as overcentralized and inefficient, but its primary liability in an ideological sense is that it represents the "substitution of planners' preferences for the peoples' preferences." In other words, consumer sovereignty is overridden by a planning bureaucracy responsible to an oligarchic government. But if the planning bureaucracy were responsible to a democratically elected government, then this situation would not represent nearly as grievous an affront to the principle of individual freedom. The central issue is definitely democracy and not the market. If an adequate degree of ideological convergence were achieved on the two issues of socialism versus capitalism and democracy versus oligarchy, then the issue of market versus planning would in all probability take care of itself.

The possibility of ideological harmonization is being intensively discussed at the present time, but in the West the discussion is mostly in terms of what has been termed here "ideological capitulation." According to the ideological capitulation scenario, the communist East will abandon socialism for capitalism, oligarchy for democracy, and planning for the market. If this scenario does in fact come to pass, it would no doubt be a marvelous transformation and it would clear away the bulk of the ideological impediments to world government. But Western analysts might be rather too optimistic about the likelihood of this scenario.

The present chapter has developed an alternative scenario based on the notion of genuine "ideological convergence" rather than "ideological capitulation." The ideological convergence scenario envisions a simultaneous movement by both East and West toward a form of democratic market socialism designated "pragmatic market socialism." This system would incorporate socialism from the communist system of thought, and democracy and market allocation from the noncommunist system of thought. As it incorporates ideas from both sides of the ideological controversy, it represents a compromise middle ground, the acceptance of which would not impose severe psychological strain on either side. If this scenario does in fact come to pass, it would also represent a marvelous transformation which would clear away in one fell swoop the bulk of the ideological impediments to world government. It is an alternative worthy of serious consideration by both sides.

NOTES

1. Russia's post-World War II emergence as the United States' primary adversary on the international stage is examined in Harry and Bonaro Overstreet (1958), Eliot R. Goodman (1960), Williamn Knapp (1967), John Lewis Gaddis (1972), Fred Schwartz (1972), John W. Wheeler-Bennett and Anthony Nicholls (1972), and Edgar O'Ballance (1982).

2. Some illustrative statements by various Western authorities concerning the role of ideology in the post-World War II Cold War situation are as follows:

Raymond Aron (1973, p. 291): "The Soviet leaders...are too much in need of Marxist categories for giving a moral foundation to their power, they have been thinking too long in these categories, to give way to skepticism so soon. They continue to believe in the irreducible hostility of the two blocs as firmly as in the inevitability of their own victory."

Zbigniew Brzezinski (1962, p. 108): "The universality-of-goals aspect of Soviet foreign policy makes it clear that, while the concept of 'national interest' may not be irrelevant to an understanding of Communist foreign policy, to be useful it must be linked to the ultimate ideological objective. As far as Communist leaders are concerned, Soviet national interest is that which increases the power and capability of the USSR to promote Communism."

R. N. Carew-Hunt (1971, pp. 104): "But before surmising, as do some analysts, that the Soviet leadership cannot possibly believe in the myths it propounds, we should remind ourselves that no class or party ever finds it difficult to persuade itself of the soundness of the principles on which it bases its claim to rule. The Soviet leaders are fortified in this conviction by the very nature of their creed, and it would be strange indeed if they had remained unaffected. It has become second nature to these men to regard history as a dialectical process—one of incessant conflict between progressive and reactionary forces, which can only be resolved by the victory of the former. The division of the world into antagonistic camps, which is an article of faith, is simply the projection unto the international stage of the struggle within capitalist society between the bourgeoisie which history has condemned, and the proletariat, whose ultimate triumph it has decreed."

Thomas Hammond (1976, p. 55): "They may not be as fanatical as the Bolsheviks were in 1917, but they still look upon the idea of a Communist world as a desirable long-run goal... They probably get a visceral feeling of pleasure at the prospect of Communism winning out in yet another part of the world."

Joseph Himes (1980, p. 20, p. 114): "Establishment of a Marxist socio-economic system in Russia launched that nation on a career of aggressive conflict... The Marxist-Leninist ideology of the Soviet Union legitimizes the resort to political and military violence of many kinds to advance the cause of Communism in the world."

R. J. Rummel (1976, p. 253): "Indeed a major source of power in conflict is man's protective need. Thus, today's contending ideologies differ in their means, such as socialism versus capitalism, but all have as their primary end the improvment of man's lot. Thus, it is not man's selfish needs that generate most large conflicts nor, I will argue, his frustrations, but his inherent goodness, his inherent protectiveness, his inherent sociality."

John Stoessinger (1965, p. 41): "More broadly, ideology has lent a Jekyll-and-Hyde quality to Soviet behavior vis-a-vis the West. In one sense, the Soviet Union has de-emphasized ideology and has acted as a nation among nations; it has used diplomacy as an instrument of national policy; and it has participated in the League of Nations and the United Nations. But on another level, the Soviet Union has always considered itself as the citadel of a revolutionary ideology destined ultimately to dominate the world. Thus, while ideology cannot be considered the cause of Soviet expansion and, hence, of the East-West struggle, it is clearly one very important cause."

Adam Ulam (1971, p. 138): "We should not, however, go to the other extreme and assume that the rulers of Russia have remained totally unaffected by the doctrines in which they have been brought up and which they have been proclaiming. The relationship between ideology and action eludes a straightforward definition, but it is naive to assume that a group of men, even when endowed of totalitarian powers and with what is to an outsider an infinite possibility of political manipulation, can remain unaffected by their habits of thought and speech, and can indulge in unrestrained Machiavellian politics."

William Welch (1970, p. 26): "Finally, there is a measure of agreement on the conclusions as to the nature of Soviet conduct and its evolution derived from contemplating this record... There is little dissent to be found in the works of the sample from the following propositions: that Soviet conduct is hardly to be described as peaceable, that its aims include the spread of communism and expansion of Soviet influence, and that in the pursuit of these aims it is active, militant, and not too moral."

3. Some illustrative references on arms control and reduction during the Cold War period include Thomas C. Schelling and Morton H. Halperin (1961), John W. Spanier and Joseph L. Nogee (1962), Hedley Bull (1965), John Newhouse (1973), Wolfram F. Hanrieder (1979), Duncan L. Clarke (1979), Gerald Smith (1980), Bruce Russett (1983), Louis Rene Bares (1983), Julie Dahlitz (1983), Strobe Talbott (1979, 1984, 1988). For the Soviet viewpoint, see A. Y. Yefremov (1979) R. Faramazyan (1981), V. Kortunov (1982), Igor Usachev (1984).

4. The popular, professional, and polemical literature which traces the history of socialist thought is of course tremendous. The range of style and treatment is enormous, from popular surveys such as Edward Hyams (1974) through college textbooks such as Ben Aggar (1979) to scholarly magnum opi such as George D. H. Cole's five volumes (1953-1960) and Carl Landauer's two volumes (1960). There are also several documentary compendiums, such as those edited by Irving Howe (1976), Dan N. Jacobs (1979), and Emile Burns (1982). As by far the single most influential codifier of socialist thinking in history, Karl Marx has attracted numerous biographers and interpreters. Representative Western biographies include Franz Mehring (1948), Robert Payne (1968), David McLellan (1968), Fritz Raddatz (1978), and Jerrold Seigel (1978), while the Soviet view of Marx's life and work is represented by P. N. Fedoseyev et al (1973). Theoretical aspects and practical ramifications of Marxism as a whole are discussed in Alfred G. Meyer (1970), R. N. Berki (1975), W. H. C. Eddy (1979), Adam B. Ulam (1979), Wolfgang Leonhard (1979), David McLellan (1979), Joseph Martin (1980), Jack Lindsay (1981), N. Scott Arnold (1990). Marx's economics have been examined by Joan Robinson (1942), Paul Sweezy (1942), Ronald Meek (1956), Murray Wolfson (1964), Ernest Mandel (1962), Michio Morishima (1971), Paul Samuelson (1971), Meghnad Desai (1979), Ben Fine and Laurence Harris (1979), John Roemer (1981, 1982, 1988), Jacques Gouverneur (1983), Allen Oakley (1984, 1985), David Gordon (1990). The Soviet Russian version of the Marxist critique of capitalism is contained in numerous titles published by Progress Publishers of Moscow: some examples include L. Leontyev (1968), Y. Vargas (1968), M. Ryndina and G. Chernikov (1974), N. Inozerntsev (1974), A. G.

Mileikovsky (1975), G. A. Kozlov (1977), G. Chernikov (1980), V. Shemyatenkov (1981), Ya. Pevsner (1982), V. Afanasyev (1983), A. D. Smirnov et al (1984), A. N. Yakovlev (1987).

5. Nassau Senior is undoubtedly the best-known of the early nineteenth century apologists for capitalism—if only because of Marx's devastating critique of his "abstinence" theory of saving in Volume I of *Das Kapital* (Volume I, Chapter XXIV, Section 3). Prior to the Bolshevik Revolution of 1917 in Russia, there had been no real-world experience of any kind with socialism in the strict sense of public ownership of capital, and criticism of the notion therefore tended to focus explicitly on various hypothetical economic incentive and coordination problems. Typical of pre-Revolutionary capitalist apologetics are works by John Stuart Mill (*Chapters on Socialism*, 1879), Eugen von Böhm-Bawerk (*Karl Marx and the Close of His System*, 1896) and John Bates Clark (*The Distribution of Wealth*, 1899). Throughout the twentieth century, much of capitalist apologetics has been implicitly—as opposed to explicitly—conveyed by a plethora of critical writings on Soviet Communism and other national versions of communism, and on the perceived excesses of social democratic policy (e.g., Swedish paternalism, British nationalized industries). Much of this latter discussion has little if anything to do—at least in a narrow logical sense—with the specific question of private versus public ownership of the capital stock. Particularly important in the development of twentieth century capitalist apologetics have been the well-known Austrian school figures Ludwig von Mises (*Socialism: An Economic and Sociological Analysis*, 1922; *Bureaucracy*, 1943; *The Anti-Capitalist Mentality*, 1956) and Friedrich Hayek (*Collectivist Economic Planning*, 1935; *The Road to Serfdom*, 1944; *The Fatal Conceit: The Errors of Socialism*, 1988). An Americanized version of the Austrian critique of socialism has been provided by Milton Friedman (*Capitalism and Freedom*, 1963; *Free to Choose*, 1979). For the present author's viewpoint on capitalist apologetics as perceived in the light of the pragmatic market socialist alternative, see Chapters 3-8 of *Socialism Revised and Modernized* (1992).

6. The literature on the twentieth century Communist social system in the Soviet Union, including all aspects (historical, economic, political, legal, philosophical, and so on) and both sources (Western and Soviet), is extremely voluminous, and it would be impractical to provide more than a few illustrative references.

Overall histories of the Soviet Union include Donald Treadgold (1964), Louis Aragon (1964), and Michel Heller and Aleksandr Nekrich (1986). The long path toward the Russian Revolution of 1917 is traced in Edmund Wilson (1947), Adam Ulam (1977, 1981), and Edward Crankshaw (1976).

The revolutionary period itself is the central focus in John L. H. Keep (1976), Harrison Salisbury (1978), Richard Pipes (1968), Oliver Henry Radkey (1963), Marc Ferro (1972), Richard Luckett (1971), W. Bruce Lincoln (1986, 1989). The nationally traumatic Stalinist period, with its purges and labor camps, is the central topic of such books as Isaac Deutscher (1967), Ian Grey (1979), Anton Antonov-Ovseyenko (1981), Robert Tucker (1977), and Joel Carmichael (1976). Internal opposition to the Soviet regime is traced in Roland Gaucher (1969). The complex foreign relations of the Soviet state during its formative interwar period are described in Kermit McKenzie (1964), Louis Fischer (1969), and Anthony Cave Brown and Charles B. MacDonald (1981). A monumental portrait of Russia during the World War II crucible has been provided by Alexander Werth (1964). Russia's post-World War II efforts to coordinate the Communist bloc of nations are detailed in Zbigniew Brzezinski (1967), Noel Barber (1974) and Donald Shanor (1975). Finally, among the English language offerings of Progress Publishers of Moscow are a number of titles which recount Soviet history and international relations from the Soviet point of view: for example, B. N. Ponomarev et al (1969, 1970), S. I. Sobolev et al (1971), Yu. Kashlev (1979), O. Bykov et al (1981), Nikolai Lebedev (1982).

Some of the many books dealing with the traditional Soviet centrally planned economy include Alec Nove (1961), Peter Wiles (1962), Nicholas Spulber (1962), Abram Bergson (1964), Edward Ames (1965), Michael Kaser (1970), Vladimir Katkoff (1973), Morris Bornstein and Daniel Fusfeld (1974), David Dyker (1976), Padma Desai (1987), John Cole and Trevor Buck (1987), Paul Gregory and Robert Stuart (1990). The various efforts since the death of Stalin to liberalize and reform the economy in the direction of decentralization and market orientation—efforts which culminated in the perestroika campaign of Gorbachev—are the focus of George Feiwel (1972), J. Wilczynski (1972), Edward A. Hewett (1988), Padma Desai (1989), Jan Adam (1989), Robert Campbell (1991). Also available are several anthologies of translations of writings by Soviet economists throughout the more recent period: Myron Sharp (1966), Murray Yanowitch (1969), Martin Cave et al (1982), Anthony Jones (1989), Anthony Jones and William Moskoff (1991).

As to noneconomic aspects, some of the important contributions to the scholarly literature include Julian Towster on political power (1948), Alex Inkeles on the formation of public opinion (1950) and on social change (1968), Barrington Moore on social control mechanisms (1954), and Myron Rush on political succession (1965). Soviet writers speak for themselves in Michael Jaworskyj's anthology on political thought (1967), and Alex Simirenko's anthology on social thought (1969). Another interesting anthology is that of Harry Shaffer (1984), which juxtaposes Western and Soviet views on various aspects of the Soviet system. Aside from the academic literature, there is an extensive popular literature on Soviet society provided by journalists (e.g., Hedrick Smith, 1976), historians (e.g., Alexander Werth, 1969), and diplomats (e.g., Foy Kohler, 1970).

Finally, reference should be made to the substantial self-apologetic literature sponsored by the Soviet regime itself, of which a considerable amount has been translated into English. On the Soviet system as a whole, see, for example, L. Grigryan and Y. Dolgopolov (1971), V. G. Afanasyev (1971), G. Glezerman (1971). On the Soviet economy, see, for example, Nikolai P. Fedorenko (1972, 1974), Y. Lazutkin (1974), T. Khachaturov (1977), A. Anchishkin (1977), L. Ya. Berri (1977), Yu. M. Shvyrkov (1980), Igor Prostyakov (1987), Leonid Abalkin (1987), Oleg Yun (1988). On the Soviet political system, see, for example, M. Perfilyev (no date), G. Shahnazarov (1974), B. Topornin and E. Machulsky (1974), and M. A. Krutogolov (1980).

7. The intellectual codification of European social democracy is generally considered to be Eduard Bernstein's *Evolutionary Socialism*, first published in German in 1899. Some effectively written English expositions of social democracy were provided in the early twentieth century by the illustrious Fabian Society members George Bernard Shaw (1928) and H. G. Wells (1931). Later British contributions in this vein include C. A. R. Crosland (1963) and Alec Nove (1983). In the United States, social democracy was pursued, with indifferent success, by the Socialist Party under the leadership of the perennial presidential candidates Eugene V. Debs and Norman Thomas. Contemporary exemplars of the American branch of social democracy include Howard Sherman (1972, 1987), Michael Harrington (1980), Samuel Bowles and Herbert Gintis (1986).

8. That the possibility of market socialism is well-recognized among economic professionals is established by the fact that the great majority of textbooks in comparative economic systems contain at least several pages' worth of explicit discussion of the concept of "market socialism," covering at a minimum the seminal contribution of Oskar Lange. Some examples include the following (chronologically ordered by date of publication): George Halm (1960), Part 5 on "The Economic Theory of Market Socialism"; Richard Carson (1973), Chapter 19 on "Traditional Market Socialism: Structure and Functioning"; Egon Neuberger and William Duffy (1976), Chapter 8 on "The Plan and the Market: The Models of Oskar Lange"; Allan Gruchy (1977), Chapter 13 section on "The Decentralized, Market-Oriented Communist Economy"; Wayne Leeman (1977), Part II on "Market Socialism"; Vaclav Holesovsky (1977), Chapter 6 section on "The

Lange Model"; Andrew Zimbalist and Howard Sherman (1984), Chapter 14 on "The Theory of Market Socialism"; Gary Pickersgill and Joyce Pickersgill (1985), Part V on "The Market Socialist Economy"; Morris Bornstein (1985), Part III on "Socialist Market Economy"; John Elliott (1985), Chapter 15 on "The Economic Theory of Decentralized Socialism"; Paul Gregory and Robert Stuart (1985), Chapter 5 section on "Market Socialism: Theoretical Foundations"; H. Bruce Gardner (1988), Chapter 10 section on "Lange's Theory of Market Socialism." A few highly real-world-oriented textbooks, such as those by Martin Schnitzer (1987) and Peter Wiles (1977), fail to mention Oskar Lange's market socialist proposal. However, with respect to these two examples, in Chapter 15 on "Yugoslavia," Schnitzer describes the Yugoslavian economy as "decentralized socialism"; and in Chapter 10 on "Short-Run Optimality in Various Market Systems," Wiles describes the essence of the pragmatic market socialist idea as "Pannonia," and cites contemporary Hungary and the Soviet New Economic Plan period (1921-1928) as examples.

9. The standard interpretation of the origin of Soviet central planning is succinctly stated by Morris Bornstein and Daniel Fusfeld (1974, p. 17): "Comprehensive central planning and administrative control were adopted in the U.S.S.R. in the late 1920's to mobilize resources for rapid industrialization." Major sources for this interpretation include Alexander Erlich (1960), Nicholas Spulber (1964), and E. H. Carr and R. W. Davies (1969).

10. Oskar Lange's well-known essay was stimulated by the publication in 1935 of *Collectivist Economic Planning*, edited by Friedrich von Hayek, a collection of papers which took a generally negative view of the possibilities for efficient economic production under socialism. Lange's response to Hayek took the form of a two-part essay, published in the October 1936 and February 1937 issues of the *Review of Economic Studies*. Shortly afterwards, Lange's essay was published in book form by the University of Minnesota Press (1938). The book, also titled *On the Economic Theory of Socialism*, contained additional contributions by Benjamin Lippincott and Fred M. Taylor. Following the war and the Communist takeover of Poland, Lange returned to his homeland, but his efforts to develop some form of liberal, market-oriented socialism there were rendered ineffective by the Stalin-era orthodox Communist ideology imposed upon Poland by the Soviet Union. Upon his death, Lange still commanded sufficient respect among mainstream Western economists—despite the fact that he had been physically and professionally removed from the Western mainstream for almost two decades—to rate a memorium in one of the field's leading theoretical journals: *Econometrica* (Walter Fisher,

1966).

11. The fundamental mainstream verdict on the Langian market socialist proposal (interesting in theory, but unpromising in practice) was handed down by Abram Bergson in a survey article on "Socialist Economics" published in 1948 in Volume I of *A Survey of Contemporary Economics*, sponsored by the American Economic Association. Bergson placed particular emphasis on the objection that a marginal cost pricing instruction could not be enforced by an easily observable success criterion, since that which marginal cost pricing maximizes, namely overall social welfare, is not directly observable. Bergson made some additional points in a second evaluative article on market socialism published in the *Journal of Political Economy* in 1967. The profound impact of Bergson's 1948 judgment on subsequent professional opinion may be guaged from the fact that most evaluations of the Langian proposal in the comparative economic systems textbook literature virtually paraphrase Bergson's analysis. Prior to Bergson's 1948 survey article, Friedrich Hayek had criticized Lange's market socialist proposal in a 1940 article in *Economica*. Bergson's critique, while not as sharp as Hayek's, seems to have had more impact on the profession of economics owing to its apparently greater objectivity.

12. A concise discussion of some of the more important technical issues relating to these various concepts of market socialism is contained in the author's 1975 survey article in *Annals of Public and Cooperative Economy*. Since the article was published, Leland Stauber has provided another interesting market socialist proposal: regional ownership market socialism (Stauber, 1975, 1977, 1987).

13. There has been a proliferation of technical work on the economic theory of the production cooperative in the journal literature following the seminal contribution of Benjamin Ward in the *American Economic Review* (1958), as evidenced by the survey articles of Alfred Steinherr (1978) and Frederick Pryor (1983). In addition, several books on the subject have been published, including Deborah Milenkovitch (1971), Howard Wachtel (1973), Ellen Comisso (1979), Norman Ireland (1982), Saul Estrin (1983), Stephen Sacks (1983). Although most of the contributors to the Western economic literature on cooperation seem to be skeptical, there are some important exeptions. For example, Jaroslav Vanek has provided a comprehensive statement of the case to be made for cooperative production in terms of contemporary economic theory (1970, 1971, 1977).

14. The author has published a considerable amount of work on pragmatic market socialism, and most of it is listed in the References for the benefit of readers who may be interested. The capital management and saving apologies for capital property income are assessed in a number of papers,

including the 1974 *RSE* article, the 1976 *ACES Bulletin* article, the 1987 working paper, and the 1988 *JCE* article. People's capitalism is assessed in the 1977 *Annals* article and the 1982 *ACES Bulletin* article. The 1979 *JEI* article argues that pragmatic market socialism could be more efficient than contemporary capitalism owing to institutional alterations that would counteract the adverse incentive consequences of the separation of owner- ship and control. The 1991 *EEJ* article argues that pragmatic market socialism could be more efficient than contemporary capitalism owing to the distribution of capital property return in proportion to labor income rather than in proportion to financial assets. The 1976 *Revista* article and the 1986 *JEI* articles both argue that pragmatic market socialism could well achieve a higher rate of capital investment and economic growth than does contemporary capitalism. The 1990 *CES* article confronts the potential Austrian argument against pragmatic market socialism on dynamic perfor- mance grounds. The 1986 *Polity* article contests the proposition that prag- matic market socialism would pose a serious threat to political democracy. An article-length summary of the case for pragmatic market socialism is contained in the 1988 *CES* article, while a book-length summary of the case is contained in *Socialism Revised and Modernized: The Case for Pragmatic Market Socialism* (Praeger, 1992).

15. The external case for pragmatic market socialism was developed in the author's 1982 *Coexistence* article and 1985 *World Futures* article. An updating of the 1982 article through the early 1990s was published in *Coexistence* in 1992.

16. Following the military adage that "a good offense is the best defense," much of the negative Marxist commentary on "bourgeois democracy" emanating from the Soviet Union is in the context of defenses of "Soviet democracy"—an institution which of course elicits as much scorn in the West as does "bourgeois democracy" in the East. Among the numerous titles from Progress Publishers which I happened to have currently available in my office, not one is devoted solely to an assault on bourgeois democracy, but no less than four are defenses of Soviet democracy which frequently invoke invidious comparisons of Soviet democracy with bourgeois democracy. Typical passages from each of the four are as follows.

M. Perfilyev (no date, pp. 37-38): "The bourgeois electoral system always guarantees the representatives of capital a majority in parliament. The sovereignty of the people in the 'free world,' with all the 'achievements of Western democracy,' is pure fiction... The voter in capitalist countries, the USA for example, has to vote for people who actually represent the interests of the exploiting class. The entire mechanics of the elections there are run by the bourgeois Democratic and Republican parties."

G. Shahnazarov (1974, pp. 130-131): "However, the opportunity the working class and other working people have of enjoying political rights and freedoms is still very far from corresponding to their numerical weight, let alone their decisive role in the life of society. The means of propaganda are still largely in the hands of the ruling class, just as they were half a century or even a century ago. The newspaper empires in the United States, the Springer concern with its stranglehold over the publishing market in West Germany—this is who provides the Western reader with information and tells him how to think."

B. Topornin and E. Machulsky (1974, pp. 22-23): "'Democratic socialism' is reformist as is evident from the stand taken by its proponents towards the capitalist state and bourgeois democracy. Right opportunist theorists renounce the concepts of class struggle, gloss over the irreconcilable contradictions between the exploiters and the exploited under capitalism, and thus advocate 'social partnership,' 'civil peace' and 'equality of workers and employers.' They regard the capitalist state as a supraclass political organization which expresses and defends in equal measure the interests of all classes and social strata, and which is used by them to gradually transform capitalism into socialism. They hold that bourgeois parliamentary democracy is 'complete democracy' and that the working class is integrated into its system... They either conceal or distort the fact that the capitalist state is now a bastion of the monopolies' political and economic rule, which bourgeois democracy disguises, protects and consolidates."

M. A. Krutogolov (1980, p. 46): "Being one of the institutions of bourgeois democracy, the multi-party system does not alter the social content of capitalism. Though [the various political parties] alternate with each other as the ruling party, they do nothing to alter the exploitative nature of the capitalist system, but rather on the contrary, do everything they can to ensure that no working class party ever comes to power."

17. A characteristic fascist statement on democracy is the following from Adolf Hitler's *Mein Kampf* (1943, p. 83): "This invention of democracy is most intimately related to a quality which in recent times has grown to be a real disgrace, to wit, the cowardice of a great part of our so-called 'leadership.' What luck to be able to hide behind the skirts of a so-called majority in all decisions of any real importance!

"Take a look at one of these political bandits. How anxiously be begs the approval of the majority for every measure, to assure himself of the necessary accomplices, so he can unload the responsibility at any time. And this is one of the main reasons why this type of political activity is always repulsive and hateful to any man who is decent at heart and hence courageous, while it attracts all low characters—and anyone who is unwilling to take personal responsibility for his acts, but seeks a shield, is a cowardly scoundrel. When the leaders of a nation consist of such vile creatures, the results will soon be deplorable. Such a nation will be unable to muster the courage for any determined act; it will prefer to accept any dishonor, even the most shameful, rather than rise to a decision; for there is no one who is prepared of his own accord to pledge his person and his head for the execution of a dauntless resolve.

"For there is one thing which we must never forget: in this, too, the majority can never replace the man. The majority is not only a representative of stupidity, but of cowardice as well. And no more than a hundred empty heads make one wise man will an heroic decision arise from a hundred cowards."

Whatever the liabilities of communism, one will search in vain through its documentation for such blatantly contemptuous attitudes toward the institution of political democracy.

18. Well before the recent collapse of the authority of the Communist Party in the Soviet Union, there were indications of political liberalization and sympathetic interest in Western democratic principles and practices. For example, G. Shahnazarov, in his 1974 Progress Publishers (Moscow) book on *Socialist Democracy*, was primarily concerned with defending the traditional Soviet political system against various Western critics. But in the course of this defense, he made a number of significant points which suggested that the future evolution of the Soviet political system might well be toward a more genuine and legitimate form of democracy. Among these points were the following:

First, to a large extent the traditional political institutions of the Soviet Union were determined by historical hostility toward socialism both within and outside Russia (p. 18): "The limiting of democracy was due primarily to internal conditions, to the fact that the revolution had triumphed in a country with a predominantly petty-bourgeois population. But there were also external causes: first armed intervention and later the persisting danger of further military invasion."

Second, there is no fundamental opposition in Marxist theory to multi-party systems (p. 29): "What exactly is the position as regards the multi-party system in conditions of socialism? To begin with it must be noted that neither in the works of the founders of scientific communism nor in documents of the international communist movement is it anywhere stated that socialism precludes a plurality of parties."

Third, potential modifications of the present political system should be examined thoroughly and objectively, because in all probability the current status quo will not remain optimal for all times (p. 141): "In mentioning all these indisputable facts, it is far from our intention to try and pretend that there are no shortcomings in the practical side of building socialism and communism. Observing Lenin's behests, the communist movement analyzes the results of its activity with the maximum objectivity and clearly sees where it has failed, shortcomings, omissions, etc. Correcting mistakes and distortions resulting from the ideology and practice of the personality cult, the restoration of socialist legality and Leninist principles in Party and government life, fruitful research into current social problems and a whole system of measures to further develop socialist democracy are clear evidence that socialist society is freeing itself from the weaknesses of childhood and becoming more mature."

19. A typical Soviet evaluation of "market socialism" is that of Y. Y. Olsevich and S. A. Khavina (1976, p. 308): "The authors of 'market socialism' models rely on complete decentralization of economic decision-making... By wishing on socialism a spontaneous market mechanism for controlling proportions, they essentially nullify the determining role of the planning principle in economic control. That would mean for socialist society the impossibility of purposefully resolving long-term economic objectives, determining the major directions of technical progress in a planned way, changing the structure of production and consumption and having a rapid growth in accumulation and consumption. The authors of the 'market socialism' theories try to square the circle: public ownership of the means of production [is combined with] the specific mechanism of spontaneous control of proportions inherent in free competition, [which is] inevitably associated with an immense wastefulness of the forces of production. These models signify rejection of the decisive advantages of socialism, a step backward."

Olsevich and Khavina do not intend to imply by this statement, however, that the market is contradictory to socialism, but rather merely that the market should be controlled and regulated by central planning under socialism. This is demonstrated by the following statement (p. 305): "In actual fact, the market (as a form of commodity circulation) is not alien to socialist relations of production; on the contrary it is inherent in them. The existence of a market in a situation of planned socialist economic development is due to the fact that products manufactured at socialist enterprises are commodities and their consumer value may be realized only through exchange. The market is the sum total of economic relations that form in the process of exchange of commodities between socialist enterprises, and between enterprises and consumers."

Moreover, Olsevich and Khavina explicitly concede that just as there exists the possibility of an under-controlled socialism, so too there exists the possibility of an over-controlled socialism (p. 301): "While Right-wing revisionism relies on the market socialist doctrine and demands the separation of the economy from the state, 'Left-'wing revisionism, on the contrary, demands that military and political state organs should control the economy directly, that the functional mechanism of the economy should be built on the principle of the military mechanisms. The effect of this 'functional mechanism' on the entire system of relations of the socialist basis is just as deleterious and destructive as the 'market socialism' mechanism, although they move in different directions."

4

PROSPECTS FOR
ECONOMIC EQUALIZATION

A. THE ECONOMIC PROBLEM

As we peer forward into an unknown and perilous future, we perceive looming up beyond the ideological conflict between communism and noncommunism a problem potentially of even more serious proportions. This problem is the economic gap—the enormous gulf that has opened up between the material living standards in the wealthiest nations, such as the United States and the Western European nations, and those in the poorest nations of Africa, Asia, and Latin America.[1] In contrast to the ideological controversy, the economic gap cannot be moderated by the relatively simple and costless expedient of people simply changing their mental attitudes. The prime hope in the noncommunist West has always been that one fine morning the communist leaders will simply wake up to the reality that the capitalist economic system is sufficiently benign to possess a legitimate right to permanent existence, and in consequence of this recognition they will thenceforward sincerely cease and desist from their support of socialist movements in the West, and will sincerely agree to an authentic, reasonable program of balanced arms reduction. Although the probability of this favorable development would probably be greatly augmented by the implementation of pragmatic market socialism in the Western noncommunist nations, as recommended in the previous chapter, in the absence of such implementation there is still a very considerable hope that the communist leaders will eventually resign themselves to permanent peaceful coexistence with the capitalistic West, thus laying the foundations for meaningful disarmament and genuine detente. In fact, the various economic reform movements currently afoot in the communist nations suggest that it is not at all impossible that these nations will themselves voluntarily rejoin the world mainstream of capitalism within the foreseeable future.

Unfortunately, however, the economic gap is a far more substantive, tangible, and concrete factor in the world today than is ideological conflict. It cannot be relegated to oblivion by mere changes of opinion. It cannot be effectively declared inconsequential and irrelevant, null and void, by the signatory flourishes of various national leaders on an historically significant disarmament pact. Even if the communist and noncommunist nations attain a sincere and permanent accommodation, the economic gap will still be there, waiting to take over the role of prime contributor to international hostility, ill will, tension, and war-risk.[2] Therefore, a truly comprehensive plan toward world peace and human welfare should address this problem in a determined and decisive manner.

Throughout this book, a consistent effort is being made at a sensible, realistic, and balanced perspective. There are no warnings of doom and disaster should these recommendations be ignored; and there are no promises of utopian bliss should they be implemented. Rather the argument is merely that the odds of favorable future progression will be appreciably augmented if the recommendations are implemented. For example, the argument of the preceding chapter was that the implementation of pragmatic market socialism in the major Western capitalist nations would appreciably augment the odds on important disarmament and sincere and permanent detente between the communist and noncommunist worlds. In this chapter, the argument will be advanced that a World Economic Equalization Program (WEEP), of a sort to be described, hopefully financed largely by economic resources liberated from military uses by an important disarmament plan, would appreciably augment the odds of a rapid and substantial rise in the material living standards of the populations of the poorer nations of the contemporary world. But no assertion is made that a WEEP is either necessary or sufficient for the solution of the economic gap problem. First, it is within the realm of possibility that the problem will eventually "cure itself," even though no concerted international effort to overcome it (such as a WEEP) is ever undertaken. In other words, world-wide living standards might eventually be equalized without a WEEP. Second, it is within the realm of possibility that the problem will *never* be cured even though a vigorous and concerted international effort to overcome it (such as the WEEP described herein) *is* undertaken. In other words, world-wide living standards might never be equalized despite a WEEP. Now that this much has been made clear, and a defense of sorts has been established against thoughtless charges of naivety, let us continue with a brief survey of the nature and implications of the economic gap.

The matter might conveniently be introduced in terms of the proverbial "good news and bad news." First, what is the "good news"? The first point to be made on the positive side of the ledger is that official estimates of the gap, such as are contained in the per capita gross national product figures for various nations published by the World Bank, generally overstate the magnitude of the gap, because they do not take into adequate account nonmarket production and transactions. Thus, living standards in the less developed nations are not quite so low as is suggested by these figures. The second point is that official figures published by the World Bank suggest that living standards are rising almost everywhere in the world. Per capita GNP as measured by the World Bank is rising in almost every country, and in some countries the rise is at quite a high rate. In many large and populous less developed nations (LDC's), living standards are already starting to approach those in the rich nations. This is especially true of those LDC's, mostly in the Mideast, which possess substantial oil reserves. The third point is that within the last few decades, population growth rates have started to taper off in most of the poor nations, even in those very populous and impoverished nations such as China and India in which population growth has been very high throughout most of the twentieth century. Diminishing pressure on new productive resources simply to support greater numbers suggests that even higher rates of progress in material living standards in the LDC's might be achieved in the future. All of this is certainly very encouraging.

But now, what is the "bad news"? First, although the official figures somewhat overstate the gap, even when careful statistical adjustments are made the gap may still be fairly described as huge—

something to which any resident of a rich country who has personally witnessed the lamentable living standards in a poor country can attest. Second, although living standards in the poor countries are increasing, living standards in the rich countries are increasing even faster, so that for the moment at least, the absolute size of the gap between the richest and the poorest nations is increasing, notwithstanding the progress being made in the poor countries. Third, while population growth in the poor countries has tapered off a bit recently, it still remains quite high, much higher than in the rich countries, which suggests that population pressure will continue to seriously retard economic progress in the poor countries. These points on the negative side of the ledger are of course not at all encouraging.

Taking all the available evidence into account, it simply cannot be taken for granted that, in the absence of any important discretionary planning, the economic gap will tend to dissipate of its own accord within the foreseeable future. If we look at the conditions over, say, the last 200 years, a period of time which has witnessed the economic rise of the rich nations, we can immediately perceive at least two extremely important factors which cannot be duplicated in the future to assist the poor nations of today to achieve a similar rise. One of these factors was the incorporation of the vast agricultural and natural resources of the North American landmass into the European economy at a critical point in its demographic and industrial development. But the basic physical resources of the earth are now for the most part identified and catalogued. There are no more extensive and rich frontiers to be opened up and exploited; the surplus populations of nations such as China and India cannot be shipped off to seek their fortunes on expansive and virtually uninhabited continents. The second factor has been the intensive utilization of fossil fuels, in particular coal and petroleum, as cheap sources of heat and power. The limits of these fixed resources are now clearly in view, and once they are exhausted, recourse must be had to more expensive sources of heat and power. We of course hope that the advance of technological progress will continue at an accelerating pace, so that the impending exhaustion of fossil fuel resources, as well as other natural resources in fixed supply, will not impose a serious drag on future economic growth. But we have no guarantee whatsoever of such a favorable outcome. Obviously there are asymptotic upper limits on the technical efficiency of production, and sooner or later the human race will be forced to confront these limits.

The question is not *whether* these resource and technical limits will be reached, but *when* they will be reached. Now it may well be that some environmentalists have been unduly shrill and alarmist in their warnings. In their desire to get attention and to share their concerns, they have tended to issue predictions of severe crisis in the very near future. The trouble with this tactic is that when these predictions are not borne out, their issuers are to a large extent discredited, and environmental concern among the general public is eventually downgraded. Generally speaking, it is folly to try to predict the future, and such predictions should be avoided by sensible individuals as much as possible. Therefore it would be unwise to make any strong forecasts as to when the human race will definitely begin to feel the environmental pinch, and/or when it will definitely encounter an environmental crisis. But it would be even more unwise to disregard the pressure which human expansion is putting on the natural environment, and to assume that everything will work out for the best in the long run. One may be blindly optimistic, and may assume that the favorable trends of the past two hundred years will be continued indefinitely, regardless of the absence of new continents and new fossil fuel reserves to be exploited and integrated into the world economy. Such blind optimism verges on foolhardiness.

So long as the economic gap persists—and we have no good reason to assume that it will not persist for a very, very long time if it remains unmolested by a major international planning effort—it will continue to constitute an inexhaustible source of irritation, friction, and hostility in human affairs. The rich nations will tend to be subject to emotions of suspicion and jealously; the poor nations will tend to be subject to emotions of indignation and envy. The poor nations will tend to label the rich nations as "selfish and uncharitable," while the rich nations will tend to label the poor nations as "greedy and grasping." Emotional overtones will tend to complicate and magnify what might otherwise be relatively minor and easily manageable conflicts in national interest between rich nations and poor nations. Such conflicts would have a propensity to incite violence and war to a much greater extent than would be the case among nations whose domestic living standards were more comparable.

No one can say exactly where the economic gap will take us in the future. Perhaps it will have no verifiable independent effect beyond the cultivation of mild feelings of hostility and mistrust in the citizens of the various nations of the world against one another—feelings too feeble and diffuse to have a demonstrably negative impact on international relations. At the other end of the possibility spectrum—looking far enough into the future—there could be nuclear attacks followed up by massive, human-wave style invasions of the rich nations by the poor nations. Somewhere in between lies the possibility of nuclear terrorism: various terrorist groups, probably operating independently of any national governments, might start detonating nuclear devices within the major cities of the rich nations in order to exact vengeance for the latter's callous disregard for the economic plight of the poor nations. Speculation on the possibility of nuclear terrorism in some extremist cause or another has abounded since the dawn of the nuclear age, but thus far no such incidents have occurred. Lest we become overly complacent, however, we should reflect on the fact that "the future" covers a very long period of time, and given enough time, almost every kind of imaginable catastrophe tends to occur—presuming the conditions for such a catastrophe are propitious.

The danger to world peace posed by the economic gap is not confined to its tendency to sour relations between the richest nations and the poorest nations. A good deal of resentment and hostility may be generated even between nations which are much closer together, in terms of economic living standards, than are the richest and the poorest nations in the world. This is particularly the case if an economic gap is added to ideological and/or nationalistic tensions. At least some of the resentment in the Arab world against Israel, for example, is quite probably due to the somewhat more comfortable living standards in Israel, particularly among the working class and the middle class, than in the other Middle Eastern nations. These resentments can also arise independently of the racial and religious characteristics of the population. For example, Iraq's invasion of Kuwait in 1991 was largely motivated by economic envy, even though the populations of both nations were racially and religiously similar. Local conflicts such as these, aided and abetted by the economic gap, may potentially bring the military superpowers of the world into a direct confrontation. Such an outcome would be particularly likely if, owing to the further proliferation of nuclear weapons which is likely to take place in the future, the local conflict threatens to precipitate, or does in fact precipitate, a nuclear war.

An effort is being made to rationalize and legitimize the natural hostility of the poor against the rich in the theory of economic imperialism.[3] The intellectual roots of this theory go back to the turn of the twentieth century, when certain Marxist ideologues, in attempting to explain the unexpectedly prolonged resistance of the advanced capitalist nations to catastrophic depression and socialist revolution, developed the basic ideas. What keeps the capitalist economies of the advanced nations going, according to these ideas, is their exploitation of the vast markets, cheap labor, and natural resources of the less developed nations of Africa, Asia, and Latin America. In its earlier days, the theory of economic imperialism was far more concerned to show that the phenomenon enabled capitalism in the economically advanced nations to survive, than to show that the phenomenon was directly disadvantageous to the populations of the less developed nations. But in the 1920s and thereafter, as the Soviet Union attempted to gain adherents to communism in these nations, the theory of economic imperialism was further developed, and a strong emphasis was added on the alleged highly negative impact of economic imperialism on the welfare of the populations of the poor nations. The proposition that international economic relations between rich and poor nations in some way or other operate to the disadvantage of the latter nations has become quite widespread, and does not in every case stem from an explicit Marxist basis.

The vast majority of economists in the rich nations are disdainful to the point of contempt toward the theory of economic imperialism. Although they will admit that crude and direct economic exploitation, backed up by military force, was fairly common during the great age of political imperialism in the nineteenth century and earlier, they assert that now that the many former colonies of advanced nations have become politically independent and sovereign nations, economic relations between rich and poor nations are on a voluntary basis, and therefore by their nature they are viewed as beneficial by both parties. They point to the development of the prosperous North American economy, which was apparently based on abundant commodity trade with and capital inflow from Great Britain and other European nations. They point out the tremendous increase in the populations of the less developed nations, an increase which, despite all its economic problems and disadvantages, demonstrates beyond reasonable doubt the vast increase in the fundamental productive capabilities of their economies during their associations, whether as colonies or otherwise, with the advanced nations over the last one hundred to two hundred years.

Most market-oriented economists of the advanced Western nations, trained as they are in the precepts of the classical economists regarding the mutually beneficial effects of international commodity trade and capital resource flows, find very little intellectual substance and merit in the theory of economic imperialism, and in the various allied theories which question, challenge or deny these beneficial effects. But the very existence of these theories is itself highly significant. The development of such theories is predictable enough in a world in which such an enormous gap exists between the living standards of the rich nations and those of the poor nations. In a world in which both rich and poor coexist and are aware of one another's presence, the poor will have a natural propensity to envy and resent the rich, and to want to attribute to the rich some degree of moral responsibility, direct or indirect, large or small, for the fact of their own poverty. The development of a literature of economic imperialism, which represents an intellectual rationalization of an emotional aversion, is very much to be expected under the present circumstances of an enormous dispersion in living standards between the rich and poor nations. It bodes ill for the future.

But even granted that the economic gap represents an obvious wellspring of trouble, the question remains: What—if anything—can be done about it? The problem of world economic development first came clearly into focus in the post-World War II era. Ever since the 1950s, the governments of the less developed nations have been appealing to the advanced nations for economic assistance to help them build up their internal productive capacity. Resources have been requested to help build social infrastructure such as roads and dams, to build factories and machinery, and to provide educational and training programs for the workforce. The potentially dramatic impact of such temporary economic assistance on the productivity of the LDC's was suggested by the Marshall Plan of the latter 1940s. For motives which combined a very noble, commendable, and even sublime altruism with a more mundane and selfish concern for maintaining national security against a growing communist threat, the United States undertook for a few years a major program of providing abundant economic resources to nations which had suffered severe structural damage during World War II. Complemented by the determined effort of the people of these nations, the program was a marvelous success. Pre-war living standards were re-attained within a few years, and since then Japan and the nations of Western Europe, the primary beneficiaries of the Marshall Plan, have surged ahead to a very high standard of life rivaling that achieved in the United States.

Since the 1970s, the economists and the governments of the LDC's have been calling for a New International Economic Order (NIEO), an umbrella term encompassing a great many specific appeals for economic help, most of which were heard long before the coining of the NIEO catchphrase.[4] Although most NIEO proposals involve relatively modest concessions such as tariff relief and price stabilization programs, at its extreme fringe is an appeal for a "world-wide Marshall Plan," a comparatively massive program of resource transfers from the rich countries to the poor countries along the general lines of the original, post-World War II Marshall Plan. To date, appeals for a world-wide Marshall Plan have been disparaged to the point of ridicule—and of course totally rejected—by the governments of the rich nations. These governments simply refuse to assume any moral responsibility for the problem of world poverty. They chide LDC governments for behaving like disreputable, wheedling beggars in making such appeals, and they inform them in no uncertain terms that the poverty of their own people is their own problem and no one else's problem.

During the 1950s and 1960s, the United States government, and those of several other major Western powers, were considerably more generous with economic assistance than they have been more recently. Two principal factors seem to have been responsible for this decline in generosity. First, and probably more important, the overall appeal of communist ideology to the populations of the LDC's, despite the assiduous efforts made by Russia and other communist nations to disseminate the theory of economic imperialism, turned out to be weaker than had been feared at the beginning of the Cold War era following World War II. Second, the slow rate of economic growth in the LDC's, together with rampant population increase, made (and still makes) the prospects for appreciable improvement in living standards in these nations appear quite bleak. Thus the continuation of substantial economic assistance programs to LDC's tended increasingly to be viewed as unnecessary in a national security sense, and in any event futile in an economic welfare sense. The rich nations—their people and their governments—have commenced to wash their hands (as did Pontius Pilate) of the fate of the poor nations, all the while insisting to themselves and to anyone else who will listen that they are doing so with a clear conscience.[5]

Implicit in the previous chapter was the argument that the failure up to now to implement pragmatic market socialism is wasting a great and historic opportunity for the people of the capitalist nations, and particularly for those of the advanced, industrialized, and wealthy capitalist nations such as the United States. The vast majority of the people of these nations would be personally and materially benefited—modestly but appreciably—by the implementation of pragmatic market socialism. Moreover, the long-term psychological benefits that might flow from the implementation of pragmatic market socialism could well dwarf the short-term material benefits. This is because the socialization of the major noncommunist Western powers would significantly moderate the intensity of the ideological conflict between the communist and noncommunist bloc of nations, thus paving the way for greater progress on disarmament, and to permanent, peaceful, and friendly coexistence. The threat to everyone in the contemporary world of an unimaginable nuclear catastrophe at some point in the future is a heavy psychological burden to bear. It substantially diminishes our ability to derive joy, happiness, serenity, and satisfaction from our lives. And it is probably a needless burden. A form of socialism is readily available, a form which has been designated herein "pragmatic market socialism," which not only possesses considerable attractiveness purely on internal or domestic grounds, but which also possesses the clear capability, though alleviating ideological conflict between communism and noncommunism and encouraging disarmament, of substantially relieving the human race of its present oppressive concern over the possibility of nuclear catastrophe.

Nor is this the only wasted opportunity. Implicit in the present chapter is the argument that were a substantial proportion of the economic resources released by a major disarmament agreement to be transferred into a world-wide economic assistance program (tentatively designated the World Economic Equalization Program—WEEP), the equivalent on a world-wide scale of the Marshall Plan which followed World War II, the impact on the economic gap might be tremendous.[6] Such a program might well virtually eliminate the gap—without the need of any reduction in the presently established living standards in the advanced nations—within a relatively brief interval of time of perhaps fifty to one hundred years. Thus the implementation of pragmatic market socialism might not only greatly ameliorate the immediate threat of nuclear catastrophe by reducing ideological conflict, but in addition it could well substantially reduce the long-term threat of such a catastrophe by means of leading indirectly to a substantial amount of economic equalization across the entire world.

According to U.S. government statistics, during the post-Vietnam War period, the United States has expended an annual average of between 5 and 6 percent of Gross National Product for national defense purchases. While the other advanced noncommunist nations are not expending quite as much on their military establishments, their defense commitments still amount to substantial percentages of their national outputs. Now of course even presuming a dramatic breakthrough on the disarmament front, it is probably not realistic to expect defense spending to drop below, say, one percent of GNP in the United States. A totally disarmed world seems almost inconceivable, and even dedicated advocates of peaceful coexistence do not normally envision this as a practical goal within the foreseeable future. However, it may be reasonable to envision a sufficiently encompassing disarmament agreement as freeing up perhaps 4 to 5 percent of United States GNP for non-military uses, and liberating proportionately smaller but still very substantial resources in the other advanced nations.

The idea of transferring resources from the manufacture of destructive weapons to the manufacture of productive machinery has a very ancient lineage: the well-known "swords into plowshares" phrase occurs in the Old Testament of the Bible. The idea became excruciatingly relevant in the post-World War II period, during which LDC governments have clamored continuously for economic assistance, while at the same time the Cold War "forced" the leading national powers to allocate tremendous economic resources to military uses. The tragic waste embodied in this situation deeply touches any person of good will who has ever seriously reflected on it. A substantial literature already exists which speculates on the immense possibilities that may be inherent in converting a major proportion of military spending into world economic development spending. The sense of desperate anguish and intense urgency in this literature seemed to crest in the early 1960s, during the relatively optimistic and progressive period when John F. Kennedy served as U.S. President.[7] But the assassination of John F. Kennedy, the ballistic missile race between the U.S. and the U.S.S.R. that continued up to the SALT agreement of the early 1970s, the costly and divisive Vietnam War, as well as many other trials and setbacks since the early 1960s, have done much to breed the current listless spirit of pessimism, resignation, and despair. The monumental waste of the international arms competition, despite the very serious world poverty problem, has now persisted for such a prolonged period of time that there is an ever-increasing tendency to simply shrug it off, with weary and callous indifference, as something which is apparently part of the inescapable ordained order of things.[8]

Nevertheless, it is quite possible that we do not, after all, have to live with the terribly wasteful and potentially deadly arms competition. The implementation of pragmatic market socialism, through its beneficial effect on the contemporary ideological conflict situation, might very quickly lead to the complete and permanent cessation of this competition. In addition to the pragmatic market socialist possibility, the various reform movements in the communist nations present other promising prospects for ideological harmonization in the relatively near future. It is also quite possible that we do not, after all, have to live with the tragedy of world poverty. If the larger part of the economic resources freed from military use by major disarmament agreements were to be shifted into the support of a World Economic Equalization Program, this massive outside support for the economic development of the poor nations might well enable a tremendous acceleration in the growth of their productive capacity and living standards. The following two sections of the present chapter investigate this possibility. Section B presents results from a computer simulation of such a Program, while Section C considers its actual functioning.

B. A WORLD ECONOMIC EQUALIZATION PROGRAM

Few if any individuals are so completely immune against the noxious vapors from the currently dominant spirit of bleak pessimism as to deny the possibility that even unprecedentedly massive support for economic development could prove to be in vain, in the sense that it would not lead to a dramatic increase in the productive capacity and living standards of the LDC's. But there is a sufficient probability that massive support would generate dramatic improvement as to make the endeavor worthwhile. If after a reasonable period of time, say ten to fifteen years, the World Economic Equalization Program were producing inadequate and unsatisfactory results, the Program would be discontinued, the rich countries would thereafter spend their resources internally, and the poor countries would be left to extricate themselves from their own poverty through their own devices. At least after making such an effort, the people of the rich nations could rest easier with their consciences, because there would be hard statistical evidence of the futility of massive economic assistance expenditures. Up to the present time, of course, there has never been anything remotely approaching "massive" economic assistance resources flows from the rich nations to the poor nations. Thus there exists no strong and direct evidence regarding the potential impact of such resource flows.

In support of the proposition that the impact of massive economic assistance resource flows on world economic development could be dramatically beneficial within a relatively brief period of historical time, at this point some research work of the present author on the question will be briefly described. This research is contained in a series of two papers, the first published in 1976 and the second in 1988.[9] These papers develop a simple model of a possible World Economic Equalization Program for use in numerical computer simulation experimentation. The model groups the nations of the world into six income brackets: in the second of the two papers these income brackets correspond to those utilized by the World Bank in its annual *World Development Reports*. The highest income bracket contains only one nation: the United States. In the lowest income bracket are nations such as Ethiopia and Bangladesh. The computer simulations encompass 35 years. A technical description of the model itself, together with discussion of its numerical implementation and the results forthcoming from it, is contained in a technical appendix to this chapter.

A very rough and informal description of the model is as follows: For each income bracket of nations, there is an annual "residual," defined as national output less domestic consumption and military spending. Of this residual, a part is devoted to internal investment in domestic "generalized capital," while the remainder is contributed into an international "transfer fund" to be used for investing in the generalized capital accumulations of the less developed nations. By "generalized capital" is denoted the value of all inputs into production other than raw labor power: therefore in addition to the value of plant and machinery it encompasses the value of educational and training inputs into the labor force. The richer the country (in terms of per capita consumption), the larger the part of the residual allocated to the transfer fund, up to a maximum of 50 percent of the residual. The nations in each bracket draw resources from the transfer fund proportionately to the size of their population and to their degree of poverty (measured by the absolute differential between their per capita consumption and per capita consumption in the richest income bracket).

The outcome of a particular numerical simulation of course depends on the assumed numerical parameter values utilized in that simulation. Using a set of numerical parameter values which are fully reasonable on the basis of currently available statistical evidence, the WEEP model produces the extraordinary results presented in Table 4.1 and illustrated by Figures 4.1 through 4.3. The basic variable used to represent the living standards of a certain income bracket is the per capita consumption of the people living in the nations of that bracket. Table 4.1 presents the projected path of per capita consumption over a 35-year period of time, for each of the six income brackets, for a situation in which a World Economic Equalization Program is not operating (the left-hand side of the table), and for a situation in which a World Economic Equalization Program is operating (the right-hand side of the table). When the WEEP is not operating, none of a region's residual is contributed into the transfer fund and hence no transfers are carried out. The left-hand side and right-hand side of Table 4.1 are portrayed graphically in Figures 4.1 and 4.2 respectively. Figure 4.1 (without WEEP in operation) shows a continuation of the widening pattern which is currently taking place. Figure 4.2 (with WEEP in operation) shows a dramatic degree of economic convergence, despite the continuation of a high rate of progress in the richest nations. At present, per capita consumption in the poorest region is only about 4 percent of that in the richest region. After 35 years of a WEEP, according to the simulation result, per capita consumption in the poorest region would be very close to 90 percent of that in the richest region.

Figure 4.3 shows a comparison of potential per capita consumption growth in the richest income bracket (the United States) both without and with a WEEP in operation (the upper two lines), and in the poorest income bracket both without and with a WEEP in operation (the lower two lines). This chart therefore graphically illustrates the profound implication of this simulation experiment: that it is fully possible that a program of massive economic assistance resource transfers from rich nations to poor nations (i.e., a WEEP) would result in a dramatic acceleration of the rate of economic progress in the poor nations at the modest cost of a very slight diminishment in the rate of economic progress in the rich nations.

TABLE 4.1

Baseline Simulation of a World Economic Equalization Model

Consumption per capita (thousand $)
Periods 1-20

| without WEEP | | | | | | with WEEP | | | | | |
| Region | | | | | | Region | | | | | |
1	2	3	4	5	6	1	2	3	4	5	6
12.3	10.0	3.7	1.7	0.7	0.5	12.3	10.0	3.7	1.7	0.7	0.5
12.5	10.2	3.9	1.8	0.7	0.5	12.5	10.2	4.0	2.2	1.9	1.9
12.7	10.5	4.1	1.8	0.7	0.5	12.7	10.4	4.3	2.6	2.7	2.7
13.0	10.8	4.4	1.8	0.8	0.5	12.9	10.6	4.6	3.0	3.9	3.9
13.2	11.0	4.6	1.8	0.8	0.5	13.0	10.9	4.9	3.4	3.9	3.9
13.4	11.3	4.9	1.8	0.8	0.5	13.2	11.1	5.2	3.8	4.5	4.4
13.7	11.6	5.1	1.8	0.8	0.5	13.4	11.3	5.5	4.2	5.0	5.0
13.9	11.8	5.4	1.8	0.8	0.5	13.9	11.8	5.8	4.6	5.5	5.5
14.2	12.1	5.7	1.9	0.8	0.6	13.8	11.8	6.2	5.0	6.0	5.9
14.5	12.4	6.0	1.9	0.8	0.6	14.1	12.1	6.5	5.4	6.5	6.4
14.7	12.8	6.3	1.9	0.8	0.6	14.3	12.3	6.8	5.8	7.0	6.9
15.0	13.1	6.6	1.9	0.8	0.6	14.5	12.6	7.2	6.2	7.5	7.4
15.3	13.4	6.9	1.9	0.8	0.6	14.7	12.8	7.6	6.6	8.0	7.8
15.6	13.7	7.3	1.9	0.8	0.6	14.9	13.1	7.9	7.1	8.4	8.3
15.9	14.1	7.6	1.9	0.8	0.6	15.2	13.4	8.3	7.5	8.9	8.8
16.2	14.4	8.0	2.0	0.9	0.6	15.4	13.7	8.7	7.9	9.4	9.2
16.5	14.8	8.3	2.0	0.9	0.6	15.6	14.0	9.1	8.4	9.8	9.7
16.8	15.1	8.7	2.2	0.9	0.6	15.9	14.3	9.5	8.9	10.3	10.2
17.1	15.5	9.1	2.4	0.9	0.6	16.1	14.6	9.9	9.3	10.8	10.6
17.5	15.9	9.5	2.7	0.9	0.6	16.4	14.9	10.4	9.8	11.3	11.1

TABLE 4.1 Continued

Consumption per capita (thousand $)
Periods 21-35

	without WEEP Region						with WEEP Region				
1	2	3	4	5	6	1	2	3	4	5	6
17.8	16.3	9.9	3.1	0.9	0.6	16.7	15.2	10.8	10.3	11.8	11.6
18.2	16.7	10.3	3.6	0.9	0.6	16.9	15.6	11.3	10.8	12.2	12.0
18.5	17.1	10.7	4.1	0.9	0.6	17.2	15.9	11.7	11.3	12.7	12.5
18.9	17.6	11.1	4.7	0.9	0.6	17.5	16.2	12.2	11.8	13.2	13.0
19.3	18.0	11.5	5.3	0.9	0.6	17.8	16.6	12.7	12.3	13.7	13.5
19.7	18.5	12.0	5.9	0.9	0.6	18.1	17.0	13.2	12.8	14.2	14.0
20.1	18.9	12.4	6.5	0.9	0.6	18.4	17.3	13.7	13.3	14.8	14.5
20.5	19.4	12.9	7.1	1.0	0.6	18.7	17.7	14.2	13.9	15.3	15.0
20.9	19.9	13.4	7.7	1.0	0.6	19.0	18.1	14.8	14.4	15.8	15.5
21.3	20.4	13.9	8.4	1.0	0.7	19.3	18.5	15.3	15.0	16.3	16.0
21.8	20.9	14.4	9.0	1.0	0.7	19.7	18.9	15.9	15.6	16.9	16.6
22.2	21.4	14.9	9.6	1.0	0.7	20.0	19.3	16.5	16.1	17.4	17.1
22.7	21.9	15.4	10.3	1.0	0.7	20.3	19.8	17.1	16.7	18.0	17.7
23.2	22.5	15.9	10.9	1.0	0.7	20.7	20.2	17.7	17.3	18.6	18.2
23.6	23.1	16.4	11.6	1.0	0.7	21.1	20.6	18.3	19.0	19.1	18.8

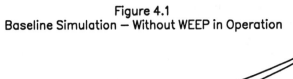

Figure 4.1
Baseline Simulation — Without WEEP in Operation

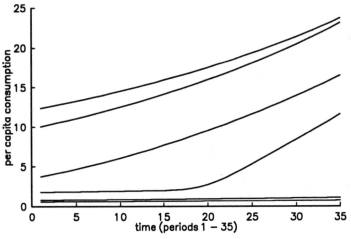

Figure 4.2
Baseline Simulation — With WEEP in Operation

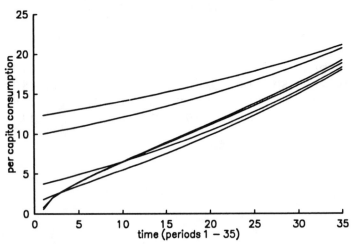

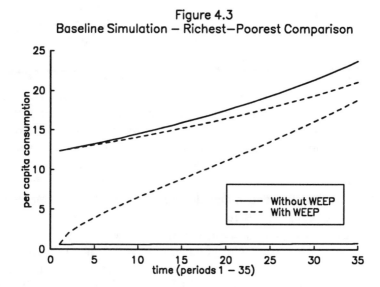

Figure 4.3
Baseline Simulation — Richest—Poorest Comparison

Thus world-wide economic equalization need not necessarily in-volve any decline at all in the living standards of the populations of the rich nations—the most that may be necessary is a marginal retardation of the rate of increase of these living standards. Surely any reasonably sensible and charitable citizen of a rich nation should be prepared to undertake such a modest sacrifice. The motivation to do so would be twofold: for the altruistic satisfaction inherent in the generosity itself, and for the self-interested purpose of ensuring that the peace, prosperity, and serenity of the rich nations is not badly disrupted and possibly completely destroyed in the future by endless conflicts with hordes of envious and dissatisfied people living in the LDC's. The question is not so much whether given that the results of the WEEP model are valid, a WEEP would be desirable. Rather the question is whether the WEEP model itself, and the specific numeri-cal parameter values used in this simulation, are valid.

One of the points to be made in favor of the validity of the simulation results is that in the absence of a WEEP, the simulation model produces results that seem reasonably plausible. Looking at Figure 4.1, we note the indication of continued economic progress for the rich nations of income bracket 1 (the United States) and income bracket 2 (comprising mainly the industrialized Western European nations such as Great Britain, France, and West Germany). Income bracket 3 (comprising nations such as Argentina and Brazil) maintains its growth but fails to converge significantly with the richest brackets. Income bracket 4 (comprising nations such as Nigeria, Turkey, and the Philippines) shows a sudden acceleration in growth reminiscent of Walt W. Rostow's take-off into self-sustaining growth, much celebrated among specialists in economic development back in the 1950s and 1960s. Unfortunately, income brackets 5 (China and India) and 6 (other low-income economies such as Ethiopia, Pakistan, and Bangladesh) show only the most marginal prospective advance with respect to per capita consumption under the no-WEEP situation. In these nations, production growth barely manages to keep pace with population growth. The population of these nations is, moreover, a very significant percentage of the total world population: to be precise, 50.28 percent in 1983 according to the World Bank's population estimates. The economic gap is bad enough at the present time: with 35 more years of progress in living standards for 50 percent of the human population, but little or no such progress for the other 50 percent (the poorest 50 percent), the situation would be substantially worse.

But that this aggravation of the economic gap, and the consequent deterioration in the long-term prospects for world peace and serenity, is not necessary, is strongly suggested by the results depicted in Figure 4.2, which shows potential results in the presence of a WEEP. Instead of languishing, income brackets 5 and 6 might be almost immediately catapulted into a pattern of rapid growth in living standards. In fact, it is a technical anomaly of the simulation model that brackets 5 and 6 would indeed soon catch up with and even slightly surpass regions 3 and 4, in the long-term drive in all four of these regions to catch up with the living standards enjoyed in the two richest income brackets (the United States, Great Britain, France, and so on). It bears reiteration that with the WEEP in operation, there would be no decrease in the absolute living standards in the rich nations, and the only sacrifice imposed on these nations would be that of a slightly reduced rate of progress in living standards. The modest sacrifice imposed on the United States (the highest income bracket) is shown by the two highest lines of Figure 4.3: the lower of these, which shows potential growth in per capita consumption with a WEEP in operation, lies only slightly below the path of potential growth in per capita consumption without a WEEP in operation.

Another measure of the potential burden of a WEEP on the United States would be the percentage of GNP contributed to the transfer fund for international economic development. For the benchmark with-WEEP simulation whose results are tabulated on the right-hand side of Table 4.1 and illustrated by Figure 4.2, the initial-year contribution would be 3.2 percent of GNP. Thereafter the contribution would gradually rise to a maximum of 4.4 percent in year 35. It is extremely significant that these figures are substantially below the average annual percent of GNP spent on national defense (between 5 and 6 percent) by the United States in the post-Vietnam War period. This suggests that contributions to an international economic development transfer fund could be financed entirely out of reduced military spending in the event of major disarmament agreements, so that they would not impinge on the U.S. population's accustomed living standards. The contributions required of the other rich nations would be proportionately smaller, and for the most part could also be met entirely out of reduced military spending pursuant to major disarmament agreements. The relatively modest percentages of GNP required of the rich nations to finance the program is another numerical indication of the basic feasibility of a World Economic Equalization Program.

We should perhaps pause for a moment to try to explain how such a drastic differential in the potential paths of world economic development with and without a WEEP can be possible. It is of course recognized by almost everyone that if the current output of all nations were lumped together and divided up equally, the uniform world-wide standard of living attainable would be very low relative to the current standards of the rich nations. It is this misleading image of "crude redistribution" which makes the results obtained in the WEEP simulation seem so astonishing and improbable. The crude redistribution image is misleading because it pertains to a hypothetical redistribution of final output, while in fact the WEEP under consideration here pertains to a potential prior distribution of new productive resources. From the fact that at most some 50 percent of the "residual" of each nation would be contributed to the transfer fund, it is impossible for the operation of a WEEP, as adumbrated in the simulation model being described here, to result in a decrease in the living standards of any nation.

Even so, one might wonder how the shift of a certain amount of new productive resources from rich nations to poor nations could have such a modest retarding effect on the economic progress of the rich nations, while at the same time it has such a terrific accelerating impact on the economic progress of the poorest nations. The answer lies in the principle of diminishing marginal productivity of capital, a principle which has been a foundation stone of modern neoclassical economics for well over 100 years. The reason why rich nations are rich is that they possess a great abundance of generalized capital (i.e., much plant and machinery, and a highly educated and trained labor force); while the reason why poor nations are poor is that they have only a very small stock of generalized capital (i.e., very limited plant and machinery, and a sparsely educated and trained labor force). The large generalized capital stock of the rich nations entails a small marginal productivity of this stock, while the small generalized capital stock of the poor nations entails a large marginal productivity of this stock. Thus depriving a rich nation of a given amount of generalized capital will reduce its output by only a small amount, while installing that same amount in a poor nation will increase its output by a large amount. Almost all professional economists will accept this general argument. What the WEEP simulation suggests, however, is that the actual numerical implications of this argument, in the context of potential world economic development, are quite possibly far more dramatic than most people, economists and others, had ever imagined could be possible.

Once again it is necessary to be somewhat cautious and circumspect in discussing such a controversial question. Needless to emphasize, it is impossible for anyone to guarantee that if a World Economic Equalization Program were undertaken, the results would be, fundamentally, as they are illustrated in Table 4.1 and Figure 4.2—in other words, that the Program would be successful. In the author's research work on this matter (described in more detail in the two papers on the WEEP model and in the technical appendix to this chapter), it has been ascertained beyond question that the Program might be a failure. Even if the basic structure of the model is retained, certain variations in numerical parameter values will produce simulation results which display little or no progress toward equalization. In addition, dubious questions might certainly be raised concerning the realism of the model itself. One vital issue, of course, involves the transferability of "generalized capital." The model assumes that $1 worth of generalized capital value installed in, say, the United States is equivalent to $1 worth of generalized capital value installed in, say, India. Skeptics, of course, will assert that $1 of generalized capital value in the United States might be equivalent to only 2 cents of generalized capital value in India. They will argue that any nation that allows sacred cows to roam around in public buildings almost certainly lacks the cultural prerequisites necessary to make full and effective use of generalized capital.

There are indeed various hypotheses, such as the "cultural attitudes" hypothesis just alluded to, which attribute the poverty of the poor nations to something other than a simple scarcity of material resources (plant and machinery) and human resources (education and training). But is certainly arguable that "people are people" and "production is production" whether the location is India or the United States. This implies that if the Indian people possessed the requisite plant and machinery, and possessed the requisite education and training, they would have no difficulty in producing just as much output as is currently being produced in nations such as the United States. But perhaps these skeptics are correct after all: perhaps the notion of world-wide economic equalization is indeed a hopeless dream. However, we have no way of knowing this to be the case at the present time, on the basis of the currently available evidence. Is it sensible to allow the mere possibility of failure to obstruct what could be a marvelously successful episode in world economic history?

C. FUNCTIONING OF THE PROGRAM

The previous section dealt with the scale of a potential World Economic Equalization Program rather than the *functioning* of such a Program. One of the most critical assumptions underlying the simulation model results which suggest the possibility of success, is that a certain value of new generalized capital investment which is not added to the generalized capital stock of a rich nation would be equal to the value of new generalized capital investment which is added to the generalized capital stock of a poor nation. But what of the possibility that the new value which is added to the generalized capital stock of the poor nation would be appreciably *less* than the new value which is withheld from the generalized capital stock of the rich nation? There are at least two very obvious possibilities tending toward this outcome. One is that the transfers would be carried out in a "leaky bucket": that the administrative overhead of the Program would be very costly, that a lot of the resource flows would be converted from producer goods to consumer goods before arriving in the poor countries, and that a very great deal would be lost to theft, graft, and other forms of dishonesty, particularly in the poorest recipient nations. The second possibility is that even those economic resources arriving in the poor countries in the form of productive capacity, both human and capital, will not be utilized as efficiently as they would be in the richer countries: such capacity would be invested unwisely, managed poorly, and would quickly lapse into disrepair and disuse.[10]

It goes without saying that every possible effort should be made to control and counteract these tendencies, because they clearly contain within themselves the potentiality of destroying the effectiveness of the World Economic Equalization Program and of condemning it to complete and ignominious failure. Needless to emphasize, the World Economic Equalization Program envisioned here presupposes that the resource transfers would be conducted in an honest, intelligent, and effective manner. The Program must clearly be much more than simply "throwing money at the problem." Its procedures would attempt to safeguard against excessive wastage and diversion, to enhance the productivity of the transferred resources, and to guarantee that the nations receiving the transfers are doing their fair share to make the WEEP a success. But clearly it would be both premature and beyond the scope of the present work to enter into a great deal of detail with regard to the actual functioning of a potential WEEP. First a decision must be made to undertake the effort, and only then is it realistic to consider the fine details of the Program's operation. The intention at this point is therefore only to enumerate a few relatively basic and commonsensical points to be observed in designing the operation of the Program.[11]

First and foremost, transfers would be strictly confined to production goods and education/training, and would never involve any commodities intended for final consumption, whether they be food, medical supplies, automobiles, television sets, or anything else not directly and exclusively employed as a production good. Transfers of consumption goods and medical supplies would no doubt be continued, particularly on humanitarian grounds following upon earthquakes, droughts, famines, etc., but such transfers must be entirely outside the purview of the WEEP. The recipient nations of productive resource transfers under the WEEP must utilize them to purchase plant and equipment, or educational and training services, from the specific donor nations providing the specific resource contributions. Thus, for example, United States donations into the international transfer fund would be spent on United States industrial products and educational services. This provision will greatly assist the political feasibility of the WEEP by making it contribute directly and obviously to the prosperity of a great many business enterprises and educational institutions in the rich nations. Once the Program has been in operation for a few years, these enterprises and institutions will have a strong vested interest in its continuation. Theoretically, various other enterprises and institutions will be losing revenue because of the WEEP's operation, but these losses would be both dispersed and, in the case of any particular enterprise or institution, uncertain, so that there would not be a strong vested interest in the discontinuation of the Program.

At the macroeconomic level, the operation of a World Economic Equalization Program would exert an obvious expansionary effect on the economies of the contributing rich nations, and indeed on the entire world economy. The benefit of an expansionary condition is higher employment while the cost is higher inflation. While opinions differ as to whether unemployment or inflation has been the greater problem during any given period in the past, it may perhaps be suggested that so long as inflation does not become extremely aggravated and so long as reasonable attention is paid to the interests of those living on fixed incomes, an expansionary condition is generally beneficial both on material and psychological grounds. The simulation model described in the previous section assumes full employment of resources even if no WEEP is undertaken, and therefore it does not incorporate the probable expansionary effect of a WEEP. In this regard, therefore, the model might actually be underestimating the potentialities inherent in a WEEP.

A large proportion of the WEEP resource transfers should be commercially allocated: that is, funds should be provided via a competitive bidding process to business enterprises or government entities under condition of assumption of some sort of repayment obligation. This principle is not only desirable from the point of view of efficient allocation of the transferred resources, but it would reduce the administrative overhead of the Program by allowing much of the transfer fund to be dispersed through existing international banking institutions. Also, funds would largely be provided to private and public borrowers in the less developed countries under various types of matching principles, so that a part of the cost of generalized capital accumulation would be borne by the populations of these nations. The matching principle would help to ensure that investment projects were being carefully evaluated prior to requests for financial assistance.

On the other hand, commercial criteria should not become excessively dominant in the allocation of the transfer fund. In some cases, the potential benefits and costs of proposed investment projects cannot be estimated with any degree of precision, and an excessive emphasis upon commercial criteria might deter some very important and worthwhile projects. A substantial proportion of the fund therefore should be distributed either in the form of free grants or in the form of loans at reduced interest rates, particularly when it is a matter of large-scale investments by government agencies in social infrastructure projects. Although it is not intended that the World

Development Authority, the overall administrative organ of the World Economic Equalization Program, be a "planning agency" in the usual sense of the term, it should at least maintain a planning department which would be particularly oriented to the study of possible large-scale social infrastructure projects. Another important departure from the commercial orientation of the WEEP would be in terms of debt reduction of recipient nations if it appears that the debt servicing burden is becoming too onerous. It is anticipated that the World Development Authority, as the ultimate lending authority (even though it might utilize existing international banks as intermediate conduits for resource flows), would be considerably more lenient with respect to debt reduction than are the contemporary international lenders, including the World Bank. This would be particularly true when it appears that the current debt servicing burden of any particular borrowing nation considerably exceeds that which had been anticipated on the basis of technically competent, good faith forecasting techniques.

In view of the overwhelming evidence that excessive population growth seriously retards progress with respect to individual living standards, determined population control efforts by LDC governments would be a prerequisite for large economic assistance resource transfers.[12] Population control is of course an extremely sensitive issue. Humanity has been endowed with an extremely strong instinct toward procreation, and this instinct is celebrated and encouraged by many of the world's great religions. At the same time, any reasonable person who appreciates the finite nature of the planet Earth, and who understands the significance of geometric growth, realizes that if the rate of population growth which has been witnessed throughout the world over the last century persists for a prolonged historical period, the ultimate result could easily be disastrous as far as individual living standards and quality of life are concerned. At the moment, there exists an uneasy stalemate between rationality and the procreative urge. Most informed individuals agree that population control is desirable, but there is not usually a great deal of urgency attached to the judgment, and official government policy and activity in the interest of population control tends to be fairly limited and lackadaisical.

Although it is not claimed that a stringent population control program is a necessary condition for the success of the World Economic Equalization Program, it is almost certain that the prospects for a successful WEEP would be considerably enhanced by more effective population control all around the world, and particularly in the LDC's. The WEEP period would therefore be a very good period in which to try to establish a reasonable degree of social control over the level and rate of change of population. The day may eventually come when the production of children will be deemed a privilege rather than a right, and prospective parents will be required to demonstrate financial solvency, as well as physical and mental competency, prior to bringing babies into the world. At this point such restrictions on the customary autonomy in this matter are regarded as a heinous abrogation of a natural right, and this may well remain the case until dramatic and irrefutable evidence is incurred of the negative effect of population pressure on economic welfare.

But the desired degree of social control over population expansion, prior to some sort of self-evident economic disaster such as a world-wide famine, may be achievable through indirect methods. There are two primary indirect methods: (1) enhancing knowledge and availability of effective contraceptive methods; (2) reducing the economic attractiveness of parenthood. The second method implies both the reduction of positive economic incentives to parenthood (mainly through the social provision of adequate retirement income to eliminate the function of children in this regard), and the implementation of various economic disincentives to parenthood (e.g., reduction or elimination of tax deductions for children, making parents legally responsible for providing education for their children through the university level, financing the educational system mainly from taxes levied exclusively on parents). These indirect methods would not eliminate the freedom of parents to produce children at their own discretion, but they would make the exercise of this freedom considerably more expensive. Such measures are justifiable on grounds that the production of children imposes a heavy expense on society as a whole, and that it is appropriate that a substantial proportion of the burden be borne directly by the parents.

Such a policy may seem harsh, but it must be recognized that it would almost certainly be in the long-term interest of the human race. If the human race is successful in establishing an upper limit on world population, possibly in the range from 8 billion to 12 billion individuals, it would considerably reduce the probability of the sort of ecological overload catastrophe that might lead to miserable living standards for a population of only 1 to 2 billion individuals. It would also considerably reduce the probability of a scenario that might be more realistic than the ecological overload catastrophe scenario: that as the human population gradually rises toward the upper carrying limit of the Earth, perhaps between 80 and 100 billion individuals, individual living standards will gradually settle down toward the same miserable level endured by only 1 to 2 billion individuals under the ecological overload catastrophe scenario. Population control will almost certainly be necessary in the long run if individual human welfare is to achieve and maintain a high level. The only question is when it will be necessary. The World Economic Equalization Program would provide a golden opportunity for the human race to take control of this situation sooner rather than later.

These and other measures should be taken to ensure the efficacy of the WEEP resource transfers in reaching the desired objectives of the Program. Predictably, skeptics will complain that if a WEEP were actually undertaken in the real world, it would constitute nothing more that a "giant pork barrel" for the personal enrichment of venal and corrupt bureaucrats. Sad to say, they may be right. But should the *possibility* of failure—a possibility which is of course inevitable where any important undertaking is concerned—be allowed to forestall even an attempt at success?

It is to be hoped that most readers will agree that the answer to this question should be a firm and resolute "No!" The answer should rather be that we should at least try, that we should definitely make the effort. A World Economic Equalization Program holds the promise of a dazzling success, an epochal advance. It offers mankind the possibility that the next generation will witness monumental progress in human wellbeing, progress on a gigantic scale never before witnessed in human history. If we are doomed to disappointment, then so be it—we will be made aware of the futility of the effort in short order. But we ought not be deterred by those cynical skeptics and petty-minded pessimists who would disparage even the mere *aspiration* toward a better world.

TECHNICAL APPENDIX

The WEEP model set out in Table A.1 represents an effort to achieve a reasonable compromise between the competing objectives of realistic economic content, and simplicity and convenience. Most variables are subscripted with an "*i*" for "region" or "income class", and a "*t*" for time period. Although in principle regions could be represented by nations, the simulations reported here are based on a very highly aggregated set of six so-called regions based on per capita income categories specified by the World Bank in its recent annual *Development Reports*.

The model's production function, equation (7), is a Constant Elasticity of Substitution form giving output Y as a function of inputs K (generalized capital) and L (population/labor). Statistical proxies are utilized for Y and L in the implementation of the model, but K, generalized capital, represents a hypothetical notion for which existing statistical proxies such as "plant and equipment" would not be appropriate. Generalized capital is the value of *all* reproducible inputs other than physical labor power. In addition to the usual plant and equipment, it would certainly include the value of educational and training inputs into the labor force, and it might also include the cost of still other inputs into the production process which are difficult if not impossible to measure precisely.

Once total output in each region has been produced according to the CES production function, it is then allocated between four uses: military output (M); consumption (C); transfer fund contribution (T); and domestic investment (I). In the WEEP-less world, no region makes a contribution into the WEEP. In a WEEP world, the richer regions would contribute into a transfer fund, from which the poorer regions would draw shares (S). Such shares would be applied to investment in generalized capital K. The rules embodied in the WEEP model for determining contributions and shares are very much of an ad hoc nature. They are meant to be commonsensically appealing; but they have no explicit justification in terms of economic efficiency or social welfare theory.

Consider first the determination of contributions. To begin with, military output M is regarded as an "obligatory" proportion of total output Y (equation 8). It is "obligatory" in the sense that in the event of a conflict, it takes precedence over consumption. Equation (9) gives "potential" consumption (C^*) as the product of population times "potential" per capita

TABLE A.1

Model Structure

Variable	Definition	Equation	(#)

Transition from period t-1 to period t:

A_t	total factor productivity	$A_t = (1 + \tau_{t-1})A_{t-1}$	(1)
τ_t	rate of change of A_t	$\tau_t = (1 + \varphi)\tau_{t-1}$	(2)
$L_{i,t}$	population/labor	$L_{i,t} = (1 + n_{i,t-1})L_{i,t-1}$	(3)
$n_{i,t}$	rate of change of $L_{i,t}$	$n_{i,t} = (1+\gamma)n_{i,t-1}$	(4)
$m_{i,t}$	military spending (proportion of output)	$m_{i,t} = (1 + \mu)m_{i,t-1}$	(5)
$K_{i,t}$	generalized capital	$K_{i,t} = K_{i,t-1} + I_{i,t-1} + S_{i,t-1}$	(6)

Period t recursive model:

$Y_{i,t}$	total output	$Y_{i,t} = A_t\,(\alpha K_{i,t}^{-\rho} + \beta L_{i,t}^{-\rho})^{-\nu/\rho}$	(7)
$M_{i,t}$	military output	$M_{i,t} = m_{i,t}Y_{i,t}$	(8)
$C^*_{i,t}$	potential consumption	$C^*_{i,t} = (Y_{i,t} / L_{i,t})^{\nu}L_{i,t}$	(9)
$C_{i,t}$	actual consumption	$C_{i,t} = \min[C^*_{i,t}, Y_{i,t} - M_{i,t}]$	(10)
$R_{i,t}$	residual	$R_{i,t} = Y_{i,t} - C_{i,t} - M_{i,t}$	(11)
$c_{i,t}$	per capita consumption	$c_{i,t} = C_{i,t} / L_{i,t}$	(12)
c^m_t	maximum $c_{i,t}$	$c^m_t = \max[c_{i,t},\ i=1,...,n]$	(13)
$r_{i,t}$	ratio	$r_{i,t} = c_{i,t} / c^m_t$	(14)
$\lambda_{i,t}$	transfer fund proportion	$\lambda_{i,t} = 0 \quad\quad\quad\ \text{if } r_{i,t} < .5$	(15)
		$\lambda_{i,t} = r_{i,t} - .5 \quad \text{if } r_{i,t} \geq .5$	

TABLE A.1 continued

$T_{i,t}$	transfer fund contribution	$T_{i,t} = \lambda_{i,t} R_{i,t}$	(16)
$t_{i,t}$	transfer fund ratio	$t_{i,t} = T_{i,t} / Y_{i,t}$	(17)
T_t	total transfer fund	$T_t = \sum_i T_{i,t}$	(18)
$d_{i,t}$	difference	$d_{i,t} = c^m_t - c_{i,t}$	(19)
$s_{i,t}$	transfer fund share ratio	$s_{i,t} = d_{i,t} L_{i,t} / \Sigma d_{i,t} L_{i,t}$	(20)
$S_{i,t}$	transfer fund share	$S_{i,t} = s_{i,t} T_t$	(21)
$I_{i,t}$	domestic investment	$I_{i,t} = R_{i,t} - T_{i,t}$	(22)

consumption, the latter obtained from a log-linear function of per capita output. Equation (10) states that actual consumption (C) is the minimum of potential consumption C^*, and non-military output $(Y - M)$: if non-military output is less than potential consumption, then actual consumption becomes non-military output. This simply says that if consumption desires (expectations, requirements, or whatever term is used) are inconsistent with the "military obligation," then it is consumption rather than military expenditure which gives way.

Deducting military spending M and consumption C from output Y will leave (if the region is at least relatively rich) a residual R. Without a WEEP, each region invests its entire residual in domestic investment I, which expands its stock of generalized capital K. With a WEEP, part of the residual may be contributed to a transfer fund. A region's contribution is determined by the conditional equation (15), which gives the transfer fund proportion (that proportion of the residual R allocated to the transfer fund contribution T), as a function of the "ratio" (r). The "ratio," defined in equations (12)-(14), is the ratio of regional per capita consumption to maximum per capita consumption over all regions. In words, the significance of equation (15) is as follows: first, if a region's per capita consumption is less than half maximum per capita consumption, it pays nothing into the transfer fund; second, if a region's per capita consumption is half or more of maximum per capita consumption, the proportion of its residual which is contributed to the transfer fund rises linearly with the ratio, up to a maximum of one half of the residual. Thus even the richest region would devote half of the residual left after consumption and military expenditures have been deducted from output, to domestic investment. A very important measure is the transfer fund ratio t, defined as the ratio of the transfer fund contribution T of a given region to its total output Y. This measure can be identified with the "proportion of GNP devoted to foreign aid," a familiar concept.

The principle of distribution of the transfer fund is contained in equations (19)-(20). The "difference" d for a region is merely the difference between maximum per capita consumption and regional per capita consumption (equation 19). This difference, weighted by population (L), is taken as the the appropriate measure of a given region's "need" for generalized capital. The share of a given region (s) in the total transfer fund is merely its own dL factor, divided by the sum of such factors over all regions (equation 20).

Table A.2 shows the numerical data used to obtain initial conditions in the regions, and the parameter values used for the baseline simulations. The World Bank publication *World Development Report 1985* (Tables 1 and 19) is the source for 1983 population, 1973-83 annual average population growth rate, and 1983 GNP per capita. In view of the considerable uncertainties regarding the measurement of military spending, both in advanced nations and LDC's, purely hypothetical numbers were used for the regional military expenditure proportions. The six regions utilized in the numerical implementation of the model are based on categories utilized in the World Bank report: region 1: the United States; region 2: all "industrial market economies" excluding the United States; region 3: "upper middle income economies" plus "East European nonmarket economies"; region 4: "lower middle income economies"; region 5: China and India; region 6: "other low income economies" (excluding China and India).

It is well known that the standard measures of national output overstate the output of advanced market economies and understate the output of traditional agricultural economies. An effort was made to adjust for this by means of using a relationship estimated by Kravis and his associates between true GNP per capita and standard measured GNP per capita (Kravis et al, 1978, equation A70). The GNP per capita figures utilized to generate initial period generalized capital by region are shown in the row labeled "Kravis-adjusted."

As mentioned above, generalized capital is not adequately measured by the "plant and equipment" values used for "capital" in the developed nations. Moreover, reliable plant and equipment figures do not exist for most LDC's in any event. The procedure for obtaining the value of first-period generalized capital for each region from data on per capita output and

TABLE A.2

Parametric Data for WEEP Model Baseline Simulation

<u>Regional Data:</u>

Variable	Region					
	1	2	3	4	5	6
1983 population (mils) (World Bank estimate)	234.5	494.4	886.2	665.1	1723.2	583.0
1973-83 annual average rate of population growth (World Bank estimate)	.010	.006	.017	.025	.018	.026
1983 GNP per capita (000 $, World Bank)	14.110	9.613	2.005	.750	.280	.200
1983 GNP per capita (000 $, Kravis-adjusted)	14.110	11.349	4.011	1.857	.784	.572
military output proportion (hypothetical)	.060	.040	.040	.035	.005	.005

<u>Baseline Simulation Parameter Values:</u>

Symbol	Parameter Definition	Value
k	region 1 initial period capital-output ratio	3.0
α	capital productivity coefficient	0.3
β	labor productivity coefficient	0.7
τ_1	initial rate of change: total factor productivity	0.015
φ	rate of change of τ	0
ν	elasticity of substitution	1.0
σ	degree of homogeneity	1.0
γ	rate of change: population growth	0
μ	rate of change: military output proportion	0
v	elasticity of per cap consumption wrt per cap output	0.95

population is as follows. First, an arbitrary judgment is made on the initial period generalized capital-output ratio for the richest region (designated k), and the corresponding value for richest region initial period generalized capital K calculated from $K = kY$. Then the initial value of A is calculated from the production function, equation (7). Finally, using this value of A, and figures on per capita output and population for the remaining regions, the implied values of initial period generalized capital K in the remaining regions may be calculated by again using equation (7).

The lower part of Table A.2 lists the parameters of the model, and shows the numerical values used in the baseline simulations. Although some of these values have quasi-empirical support, it has to be admitted that as a whole, the set of parameter values is very much of a hypothetical nature. Thus the importance of the sensitivity analysis reported in Table A.4.

However, in its defense it may be said that the set of parameter values shown in Table A.2 does produce a simulation which passes a very crude validation test. The World Bank *World Development Report 1985* gives for each of the six regions the average annual growth rate in GNP per capita from 1965-1983. These rates may be compared with the average annual growth rate in output per capita produced by the Table A.1 model without WEEP (that is, the Table A.1 model minus the lower part of equation 15), using the Table A.2 parameter values, over the first 20 periods:

Region	World Bank estimate	Model estimate
1	1.7	1.8
2	3.0	2.4
3	3.8	4.9
4	2.9	2.4
5	3.2	0.9
6	0.7	0.7

The World Bank estimates and the model estimates are in agreement on a kind of "inverted-V" pattern of growth rates: lower for richest and poorest regions, higher for intermediate-income regions. The most glaring inconsistency between the two sets of growth rate estimates pertains to region 5 (China and India): the World Bank estimates a GNP per capita growth rate of 3.2 percent per annum over the last two decades, while the model indicates only a 0.9 percent growth rate. Against the validity of the World Bank estimate is the point that if the 3.2 percent growth rate for China and India were valid, it would constitute a glaring inconsistency with the "inverted-V" pattern established by the other five regions.

Table A.3 compares baseline simulations of the model displayed in Table A.1, using the numerical parameter values displayed in Table A.2, over 35 periods. The first simulation represents growth in the absence of a World Economic Equalization Program (WEEP): in this case each region retains its entire residual R for domestic investment I. The second simulation represents growth in the presence of a WEEP: in this case the richer regions contribute a part of their residuals to a transfer fund T from which the poorer regions draw shares S, which are then allocated to generalized capital accumulation.

Table A.3 displays, at five-year intervals over the six regions, four key variables: (a) per capita consumption; (b) ratio of regional per capita consumption to maximum per capita consumption; (c) transfer fund ratio; and (d) transfer fund share ratio. Looking first at per capita consumption, the drastic effect that a WEEP might have on world income distribution is strikingly evident. A WEEP would indeed have a retarding effect on growth in per capita consumption in the two richest regions; however, it would be fair to describe the retarding effect as "modest." In the richest region (the United States), for example, per capita consumption would rise over the 35 years of the WEEP planning period from 12.4 to 21.1, instead of from 12.4 to 23.7, which would be the expectation without the WEEP. Meanwhile, the WEEP would have a significant accelerating effect on the per capita consumption of the poorer regions. For the poorest regions, this acceleration might well be termed "tremendous." In the poorest region, the expected rise in per capita consumption without the WEEP is barely perceptible: from 0.6 to 0.7; while with the WEEP the expected rise would be from 0.6 to 18.8. From the ratio data in part (b) of Table A.3, it is seen that 18.8 is .893 of the richest region per capita consumption of 21.1.

In a fundamental sense, the burden of a WEEP on the developed nations is manifested in the retardation they would experience in per capita consumption growth. This burden is estimated by comparing the time-paths of consumption per capita with and without the WEEP shown in part (a) of Table A.3. But in view of the attention paid to the ratio of foreign aid contributions to GNP, the "transfer fund ratio"(t) in the WEEP model is an interesting alternative measure of the burden. This ratio is shown in part (c) of Table A.3. According to the baseline with-WEEP simulation, a WEEP would entail an initial-period contribution from region 1 (the United States) of 0.032 of total output, and this contribution would gradually rise through the planning period to a maximum of 0.044 in period 35. In percentage terms, these figures represent "3.2 percent of GNP" and "4.4 percent of GNP."

TABLE A.3

Baseline Simulation Results
without WEEP (w/o) and with WEEP (w)

	Region 1		Region 2		Region 3		Region 4		Region 5		Region 6	
	w/o	w	w/o	w	w/o	w	w/o	w	w/o	w	w/o	w
a)	per capita		consump.									
1	12.4	12.4	10.1	10.1	3.7	3.7	1.8	1.8	0.8	0.8	0.6	0.6
5	13.3	13.1	11.1	10.9	4.7	4.9	1.8	3.5	0.8	3.9	0.6	3.9
10	14.5	14.1	12.5	12.1	6.0	6.5	1.9	5.5	0.8	6.5	0.6	6.5
15	15.9	15.2	14.1	13.4	7.7	8.4	2.0	7.5	0.9	8.9	0.6	8.8
20	17.5	16.4	16.0	14.9	9.5	10.4	2.7	9.8	0.9	11.3	0.6	11.1
25	19.3	17.8	18.1	16.6	11.6	12.8	5.3	12.3	1.0	13.8	0.7	13.5
30	21.4	19.4	20.4	18.6	13.9	15.4	8.4	15.0	1.0	16.4	0.7	16.1
35	23.7	21.1	23.1	20.7	16.5	18.3	11.6	18.0	1.1	19.2	0.7	18.8
b)	ratio											
1	1.00	1.00	.813	.813	.303	.303	.145	.145	.063	.063	.046	.046
5	1.00	1.00	.835	.833	.351	.375	.139	.267	.061	.302	.044	.300
10	1.00	1.00	.861	.859	.417	.464	.132	.389	.057	.465	.042	.459
20	1.00	1.00	.911	.908	.543	.634	.155	.598	.053	.688	.037	.676
25	1.00	1.00	.934	.933	.600	.716	.275	.691	.051	.772	.035	.758
30	1.00	1.00	.955	.958	.651	.794	.394	.776	.048	.846	.033	.830
35	1.00	1.00	.975	.980	.696	.868	.490	.854	.045	.909	.031	.893
c)	transfer		fund		ratio							
1	—	.032	—	.023	—	0	—	0	—	0	—	0
5	—	.033	—	.026	—	0	—	0	—	0	—	0
10	—	.035	—	.030	—	0	—	0	—	0	—	0
15	—	.037	—	.034	—	.003	—	0	—	.009	—	.008
20	—	.038	—	.038	—	.010	—	.008	—	.022	—	.020
25	—	.040	—	.042	—	.018	—	.017	—	.034	—	.032
30	—	.042	—	.047	—	.028	—	.027	—	.046	—	.043
35	—	.044	—	.052	—	.037	—	.037	—	.057	—	.054
d)	transfer		fund		share		ratio					
1	—	0	—	.027	—	.177	—	.164	—	.472	—	.160
5	—	0	—	.028	—	.199	—	.181	—	.441	—	.152
10	—	0	—	.028	—	.210	—	.193	—	.418	—	.151
15	—	0	—	.027	—	.218	—	.204	—	.400	—	.151
20	—	0	—	.025	—	.223	—	.214	—	.384	—	.154
25	—	0	—	.023	—	.227	—	.224	—	.368	—	.157
30	—	0	—	.019	—	.231	—	.237	—	.351	—	.162
35	—	0	—	.013	—	.234	—	.254	—	.329	—	.169

According to Table 18 of the 1985 *World Development Report,* in 1984 the United States contributed 0.24 percent of GNP (less than one quarter of 1 percent) to "official development assistance." It would appear that there is a long way to go between current practices with respect to economic development contributions, and the World Economic Equalization Program under consideration here. However, it is important to recognize that a potential WEEP would not require extravagant percentages of GNP in order to function. Around three to four percent of GNP seems a manageable figure. It is in fact very considerably less than the United States is currently spending on its military establishment.

The baseline simulation results are remarkably encouraging. In fact, it would seem that if it were assured that the baseline with-WEEP simulation was a valid representation of a practical possibility, only a small minority of extremely short-sighted and selfish individuals in the richer regions would be opposed to a WEEP. Surely the great majority of their populations would find the increase in international stability and security, and the sense of altruistic achievement, to be derived from a WEEP, to be well worth the modest sacrifice in material consumption it would entail. The real question pertains to practicality. Most advanced nation economists have absorbed a sufficient amount of pessimism about economic development that they would feel impelled to object that the baseline with-WEEP simulation result is "too good to be true." Therefore it is appropriate to examine the robustness of the result with respect to various alternative sets of parameter values.

There are ten different parameters listed in the bottom section of Table A.2. Even if one were to confine oneself to numerical values which possess some degree of "substantiation," either in the form of empirical evidence (for example, econometric estimates of the rate of growth of total factor productivity), or of common usage on a priori grounds (for example, the common assumption that production functions are linear homogeneous), the number of different combinations of numerical parameter values is enormous. Thus "exhaustive" sensitivity analysis is clearly impractical. Of necessity, sensitivity analysis must be confined to a few experiments whose implications are merely suggestive.

Table A.4 gives results from a few such experiments. The body of the table consists of pairs of numbers: the first is the consumption per capita in region 1 (the United States) in the 35th period (with a WEEP); the second is the ratio of region 6 per capita consumption to region 1 per capita consumption in the 35th period. Thus the first number represents the absolute standard of welfare attained in the richest region at the end of the planning interval, while the second number represents the relative standard

Table A.4

Sensitivity Analysis of WEEP Model Results
to Parametric Variation

$c_{1,35}$ / $r_{6,35}$ for various combinations of numerical parameter values

a) technical production coefficients

k:	3.0	4.0	5.0	6.0	7.0
α β					
.3 .7	21.1/.893	20.4/.811	20.0/.748	19.7/.699	19.5/.658
.4 .6	21.5/.752	20.5/.635	20.0/.552	19.6/.490	19.3/.442
.5 .5	22.0/.551	20.7/.421	19.9/.344	19.4/.292	19.2/.256
.6 .4	22.5/.358	20.8/.258	19.9/.205	19.3/.173	18.9/.151
.7 .3	23.0/.232	21.0/.166	19.9/.133	19.2/.113	18.7/.101

b) total factor productivity

τ_I:	0.000	0.005	0.010	0.015	0.020
φ					
− 0.04	12.4/.777	13.7/.803	15.1/.828	16.7/.854	18.5/.879
− 0.02	12.4/.777	14.1/.808	16.1/.839	18.3/.870	20.9/.901
0.00	12.4/.777	14.8/.815	17.7/.854	21.1/.893	25.2/.931
0.02	12.4/.777	15.9/.826	20.3/.875	26.1/.925	33.5/.974
0.04	12.4/.777	17.7/.841	25.3/.906	36.2/.971	52.1/1.04

c) returns to scale/elasticity of substitution

ν:	.5	.6	.7	.8	.9
σ					
.7	18.6/.684	18.9/.735	19.2/.791	19.6/.852	19.9/.918
.8	18.7/.660	19.1/.711	19.4/.766	16.6/.828	20.1/.898
.9	18.9/.629	19.2/.676	19.6/.730	20.0/.791	20.4/.862
1.1	19.2/.533	19.6/.592	20.1/.635	20.5/.686	21.0/.746
1.2	NS	NS	NS	20.7/.627	21.1/.679

d) disarmament/population growth deceleration

μ:	0.000	− 0.025	− 0.050	− 0.075	− 0.100
γ					
0.000	21.1/.893	21.8/.884	22.2/.880	22.5/.879	22.6/.878
− 0.025	21.7/.906	22.4/.898	22.8/.895	23.1/.893	23.2/.892
− 0.050	22.1/.913	22.8/.905	23.2/.902	23.4/.900	23.6/.900
− 0.075	22.3/.916	23.0/.908	23.4/.905	23.7/.904	23.8/.903
− 0.100	22.4/.917	23.1/.910	23.6/.907	23.8/.906	24.0/.905

of welfare achieved at that time by the region which is presently the poorest. The body of the table consists of four sections, each of which contains results for variations in two related parameter values.

Of all the parameters used in the WEEP model, it is k and α which are the most hypothetical in nature, because they pertain to the relationship between output and the unmeasured variable "generalized capital." (The capital productivity coefficient α and the labor productivity coefficient β are assumed to add up to 1: thus the β value may be deduced from the α value.) It is intuitively obvious that the WEEP approach to economic development would be ineffective if the real reason for regional output differentials is differentials in total factor productivity (A) rather than differentials in generalized capital endowments (K). The results in part (a) of Table A.6 demonstrate that ineffectiveness would also result from parameter values for α and k which substantially exceed the baseline simulation values. The worst case shown in the table combines an α value of 0.7 with a k value of 7.0: in this case, region 1 per capita consumption would rise to only 18.7 (versus 21.1 in the baseline case), while the region 6 ratio would rise to only 0.101 (versus 0.893 in the baseline case). Clearly there exists the possibility—even granting the validity of the model itself—that the true value of k might be sufficiently high, and/or the true value of α might be sufficiently high, that a real-world implementation of the WEEP would have a negligible impact on the interregional distribution of output, consumption, and welfare.

Part (b) of Table A.4 pertains to variations in the parameters which affect total factor productivity (A). The results shown suggest that the development of total factor productivity will have a strong impact on the level of absolute welfare achieved in the richest region, but were a WEEP implemented, the effect of variations in the future course of total factor productivity would not have a numerically substantial impact on the amount of equalization attained. Even under the worst assumptions examined, the degree of equalization would be very substantial

Part (c) of Table A.4 examines variations in two parameters of the CES general case: the returns to scale parameter (ν); and the elasticity of substitution parameter (σ). The Cobb-Douglas sub-case ($\sigma = 1$) is not included in this part of the table, because of the technical complications of doing so. In particular, in the CD sub-case, the parameter $\nu = \alpha + \beta$, and there are an infinite number of combinations of α and β which sum to any given value of ν. Another technical complication was encountered in running simulations using various combinations of ν and σ: for certain combinations of values a positive initial-period solution for K over all regions does not exist. These combinations are indicated by "NS" for "no solution." The results obtained indicate that an increase in the returns to scale parameter (toward the constant returns level of 1.0) augments both richest region absolute welfare and poorest region relative welfare, while an increase in the elasticity of substitution parameter increases richest region absolute welfare but tends to work against poorest region relative welfare.

Finally, part (d) of Table A.4 explores two possibilities which are much discussed, and generally desired, by students of the contemporary human condition: disarmament, and population growth deceleration. In the baseline case, it is assumed that there will be no changes in the present rates of military spending, nor in the present rates of population growth. Respectively these assumptions are embodied in $\mu = 0$ and $\gamma = 0$. Part (d) of the table shows period-35 results under conditions of some combination of disarmament and population growth deceleration: these conditions are embodied in negative values of μ and γ. It is observed that both eventualities have a generally positive effect on the outcome, which is of course to be expected. What is surprising, however, is that quantitatively the effect is quite modest. This might be regarded as a favorable indication, in that it suggests that a successful WEEP might be a possibility even in the absence of major disarmament and/or major population growth deceleration. On the other hand, it is so widely assumed that both of these eventualities constitute necessary (but not sufficient) conditions for important economic progress on a world-wide scale, that the model indication that they are in fact not necessary conditions for this, might be taken as evidence against the validity of the model.

The results displayed in Table A.4 represent only a tiny sampling from a vast population of potential sensitivity experiments, and as such they can merely be suggestive of the very wide array of possible outcomes. The possibility that an actual WEEP would be ineffective is clearly demonstrated by the results contained in part (a) of the table: any specified degree of ineffectiveness may be produced simply by taking the k and/or the α parameter to be sufficiently high. Be that as it may, taken as a whole, Table A.4 suggests that the fundamental implication of the baseline with-WEEP simulation is not excessively frail. In general, the degree of equalization potentially achievable via the WEEP does not taper off drastically as less favorable parameter values are assumed. Also it ought to be stressed that there is no more justification for assuming that the true parameter values would be less favorable to a WEEP than the assumed baseline values, than there would be for assuming the true parameter values would be more favorable. Even the best empirical evidence presently available can give us no more than vague hints as to the true values of these parameters.

NOTES

1. The observations contained in this chapter on the world poverty problem and potentialities for world-wide economic development represent a judgmental distillation from a very substantial literature. A few illustrative references, in chronological order, are as follows: Peter T. Bauer and Basil S. Yamey (1957), A. N. Agarwala and S. P. Singh (1963), Everett Hagen (1968), Barbara Ward et al, eds. (1971), Gustav Ranis (1972), Paul Alpert (1973), Cornell Capa and J. Mayone Stycos (1974), Alistair I. MacBean and U. N. Balasubramanyan (1976), Albert Fishlow et al (1978), David Colmans and Frederick Nixson (1978), Erik Dammann (1979), William W. Murdock (1980), Michael P. Todaro (1981), Jacques Loup (1983), Ashok Bapna (1985), Nicholas Stern (1989).

2. Almost without exception, authorities on the world economy agree that widespread poverty in the LDCs constitutes a "threat to peace." The following statement from Paul Alpert (1973, p. ix) is typical: "A conflict of far greater scope is emerging as the major threat to peace, continued progress, and the very survival of our civilization. This is the conflict between the rich minority and the vast, rapidly growing majority of the underdeveloped poor in Asia, Africa, and Latin America, the proletariat of humanity." For the most part, however, analysis of the threat is brief and superficial, as for example in Goran Ohlin (1972, p. 63): "The argument that the gap is a threat to international security is sometimes taken to suggest that the rich countries, as small islands of prosperity, will find themselves attacked by the populous underprivileged nations around them. This appeal to the fears of the prosperous does not have much warrant in history. Technology may of course change that and many other things. A more down-to-earth argument is that many developing countries represent international danger spots where political instability threatens to involve the great powers in escalating conflicts." For a comparatively rare full-scale analysis of these possibilities, see Mario'n Mushkat (1982).

3. Principals among the turn-of-the-century Marxists who initiated the theory of economic imperialism were John Hobson, Vladimir Lenin and Rosa Luxembourg. Some illustrative references from the contemporary literature on economic imperialism are as follows: Pierre Jalee (1968, 1969), Robert I. Rhodes (1970), Arghini Emmanuel (1972), Vasily Vakhrushev (1973), L. L. Klochkovsky (1975), Ranjit Sau (1978), Keith Griffin and John Gurley (1985).

4. Typical expositions of the ideas represented by the phrase "New International Economic Order" (NIEO) are those of William G. Tyler (1977), Jyote Shankar Singh (1978), Jorge Lozoya and Rosario Green (1981), Davidson Nicol et al (1981), Pradip K. Ghosh (1984). The dismis-

sive early appraisal of the NIEO by the mainstream Western economist, Keith B. Griffin, still seems on target today (1978, p. 114): "The specific proposals that have been put forward to create a new international economic order are very modest and any measures likely to be implemented are unlikely to result in a significant transfer of income to the Third World."

5. During the post-World War II era, perhaps the leading intellectual champion of pessimism concerning the prospects for economic progress in the Third World has been Peter T. Bauer of the London School of Economics. According to Bauer, the imbedded institutional, cultural, and attitudinal characteristics in many if not most LDC's are such as to pose high and quite possibly insurmountable barriers to significant economic advance, at least as "economic advance" is generally defined within the advanced, industrialized nations. A corollary of this proposition is that economic development assistance from the advanced nations will have either no influence or a perverse influence on the economic condition of the recipient nations. This message has been tirelessly reiterated and elaborated in great detail in numerous articles and in no less than five books published between 1957 and 1984: *Economic Analysis and Policy in Underdeveloped Countries* (1957), *Indian Economic Policy and Development* (1961), *Dissent on Development* (1972), *Equality, the Third World, and Economic Delusion* (1981), and *Reality and Rhetoric: Studies in the Economics of Development* (1984). The negativity of Bauer's position was relatively unpopular in the 1950s and 1960s, but as the general ideological pendulum in the West swung inexorably toward conservatism in the 1970s and 1980s, Bauer became something of a darling of the increasingly influential neoconservative movement. See, for example, the festschrift in Bauer's honor sponsored by the Cato Institute (James A. Dorn, editor, *Cato Journal*, 1987).

6. As perhaps the most transcendent episode of public altruism (and/or enlightened self-interest) in world history, writing on the Marshall Plan tends to be rhapsodic, as for example in Harry Bayard Price (1955) and Robert J. Donovan (1987). And despite the currently prevailing pessimism in the developing nations regarding the economic destiny of the Third World, there still occurs sporadic support for a major economic assistance effort along the lines of a worldwide Marshall Plan. For example, in a *Time* Essay ("The Case for a Global Marshall Plan") published in 1978, George Church wrote: "Yet a new version of the Marshall Plan that rebuilt Europe after World War II may well be the most workable solution. Only such a plan could overcome the widespread feeling among voters that much aid to LDCs is wasted because it consists of piecemeal efforts by the givers to finance uncoordinated projects. It is often forgotten that the Marshall Plan

involved far more than the mere ladling out of money: it committed the U.S. to aid countries that drew up detailed and effective plans to use the cash and goods for rebuilding. This coordinated planning is vital—especially since the task of promoting growth in the poor countries will be much harder than the reconstruction of Europe was; postwar Europe had the skilled work force and industrial base that LDCs lack. A new Marshall Plan ought to commit the U.S., Europe and Japan not only to give more, but to give more according to a comprehensive and effective plan." See also Charles A. Cerami, *A Marshall Plan for the 1990s* (1989).

7. Although optimism in the advanced nations regarding the prospects for worldwide economic development have never been extremely high in an absolute sense throughout the post-World War II period, in a relative sense optimism—in the United States at least—seems to have crested in the early 1960's, as evidenced by such popular works as Seymour Melman's *The Peace Race* (1961), Amitai Etzioni's *The Hard Way to Peace* (1962), and Jacob Rubin's *Your Hundred Billion Dollars* (1964). Perhaps it had something to do with the fact that the young and vigorous John F. Kennedy was occupying the White House. By 1970—owing to such vicissitudes as assassination (John F. Kennedy, Robert Kennedy, Martin Luther King), racial rioting in the cities, and the Vietnam quagmire—the progressiveness, optimism, and idealism of "Camelot" seems to have been thoroughly expunged from American life and thought.

8. As of 1973, when the Overseas Development Council published the results of a survey of the United States population on economic development and foreign aid under the authorship of Paul Laudicina, most of the U.S. population had apparently adopted the pessimistic attitude being put forward in the academic world by P. T. Bauer and various like-minded colleagues. According to this survey, the U.S. population had resigned itself to the poverty of the Third World, as manifested by the fact that only 15 percent of the U.S. population believed that "poverty could be eliminated in the world within 50 years" (p. 8). Moreover, the U.S. population did not perceive any moral responsibility to help the Third World overcome poverty, as manifested by the fact that only 17 percent of the U.S. population felt that the U.S. government was "doing too little to fight world poverty" (p. 21).

9. These two articles are: "A World Economic Equalization Program: Results of a Simulation" (*Journal of Developing Areas*, 1976); "A World Economic Equalization Program: Refinements and Sensitivity Analysis" (*World Development*, 1988). The WEEP model discussed herein is hardly typical of conventional world development models, as exemplified by Bert Hickman (1983) and Stuart A. Bremer (1987). The WEEP model is simul-

taneously smaller but more general than the usual model, since the usual model is focused on a much more specific and marginalist policy proposal than that of a worldwide economic development program. The author's hope, of course, is that the WEEP model discussed herein will provide a prototype for larger and more elaborate models in future research—but larger and more elaborate models which do in fact boldly tackle a really fundamental policy initiative along the lines of a WEEP.

10. An extensive economic literature exists on the impact of foreign aid on economic development, for example: Gustav F. Papanek (1972, 1973), Colin Stoneman (1975), Volker Bornschier et al (1978), Paul Mosley (1980, 1987), R. H. Cassen (1986), Roger C. Riddell (1987), C. J. Jepma (1988, Part 3). Although some statistical support has been found for a positive effect of aid on development, that support is neither reliable nor strong. It is necessary to keep in mind various statistical problems (specification, identification, etc.) which may hamper the correct estimation of the relationship. A very fundamental identification problem exists in that the amount of contributed foreign aid up to this point may have been too limited, and its distribution too uncoordinated, piecemeal, and politically motivated, to have been effective. In the final analysis, the statistical evidence obtained to date does not provide much assistance in evaluating the potential impact of an economic assistance effort on the giant scale of the World Economic Equalization Program considered here.

11. Although most of the economic development literature is descriptive and explanatory rather than prescriptive, some substantial contributions have been made oriented specifically to policy, such as Lester B. Pearson (1969) and Gunnar Myrdal (1970). Such contributions as these would provide a firm conceptual basis for the functioning of a potential World Economic Equalization Program.

12. The effects of rapid population growth on the natural environment and individual living standards are addressed in a very large literature, much of it explicitly alarmist in nature. Some illustrative references on the issue include Robert C. Cook (1951), Elmer Pendell (1951), J. O. Hertzler (1956), Ansley J. Coale and Edgar M. Hoover (1958), Carlo Cipolla (1962), Philip Hauser (1963), Alfred Sauvy (1963), Larry K. Y. Ng (1965), Goran Ohlin (1967), Paul Ehrlich (1968), Tadd Fisher (1969), Anthony Allison (1970), Dean Fraser (1971), Dennis Meadows et al (1972), Timothy King et al (1974), Michael E. Endres (1975), Richard Easterlin (1980), T. Paul Schultz (1981), Pradip K. Ghosh (1984), Georgia Lee Kangas (1984), Allen C. Kelley (1988). For a dissenting viewpoint to the effect that humanity need not be especially concerned about population growth—at least into the foreseeable future—see Julian Simon (1977, 1981).

5

STATE AND WORLD STATE

A. THE PROBLEM OF NATIONALISM

The previous two chapters have considered means by which the ideological and economic obstacles to supernational federation might be ameliorated or even completely overcome in a reasonably abbreviated period of historical time. It might be argued by a skeptic that all of the above discussion—whatever its inherent merits or demerits—is nevertheless irrelevant and beside the point, because even if we imagined a world that was both ideologically and economically homogeneous, the force of nationalism would still stand as an insuperable barrier to the formation of a Federal Union of Democratic Nations. The purpose of this chapter is to dispute this potential argument against supernational federation.

While one has to concede that nationalism is a potent force in the contemporary world, and that to some extent it is indeed an independent impediment to supernational political unity rather than being merely an outgrowth of ideological, economic, and other incentives to conflict, the fact remains that nationalism is a controllable phenomenon.[1] It is not some primitive, quasi-mystical force totally beyond the dictates of reason and rationality, which will forever preclude the development of political loyalty to a state entity higher than the contemporary nation-state. As a matter of fact, in historical context, nationalism has been a stabilizing and unifying force to a greater extent than it has been a destabilizing and disunifying force. Those who would today argue that nationalism will forever prevent the formation of a viable world state because mankind is incapable of developing anything beyond national loyalties are comparable to those who several hundred years ago would have argued that local and regional loyalties would forever prevent the formation of a viable nation-state. Indeed, a healthy degree of nationalistic pride might even, in some ways, facilitate the formation and development of a world state. At some point a bandwagon effect might take hold, so that people will demand that their particular nation take up its rightful place in this great human endeavor—and not be left behind with the handful of unprogressive, reactionary, and backward-looking nations who continue to decline membership in the Federal Union.

We should consider the issue of nationalism in the light provided by the ideas and proposals put forward earlier in this book. First and foremost, the supernational federation proposed herein would be a relatively loose and flexible type of state organization. It is not expected that the power and authority of the supernational federation toward its citizens would be anywhere near as strong and extensive as is the power and authority of a typical contemporary nation-state toward its respective citizens. Nor is it expected that the loyalty of its citizens toward the supernational federation would be anywhere near as deep and abiding as is the loyalty of the typical contemporary citizen toward his or her respective nation-state today. Secondly, it is anticipated that some significant degree of progress will have been made toward the reduction of various ideological and economic barriers to supernational federation. The ideological gap and the economic gap tend to aggravate nationalistic loyalties, making them less amenable to reason and rationality. When it is argued here that nationalism, in and of itself, is not an insuperable obstacle to world union, it is understood that the world union involved would be quite loose and tolerant, and also that some progress will have been made toward the reduction of ideological and economic differences—and that there will be a good prospect toward the further reduction of these differences within the near future.

An objective and dispassionate examination of nationalistic spirit reveals it as closely allied to the emotion of personal pride in the individual human being. Part of any human being's basic identity is membership in some politically organized social group. Just as a psychologically healthy individual will take a reasonable degree of pride in himself or herself as an individual, so too he or she will take a reasonable degree of pride in various groups in which membership is held. Of these groups the nation-state is one of the most important—if not *the* most important—at the present stage of development of human civilization. It is perhaps the most important because of the combination of large scale and tight integration, which makes it the most powerful single group—in terms of raw force—in which the typical individual holds membership.

There is a happy medium, in the individual human being, between private orientation and social orientation. We do not expect most human beings—ourselves included—to become saints who make unusual and extreme personal sacrifices in order to assist and benefit others. At the same time, we expect most human beings to refrain from constant, single-minded pursuit of short-term personal self-interest. We expect human beings to show some toleration, respect, and consideration for other human beings. That such toleration, respect, and consideration is not completely automatic and natural is demonstrated by our fundamental social institutions.

Perhaps the most fundamental characteristic of any organized human society is a system for the promulgation and enforcement of laws regulating individual human conduct. In modern civilization, we establish legislative bodies to promulgate laws, police forces to apprehend offenders, courts in which to try and sentence offenders, and prisons in which to incarcerate convicted offenders. The activity of the formal law enforcement system is supplemented by the efforts of educational and religious institutions. The educational system continues the socialization process commenced in the home, by which children are made aware of the need to curb the pursuit of their own self-interest in the interests of others. Secular socialization in the home and in schools tends to emphasize the utilitarian purposes of moral and lawful behavior—it is normally in the individual's own long-term self-interest to do good because those who treat others well tend to be treated well themselves. Religions warn that evil behavior (most of which is also illegal) will be subject to various supernatural sanctions, either in this world or in some afterlife—even if the offender manages to evade the temporal law enforcement system. In a sense, religion also proposes utilitarian purposes of pursuit of long-term self-interest in doing good, but the distinction with secular socialization is that religion posits supernatural rather than natural sanctions for wrong-doing. Both secular and religious socialization endeavor to achieve an internalization of moral standards—to get the individual to regard virtue as a value in and of itself, rather than simply as a means to the end of long-term self-interest. Whether "genuine" internalization of morality and virtue ever occurs in the human being is an intriguing but probably irrelevant question.

Despite all this effort on the part of the law enforcement system, the educational system, and the religious system, substantial immoral and criminal behavior continues to be a fact of life even in the most advanced and civilized societies. This behavior manifests a cancerous overdevelopment of the normal and acceptable emotion of personal pride and self-esteem in these particular individuals. The criminal disregards the interests of others—and the interest of society as a whole—in the pursuit of his or her own short-run personal self-interest. Whether this disregard is voluntary or involuntary (the free will issue) is another intriguing but probably irrelevant question.

Just as the normal emotion of personal pride and self-esteem in the individual human being can become overdeveloped and lead to immoral and criminal behavior by that individual, so too the normal spirit of nationalism among the population of a nation can become overdeveloped and lead to hostile, belligerent, and aggressive behavior by that nation. The twentieth century has witnessed a horrifying example of the consequences of virulent nationalistic inflammation in the brief but terrible history of Nazi Germany from 1933 to 1945.[2] Adolf Hitler's perverted dream of a Germanic world empire came terrifyingly close to realization. Had the 1941 German invasion of the U.S.S.R. been successful and the vast natural resources of the Russian land mass been put at the disposal of the German war machine, Germany might well have become an unstoppable force. Of course it was not merely the chauvinistic notion of a Teutonic master race ruling the world which explains the horror of the Nazi period in twentieth century history. It was also the fact that that rule would have been almost unimaginably brutal and despotic. The fascist sociopolitical philosophy totally renounced and condemned the ideas and values which had been growing steadily more accepted and dominant among educated and progressive people since the eighteenth century European Enlightenment: the importance of the individual, the state as a social contract, the benefits of democratic accountability of government, toleration of social and religious diversity, the desirability of humane and compassionate attitudes in people, the primacy of reason and rationality over tradition and emotion. The tangible consequences of the fascist philosophy in Nazi Germany included the rapid suppression of individual rights and political democracy and their replacement by a totalitarian dictatorship, the designation of innocent Jewish people as scapegoats for the release of generalized hostility—a designation which led first to social persecution and eventually to physical extermination, and the militarization of the nation for purposes of aggressive, imperialistic expansion. There can be little question that had Adolf Hitler's ambitions been achieved, human civilization throughout the world would have experienced a very nasty period indeed. Perhaps there would eventually have been a recovery—and perhaps not. In any event, after six years of the most devastating warfare in human history (1939-1945), the Allied powers finally prevailed over the Axis, and since then fascist thinking has been relatively muted in human affairs.

To some unknown extent the intensity of the Nazi nightmare from 1933-1945 may be attributed to the demonic charisma of Adolf Hitler. But Hitler's personal attitudes and powers of persuasion over the German people were grounded in history. Among the factors instrumental to his success was the wounded national pride of the German people following Germany's defeat in World War I. The German people tended to regard the Treaty of Versailles as an outrageous imposition on their national honor. Only the power of nationalism can explain their defiance and unwillingness to accept defeat. From the perspective of long-term military history, World War II was merely a continuation of World War I. The intensification of nationalistic spirit in Western Europe and throughout the world in the nineteenth century was a major factor in the eventual breakdown of the balance of power and the initiation of the devastating world wars which blighted the first half of the twentieth century.

Of course nationalism alone does not account for the first half of the twentieth century. Ideological controversies exacerbated nationalistic emotions. Although the emergence of fascism after World War I intensified the ideological conflict between supporters and opponents of modern forms of constitutional democracy, that conflict in fact long predated World War I. At the same time that fascist ideologues rejected political democracy, thus bringing Germany into national conflict with Great Britain, France, the United States, and many other nations, they also rejected communistic socialism, thus bringing Germany into national conflict with the U.S.S.R. It was the combination of fundamental ideological controversy with nationalistic sentiment that proved highly incendiary, and led to the attitude of chauvinistic arrogance which brought Germany and the other fascist nations into military conflict with the rest of the world.

The implication of nationalism with fascism generally, and with the brutality and callousness of National Socialism in Germany in particular, has rendered the contemporary mentality properly wary and skeptical of nationalism. Nationalism is now clearly recognized as a serious problem, as an aggravator and intensifier of disagreements and conflicts of interest, as the instrument through which peoples and their governments tend to become unreasonable and bellicose. Of course, conflict and war have existed throughout recorded human history—long before the rise of modern nationalism. The fundamental problem is the persistence of substantial hostility and greed within the individual human being—despite society's best efforts at socialization of its members. The expression of hostility and greed at the individual level tends to be personally costly and unproductive owing to the formal and informal social enforcement system. But under the appropriate circumstances, the individual may be able to express hostility and greed through the group. Tribalism is as old as human history, and is merely a transference of the inherent primacy of the self within the individual to a higher social level. Nationalism is simply the contemporary form of tribalism in human affairs.

This recognition does not mean that nationalism, in and of itself, must necessarily be eradicated from human mentality in order to achieve permanent peace. Just as the normal person possesses a healthy level of personal pride and self-esteem, and does not allow this level to become so overdeveloped as to lead to immoral and criminal behavior, so too under normal circumstances the population of a nation does not allow its nationalistic pride and self-esteem to become so overdeveloped as to lead to hostile and aggressive behavior. At the same time that nationalistic pride need not cause aggressive behavior against other nations, it serves as a powerful deterrent to conflict within the nation. It inculcates proper attitudes of mutual respect and good will, so that conflicts of interest between various individuals and groups within the nation are resolved fairly and peacefully. Just as pride and self-esteem in the individual—properly restrained—can be a positive and beneficial influence on individual welfare, so too a properly restrained nationalism can be a positive and beneficial influence within human civilization, both national and international.

In historical perspective, the development of nationalistic spirit has been associated with three major motivations. Although individual cases often display a combination of these motivations, they are logically separate. First, nationalism has been associated with religious and ideological ideas and aspirations toward the general reform and progress of human civilization. Second, nationalism has been associated with motives of unification and expansion. Finally, nationalism has been associated with a desire for liberation from governments which are perceived to be remote and oppressive. In considering the prospects for supernational federation in the light of nationalism, we observe that the first two of these motivations could indeed enhance the possibility of supernational federation—in the future the world state could be viewed as an instrument for the pursuit of these objectives just as in the past the national state has been viewed as an instrument for their pursuit. Nationalistic spirit only necessarily poses an obstacle to world union to the extent that it is associated with motives toward liberation from remote and oppressive governance. This alerts us—once again—to the fact that to be feasible, the world government must be neither remote nor oppressive. But the Federal Union of Democratic Nations put forward in this book would in fact be neither remote nor oppressive. In reality, therefore, the force of nationalism in the contemporary world, potent though it undoubtedly is, need not constitute an insuperable obstacle to supernational federation. Let us consider in turn each of the three motivations which have historically been associated with the development of nationalism.

There are several striking instances in modern history in which internal social transformation has heightened national consciousness. In the enthusiasm generated by drastic revolutionary reform of society, the nation is perceived by its citizens as setting a noble example for the rest of humanity to emulate. At the same time, revolutionary transformations may very well set the nation apart from the rest of the world, subjecting it to intense suspicion and hostility from other nations which have not yet experienced these transformations. In extreme cases, the revolutionary transformation of a nation has started a chain reaction leading to prolonged and bitter international warfare.

An early example of this pattern was the English revolution and civil war of the 1640s, which saw the deposition and later execution of Charles I. While the deposition and elimination of monarchs by alliances of nobles had been fairly common during the medieval period, the English revolution of the 17th century was qualitatively different in that the revolutionaries were bourgeois rather than aristocratic, and they were largely motivated by generalized ideological aspirations toward religious freedom and constitutional governance rather than mainly by a simple selfish desire to rid themselves of constraints imposed on their personal wealth and power by the king. Of course the English revolution and civil war of the 1640s did not lead directly and immediately to religious freedom and constitutional democracy as they are known today in Great Britain and elsewhere. During this period Parliament was hardly an organ of the popular will, but was rather heavily dominated by the wealthy, landed gentry. Moreover, the early Puritan enthusiasm was quickly dissipated in conflict and dissension, and Oliver Cromwell's tenure as head of state was widely regarded as a form of despotism not much better than that of Charles I.

Following Cromwell's death, the Stuart monarchy was restored (1660), and the conflict between Parliament and the king which had degenerated into civil war in the 1640s was resumed. But the lesson implicit in the execution of Charles I in 1649 was not lost. Parliament was bolder, and when its conflict with the king reached a critical point in 1688, the Stuart monarchy was permanently abrogated in a relatively bloodless revolution (the "Glorious Revolution"), and the

House of Orange (in the persons of William and Mary), was brought in to assume the throne. By clearly demonstrating the power primacy of Parliament over the king, the Glorious Revolution was decisive in the historical transition of Britain from absolute monarchy to constitutional monarchy, and was thereby an important milestone in the development of modern concepts of democracy.

During this entire period from 1640 to 1688, despite the various disappointments and setbacks along the way, British national consciousness was gradually and significantly raised through the growing perception by its citizens of Britain as being on the leading edge of social improvement. Through its demonstration of the benefits of setting various formal and informal limitations on the power and authority of the king, and of establishing religious toleration as the law and policy of the land, Britain was setting a noble example for the rest of the world to follow. This period provides an example of the first motivation toward heightened nationalism in an almost unalloyed form. Throughout the period from 1640 to 1688, Britain was an independent nation, so that there was no question of liberation from the rule of a larger, imperial government. Similarly the boundaries of Britain remained unchanged, and so did the various difficulties among its various constituent parts (England, Wales, Scotland, and—at that time—Ireland). So there were no aspects of unification and expansion operative during the period.

The War of Independence in the American colonies (1776-1781), and the subsequent history of the United States through the nineteenth century, on the other hand, provides a more complicated example of interaction among all three principal motivations to nationalism. The initial impetus to the American revolution was provided by the third motivation: the colonists wanted to achieve independence from the remote and oppressive British imperial government in London. Not only was that government physically distant, requiring weeks and even months for the passage of communications, but through its policy of taxation without representation, it was also increasingly regarded as intolerably oppressive. But once the decision to fight for independence had been made, high principles from the European Enlightenment were immediately invoked. The U.S. Founding Fathers envisioned a democratic republic from which all types of artificial aristocratic distinctions and oligarchic governance would be banished, a nation in which religious and political freedom would be constitutionally guaranteed, a land in which the rights and dignity of the individual citizen would be zealously cherished and safeguarded. The War of Independence was transformed into a struggle for liberty and justice for all, to establish upon the earth a new and improved form of human civilization. Without doubt these visionary ideas played a major role in sustaining the determination and enthusiasm of the colonists in their protracted struggle to gain independence from Britain. Having attained independence and having established a new form of representative democracy in conformance with the most progressive elements of the eighteenth century Enlightenment, the citizens of the early United States republic turned their eyes westward toward the huge North American land mass lying between themselves and the Pacific Ocean. One glance at a map sufficed to verify that any single political entity which could encompass that vast land area would automatically become a very formidable force in worldwide human civilization. Thus the notion of "manifest destiny"—of a single nation spanning the entire continent—dominated the American mentality throughout the nineteenth century and into the twentieth.

The development of American nationalism represents an amalgam of all three components of nationalistic motivation. Although it was initially animated by a simple desire for liberation from a government perceived to be remote and oppressive, this motivation was soon supplemented and superceded by the two other motivations: the ideological motivation and the expansion-unification motivation. From the very beginning, the citizens of the United States regarded their form of government as politically superior to most other governments in the world, and their form of society as morally superior to most other societies in the world. The United States was perceived as providing a glowing example of the best possible form of human civilization. With this very positive self-image, it is not surprising that there were few qualms expressed and little hesitation witnessed throughout the long and difficult process through which much of the North American land mass was incorporated into the United States throughout the nineteenth century. Whether the means were monetary (as in the case of the Louisiana Purchase) or military (as in the wars with Mexico and the Indian tribes), they were generally regarded as fully justified in the cause of raising up before all mankind a higher form of social organization. It was not simple lust for territorial expansion and greater power which explains the strong growth of nationalistic sentiment among the citizens of the United States during the nineteenth century; it was the combination of this lust with higher humanitarian purposes of service to all mankind.

The year 1789—only one year following the ratification of the United States Constitution—witnessed the outbreak of the French Revolution, one of the most portentous events in modern history. The makers of the French Revolution were ideologically inspired by the American example, but they soon learned from hard experience that it would be much more difficult to establish a tolerant, liberal, and democratic republic within an old and established European nation-state than it had been within a lightly-populated frontier region relatively unburdened by history and tradition. Although the basic concepts and policies of the French Revolution appealed to the great majority of the French population—and indeed of the entire European population, they also aroused stubborn resistance from the large and entrenched aristocracy both inside and outside France. Amidst drastic polarization, the moderates were swept away and radicals and reactionaries came to dictate events. Within a few years of the enthusiasm and optimism of 1789, France, having executed its deposed king Louis XVI, was in the throes of the radical revolutionary Terror at home, and meanwhile embroiled in a major European war abroad. Although the Terror subsided quickly following the Thermidorean reaction of July, 1794, the war persisted steadily, with periodic interruptions, through to the defeat of Napoleon at Waterloo in 1815.

In ferocity and extent, the wars of the French Revolution and the Napoleonic era constituted the worst period of conflict in European history since the Thirty Years' War (1618-1648). These two periods of conflict had in common the fact that ordinary, mundane motives of power, wealth, and prestige were heavily supplemented by higher principles and ideals. They were both ideological conflicts in a general sense: in the case of the Thirty Years' War different religious beliefs and practices were at issue, while in the case of the "French wars" the issues were largely secular, pertaining to proper social organization and policy. Supporters of the principles of the French Revolution conceived a better world free of the archaic distinctions and unjustified privileges of the old regime; opponents of these principles saw them as threatening to lead to mob rule, anarchy, the destruction of culture and learning, and the collapse of civilization. In the perceptions of the participants it was not merely individual and national self-interest that were at stake; rather it was the welfare of the entire human race.

The Thirty Years' War was a violent and bloody step on the path to contemporary concepts of religious liberty and toleration, and the French wars from 1792 to 1815 were a violent and bloody step on the path to contemporary concepts of political freedom and democracy. But in neither case was the progress made in a quick and easy manner. Just as the English Civil War of the 1640s produced a dictator in the form of Oliver Cromwell, so too the French Revolution produced a dictator in the form of Napoleon Bonaparte. In Britain the restoration of 1660 brought back the Stuart monarchy; in France the restoration of 1815 brought back the Bourbon monarchy. But despite the disappointments and retrogressions, permanent progress had been made. Neither France, Europe, nor the world were ever quite the same following the events of 1789 and the early 1790s. The medieval principles and practices of hereditary aristocracy and absolute monarchy had been dealt a mortal blow, although the better part of a century was to pass before the fact became indisputably obvious.

Another aspect of the period which was not fully obvious at the time was the significant rise of nationalistic spirit among all the warring nations. For a time France herself was carried away by a messianic impetus toward humanitarian imperialism: the odious old regime would be swept away not merely in France but throughout Europe as well. Meanwhile, supporters of the old regime endeavored to enlist nationalism in their defense, by representing revolutionary France as a grasping, bullying upstart mainly concerned to widen the scope of its own power and influence. England, Spain, and Russia experienced growing nationalism through their military efforts against Napoleonic France, and similarly the struggles of the various Italian and German principalities against Napoleon were a major factor in the eventual national unifications of Italy and Germany later in the nineteenth century.

Moving forward to the twentieth century, we encounter dramatic examples of the interaction between nationalism and ideological concepts regarding desirable social institutions and policies. On the allied side in World War I, the German and Austrian governments—in which hereditary monarchs continued to wield considerable authority—were regarded as undemocratic and reactionary. Meanwhile, constitutional democracy as practiced in England and France were regarded in Germany and Austria as producing contemptibly weak and fickle governments. This is not to say that ideological lines were clearly drawn in World War I—England and France were allied with the Russian imperial government, which was in fact far more conservative and autocratic than either the German or Austrian governments of the same period.

The Russian Revolution of 1917 took Russia out of World War I, and led ultimately to the formation of the Union of Soviet Socialist Republics, a large, populous, and powerful nation-state with a strong commitment to worldwide socialist revolution. The rapid transformation of Russia from a politically backward monarchy to a socialist republic with messianic aspirations had a tremendous impact upon subsequent world history. Prior to the Russian Revolution, the issue of socialism versus capitalism had seemed relatively remote and academic. Conservatives tended to discount the possibility of socialist revolutions, on grounds that no people would be sufficiently foolish to attempt to implement an economic system that was so clearly unworkable. The Russian Revolution suggested that under certain circumstances, the people might indeed make a socialist revolution, and the persistence of the U.S.S.R. into the 1920s and beyond suggested that a socialist economic system might indeed possess sufficient viability at least to survive. In the aftermath of World War II, through the direct or indirect intervention of the U.S.S.R., several more nations were added to the socialist camp including, among others, China and the nations of Eastern Europe. For a while after World War II, it appeared as though the Russian messianic aspiration toward worldwide socialization, implanted by the revolution of 1917, might be on the verge of realization.

The fear of socialist revolutions aided and abetted by foreign powers has been extremely potent throughout the twentieth century, and it has led directly to conservative political reactions in many nations. The most drastic and portentous reaction occurred in Germany in the 1930s, bringing to power Adolf Hitler, and causing a very large and powerful nation-state to embrace a form of extreme fascism no less virulent and inhumane than the communistic socialism of Joseph Stalin in the Soviet Union during the same period. Hitler's appeal to German nationalism encompassed motives of revenge against the humiliation of the Versailles Treaty, the higher humanitarian purpose of preserving all human culture and civilization from the horrors of communistic socialism, and the simple, unadorned lust for territorial expansion. The German people revived an ancient vision of a German empire encompassing the enormous Eurasian land mass—what lent this vision its intense urgency during the period of the Third Reich was the strong belief that such an empire would represent a welcome, humanitarian deliverance of the populations of this region from the barbarity and deprivation of communism. The perceived complementarity of self-interest and wider social interest explains the extreme and intense chauvinistic enthusiasm developed among the German people from 1933 to 1945.

While Nazi Germany represents an extreme example of over-development of nationalistic spirit, the intensification of nationalism during the twentieth century owing to ideological factors has been very widespread. In Russia, the nation-state has been perceived as the instrument through which the economic exploitation and social degradation of capitalism might finally be abrogated, once and for all, throughout the world. In the United States, the nation-state has been regarded as the chief means of defense against such socioeconomic obscenities as totalitarian fascism and totalitarian communism. Much the same perceptions and motivations have been operative in many of the world's largest nation-states throughout the twentieth century. Indeed, it is safe to say that the twentieth century has witnessed the full flowering of the identification of narrow national interests with wider ideological purposes—an identification prefigured in the English revolution of 1640-1648.

Turning now to the second major correlate of the growth and

development of nationalism, the unification-expansion motivation is based on the universal human aspiration toward membership in large and powerful social groups. Over the last two centuries of human history, this motivation has often overridden considerations of regional autonomy and local interest. It explains why, after having thrown off the dominion of the British imperial government, the American colonists ultimately opted to unite their respective states in a relatively centralized federal state. It explains the eventual amalgamation of the previously sovereign and independent principalities of Italy and Germany into nation-states in the nineteenth century (respectively in 1861 and 1871). These are perhaps the most dramatic examples, but there have been numerous analogous cases.

Once the unification motivation has brought a nation-state into being, the expansion motivation comes strongly into play if the occupants of adjacent territories are relatively weak and unorganized. The nineteenth century saw the coast-to-coast expansion of the United States and Canada across the North American land mass—an expansion that was beyond the power of the Indian tribes to consistently and successfully resist. Much the same pattern was also demonstrated on the other side of the world as the Russian empire expanded across the Eurasian land mass toward the Bering Sea. The expansionary motivation does not necessarily require adjacent lands. The Asian and African empire-building of Britain, France, and other metropolitan European nations from the seventeenth century onward is still another manifestation of the inherent human impulse toward territorial expansion. As was, of course, the German effort to carve out an empire from the huge territory of the U.S.S.R. from 1941-1945. As the nation-state is the prime instrument through which the individual attains his or her membership within a large and powerful social group, episodes of unification and expansion—whether abrupt or prolonged as the case may be—are associated with an intensification of nationalistic sentiment.

Looking at the first two correlates of nationalism—the ideological purpose and the unification-expansion purpose, we recognize the possibility that just as in the past these purposes have been instrumental in the development of various national loyalties, so too in the future they might be instrumental in the development of supernational loyalty. A world state might be viewed as an instrument through which social progress might be achieved throughout the world. And a world state—that is, a supernational federation in which a large majority of the nations of the world would participate—would fulfill natural human aspirations toward membership in a large and powerful social group. Just as in the past, people have gazed at maps and been inspired by the vision of a single, national political entity covering a very large area, so too in the future people may gaze at maps and be inspired by the vision of a single, supernational political entity covering an even larger area.

Obviously, if either of these two motivations were to get out of hand, the supernational federation might become an evil and perverse force in human affairs. Neither social progress in the nonmember nations, nor the physical expansion of the supernational federation, can be pursued by means of coercion and force. The member nations of the supernational federation, and the supernational state itself, will endeavor to achieve a standard of wise and humane government which the populations of the nonmember nations will desire to emulate by assimilation, by becoming members themselves of the federation. And needless to say, the supernational federation must absolutely renounce any aspirations or intentions to recruit new member nations by the traditional means of imperialistic conquest. If any appreciable proportion of the human population comes to perceive the supernational federation as an arrogant and bellicose empire comparable to such historical cases as the ancient Roman empire, then the cause of supernational federation will be lost.

The need for patience, caution, and nonviolent policy on the part of the supernational federation in its dealings both with member and nonmember nations is underscored by the important role of the third factor in the development of contemporary nationalism: the desire for liberation from remote and oppressive governance. This is the area in which direct conflict might legitimately be perceived between nationalism and the possibility of supernational federation. Modern history has witnessed many striking examples of the breakup of large political entities into a number of sovereign and independent nation-states owing to perceptions of oppression among the populations of these nations-states. The United States of America, for example, had its inception in such perceptions. These perceptions were critical in the various Latin American revolutions which dismantled the Spanish empire in the Americas in the early nineteenth century. Two other large and important empires, the Ottoman and the Austro-Hungarian, remained in a state of turmoil and decline throughout the nineteenth century owing to the restiveness of the various national populations within their boundaries—although it took the cataclysm of World War I to bring about their final dismemberment and dissolution. In the twentieth century an analogous restiveness brought about the definitive termination of the British, French, and other European empires in Africa and Asia. Over the past few years, we have witnessed yet another example of the continued potency of nationalistic sentiment in the breakup of the Union of Soviet Socialist Republics.

In each of these cases, nationalistic separatism arose—and eventually triumphed—in response to perceptions of remote and oppressive governance. Of course it is widely believed at the present time that a supernational government would necessarily be remote and oppressive. There is a strong tendency to imagine that owing to the divisiveness within the human race at the present stage of its history, the only conceivable kind of world state would be a ruthlessly totalitarian state. To a large extent this negative image stems from the difficult course of human history during the twentieth century: the two World Wars, the Cold War, the totalitarian regimes of Hitlerite Germany and Stalinist Russia. It also stems from the fact that because of this difficult course, the modern nation-state has become extremely potent and important in the twentieth century—even more so than in the nineteenth century. It has become difficult for humanity to conceive of alternative environments, of alternative concepts of state authority.

But as the end of the twentieth century nears, there are many favorable signs. The totalitarian fascist powers were defeated in World War II, thus immensely enhancing the cause of political democracy in human affairs. Horrified by the destructive potential of nuclear weapons, humanity has drawn back from the precipice of World War III—despite a virulent ideological conflict between the communist and noncommunist nations. The extremely totalitarian communist regimes of the Stalinist era moderated greatly during the succeeding decades—even prior to the sweeping reform movements of the last few years. At the same time, humanity has developed formidable economic capacities. An appreciable proportion of the human race now enjoys a standard of living that would have been unimaginable 100 or 200 years ago. We also know far more now than we did 100 or 200 years ago about the probable causes of economic poverty, and about the prospects for economic progress and equalization on a worldwide scale.

A new world order is emerging, and as humanity adjusts to this new world order the possibility is growing that within the near future, the feasibility of supernational federation will be recognized. The kind of government needed at the supernational level at this stage of human development would be a genuine and legitimate state entity— but all the same much less powerful and important in relation to its citizens than the typical nation-state of today. In Chapter 2 of this book, the basic features of a Federal Union of Democratic Nations were sketched out. This plan clearly represents a viable compromise between the level of authority represented by the contemporary nation-state and that represented by the contemporary United Nations. The Federal Union would constitute a significant step forward beyond the United Nations, but would at the same time be sufficiently constrained to permit its foundation and development in the nationally oriented contemporary world.

The study of nationalism in human history clearly shows that in order to be viable in a world still very nationalistically oriented, a world state *must not* be regarded as remote and oppressive by any substantial proportion of its citizens. As to the specific issue of remoteness, this potential problem has largely been abrogated—relative to 100 or 200 years ago—by the amazing technological progress in the area of transport and communications. There would be no difficulty in maintaining close contact between the individuals and agencies of the supernational government and their constituent citizens. During the twentieth century, the science of opinion polling has also made great progress, and no doubt this science would be relied upon extensively in making judgments as to what the Federal Union should do and should not do.

The maintenance of close and continual communication between the Federal Union and its citizens will help to forestall feelings of oppression among the latter. In addition, the proposed Federal Union would display numerous features explicitly intended to inhibit tendencies toward oppressiveness—ranging from the national right of secession to the dual voting principle in the Chamber of Representatives. Of course, among the strongest guarantees of nonoppressiveness is the fact that the government of the supranational federation would be democratically elected by the population of the Federal Union. When we think of oppressive regimes throughout history, from the ancient Roman empire through to Stalinist communism, a unifying feature is the absence of democracy, of democratic accountability of the government to the population which it governs. By means of close contact and communication, democratic elections, formal constitutional guarantees, and the good sense and wisdom of the leaders of the supranational federation who will hopefully remain aware of the strong possibility of disaster should they overstep their political and moral authority—it may be anticipated with a reasonable degree of confidence that the Federal Union of Democratic Nations will avoid becoming an instrument of oppression.

To summarize, a careful consideration of the role of nationalism in modern human history suggests that the nationalistic spirit is not as strong an obstacle to supranational federation as might at first be thought. In fact, of the three major correlates of nationalism, two may actually assist in the foundation and development of a supranational federation. Such a federation might be viewed as a means of achieving a higher quality of human civilization throughout the world, owing to the fact that it would work steadily toward the paramount goals of political democracy and economic prosperity. Such a federation would also be territorially extensive, which would enhance feelings of security and self-esteem among its citizens. The third correlate of nationalism—the desire for liberation from remote and oppressive governance—is the only one of the three that would tend automatically, even if illegitimately, toward resistance to the notion of supranational federation. Against this automatic tendency we can do no more than muster rational argumentation as to why *this particular* form of supranational government would not in fact become oppressive. There is a certain mentality that would argue that against certain "instinctive assumptions," rational argumentation is powerless—and that the feeling that a world state would be oppressive is indeed among such "instinctive assumptions." It is to be hoped that this expectation will not be borne out. In any event, additional thoughts will be offered in the remainder of this chapter, pertaining to the concept of the state, and to the potential functions and purposes of a world state in human affairs, which continue to suggest that a world state would most likely represent a positive rather than a negative force in the continued progress of human civilization.

B. THE CONCEPT OF STATE ORGANIZATION

A "state" is a political organization of human individuals: in the general sense it refers to the entire commonwealth of citizens, while in the specific sense it refers to the government organs and agencies which exercise authority over the commonwealth of citizens. Essential to the concept of the state is the concept of sovereignty.[3] Within the territory which it encompasses, the state is the sole repository of political power, and it recognizes no other authority to which it is subject. It permits no competition for the loyalties of its citizens, and it accepts little or no limitation on the extent of its authority over its citizens.

In human thought and imagination, the state has always been an intimidating, awe-inspiring, and magisterial concept. In the minds of its citizens the state possesses attributes comparable to those of a father in the minds of his children. As does a father, the state embodies formidable power and authority. Ideally, this power and authority is utilized wisely and benevolently: to protect and benefit the citizens of the state. But just as a father may, under adverse conditions, become the oppressor of his children, so too the state may become the oppressor of its citizens. Therefore, human individuals experience ambivalent feelings about the state: gratitude, respect, and love on the one hand; apprehension, fear, and hate on the other.

As does the word "state," the word "sovereignty" has an appropriately sonorous ring: it tends to evoke deep and abiding emotions, to elicit intimations of fundamental issues of survival and wellbeing, to generate what might be termed a "mystical" frame of mind in the individual. Once in this frame of mind, it is relatively easy to imagine that the concept of national sovereignty constitutes an insuperable obstacle to supernational federation. Such a federation would constitute an abridgement of and an infringement upon the national sovereignty of its member nation-states. But nation-states cannot permit such a "competitor" for their traditional authority to exist and yet remain nation-states. By the same token, a world state—in order to constitute a proper state entity—could not tolerate the limitations upon its own sovereignty represented by the sovereignty of its component nation-states. It simply could not allow such significant restrictions on its authority, and it simply could not permit so much competition for the loyalties of its citizens. Therefore, one or the other would have to go: either the concept of national sovereignty or the concept of supernational sovereignty. Since it is impossible to imagine the nation-states of today surrendering their national sovereignty, we are forced to conclude that a world state is infeasible.

Such thinking is muddled and fallacious. It manifests an excessively rigid mentality that perceives only black and white rather than shades of gray, that focusses only on the extreme endpoints of the spectrum of possibilities rather than looking for the happy medium. The formation of a world state would not necessarily manifest the abrogation of national sovereignty, nor would the continuation of national sovereignty necessarily imply an absence of sovereignty on the part of the world state. The world state and the component nation-states would each have their respective areas of sovereignty: areas in which they would indeed exercise absolute and undisputed authority. In some areas the world state would possess sovereign authority, and in other areas the individual nation-states would possess sovereign authority.

At first it may seem paradoxical to think about "areas" of sovereignty and "limitations" on sovereignty—such restrictive notions seem basically contradictory to the essential concept of sovereignty. But we must take a more sophisticated view of reality. It would be intellectually crippling to cling to the notion that "sovereignty" is an absolute rather than a relative concept. In actual fact, the notion of "sovereignty" to a state is quite closely analogous to the notion of "freedom" to an individual. "Freedom" is of course a marvelous abstraction: it expresses the deepest and most sublime human aspirations toward individual autonomy, discretion, and self-determination. Every rational human being desires to have as much freedom for himself or herself as is conceivably possible.

But at the same time, every rational human being also recognizes the many practical and unavoidable constraints which must restrain autonomy, discretion, and self-determination. Some of these constraints are imposed by nature: human beings cannot fly like birds, they cannot breathe water like fish, they require food, drink, and shelter to survive, and despite their best personal efforts to implement the instinct of self-preservation indefinitely, they are all eventually subject to the physical dissolution of death. Some of these constraints are imposed by economic realities: the person of average means, even in the most prosperous nations, is not able to live in a large mansion on an extensive estate, is not able to eat steak and lobster every day, is not able to take six-month tours around the world. Some constraints are imposed by the social enforcement system: theft, rape, murder, and many other actions that may appeal to certain persons at certain times, will normally eventuate in confinement and the spartan living conditions of prisons. Some constraints are imposed by the political system: even in the most democratic polities, no individual citizen can autonomously specify who shall be the head of state—such as himself/herself or some close friend or relative.

Such constraints, however, do not constitute flat contradictions to a *sensible* understanding of freedom. It is fully sensible to interpret "freedom" as involving simply a *substantial* amount of personal autonomy, discretion, and self-determination—even if that amount is indeed far short of what could be imagined. We may certainly think of ourselves as free—even though we may be subject to physical limitations and mortality, even though we may be able to afford a relatively modest standard of living, even though we must avoid criminal behavior or suffer the consequences, even though our own personal influence in determining the social leadership may be minimal. It is the same thing with national sovereignty—or in more general terms, with *any* type of state sovereignty. Just as it is possible to legitimately describe a person as free even though there may be many practical constraints operative upon his or her individual autonomy, discretion, and self-determination, so too it is possible to legitimately describe a state as sovereign even though there may be many practical constraints on the power and authority of that state, and even though that state must share the loyalty of its citizens with other state entities.

A realistic appreciation of history and contemporary civilization clearly manifests that "state sovereignty," whether that state is a nation-state or some other form, is in fact significantly limited both internally and externally. Internally, the government cannot ignore the interests and desires of its citizens, or it runs the risk of being ousted by election or overturned by revolution. Even if elections are not on the social agenda, there are still limits on the degree of control exercised over the citizen body by even the most brutally despotic regimes. A completely coerced obedience obtained solely through brute force is highly dangerous and unreliable. If disaffection becomes too widespread among the population, then that disaffection will tend to percolate upwards into the highest corridors of power. And when that happens, the despot loses his personal security, no matter how unassailable he may appear to be from the outside.

The twentieth century despotisms of Hitlerite Germany and Stalinist Russia did not rely entirely upon secret police, concentration camps, and executions. Rather these tools of forcible coercion were heavily supplemented by an extraordinary propaganda campaign conducted through the media of mass communications. Tremendous efforts were exerted by both of these totalitarian regimes to pursuade the citizens that they were being governed in accordance with their own best interests. Had Hitler and Stalin relied exclusively upon forcible coercion, they would not have been nearly as successful as they were. In all likelihood, they would have been quickly eliminated by some highly placed lieutenant anxious to achieve a better level of voluntary support and cooperation from the citizen body. We can probably go even further to say that had not Adolf Hitler and Joseph Stalin *genuinely and sincerely* believed that they were exercising their personal political power in the best interests of the citizens of their respective nations, then they would probably have been quickly eliminated.

The externally imposed limitations on the sovereign power of a state—including a nation-state—are just as important as the internally imposed limitations. The two afore-mentioned twentieth century dictators, Adolf Hitler and Joseph Stalin, were made acutely aware of this as their respective nations fought it out on the Eastern front from 1941 to 1945. The exercise of sovereign power has frequently brought states into armed conflict throughout human history, and the possibility of armed conflict constitutes a major constraint on the autonomy, discretion, and self-determination of state entities. This major constraint is just as operative upon the modern nation-state as it has been upon earlier state entities. No national government can afford to entirely ignore or disregard the strong national interests of other national governments—sovereignty or no sovereignty.

All this is not to deny the existence and significance of the concept of sovereignty. It is rather merely to point out that in practice, sovereignty does not imply absolute and unlimited power and authority. Just as there are internal limitations on the freedom of a human individual inherent in our physical nature, so too there are internal limitations on the sovereignty of the state inherent in the private interests and desires of its citizens. Just as there are external limitations on the freedom of a human individual inherent in the fact that we live in societies composed of many other human individuals such as ourselves, so too there are external limitations on the sovereignty of the state inherent in the fact that they exist in societies composed of many other states such as themselves. But just as these internal and external limitations on the practical freedom of the individual do not abrogate the sensibility of the concept of "freedom," so too these internal and external limitations on the practical sovereignty of the state do not abrogate the sensibility of the concept of "sovereignty."

The proposed Federal Union of Democratic Nations would be a *federation* of nation-states. A distinction is made in political science between the "unitary" nation-state and the "federal" nation-state.[4] In the federal type of nation-state, regional and local governments remain conceptually distinct from the national government, and they exercise an appreciable amount of independent autonomy. That is, in certain areas of policy and procedure, they can take actions of which the national government might strongly disapprove. In the unitary type of nation-state, on the other hand, regional and local governments are considered to be branches of the national government, and in principle they are absolutely subservient to the national government. Therefore, in principle, they are unable to take any actions of which the national government strongly disapproves.

The difference between the unitary and federal form of the nation-state, so clear in principle, is much less clear in practice. That is to say, there is extremely little obvious and systematic difference between actual practical governance as between federal and unitary nation-states in the contemporary world. In a word, the differences seem to be more of a formal-legal nature rather than of a substantive nature. In Britain—an example of a unitary nation-state—decisions of the various local governments are rarely overturned or challenged by the national government in London. Moreover, substantial regional autonomy exists in each of the component regions of Great Britain: England, Wales, Scotland, and Northern Ireland. While Britain provides an example of a highly decentralized "unitary" nation-state, at the opposite end of the spectrum the Soviet Union during the heyday of Stalinism provided an example of a highly centralized "federal" nation-state. In the Stalin-era U.S.S.R., the various republics of the federation in principle exercised a great deal of regional autonomy, but in practice this autonomy was almost entirely overridden by the paramount authority of the tightly centralized Communist Party. The artificial quality of the distinction between federal and unitary nation-states is also suggested by the close parallel between the practical operations of government as between Great Britain and the United States, although the former is a unitary form and the latter a federal form. Just as the unitary form of national government in Great Britain does not impinge too strongly on a reasonable degree of local autonomy, by the same token the federal form of national government in the United States does not imply unlimited local autonomy. The U.S. federal government regularly intervenes at the local level in the national interest—as, for example, in its efforts to abolish segregation in the Southern states during the civil rights movement of the 1950s and 1960s.

Whether we conceptualize a state entity as being unitary or federal, we confront the same issue of finding the appropriate distribution of authority as between the central government and the local governments. Authority should not be excessively centralized, lest the specific interests of the local population be inadequately appreciated and incorporated into policy. This point of view finds expression in the concept of *subsidiarity*: whatever function of government is best handled at the lower level of government *should* be handled at that level. While the principle of subsidiarity is unobjectionable in principle, in practice there is often disagreement as to whether some governmental function is "best handled" at a higher or a lower level. There are some practical benefits of uniformity and homogeneity, and these benefits point to the efficiency of making decisions and policies at a higher level of government. There is also the possibility that if left unmolested, some decisions and policies of lower levels of government would be so severely prejudicial to the interests of certain of their citizens as to constitute violations of natural rights. The question is how strong the evidence needs to be that some function of government is best handled at a higher level of government in order for it to be properly handled at that higher level. Political conservatives tend to believe that there should be a heavy preponderance of evidence in favor of handling the function at the higher level of government before actually doing so; liberals tend to believe that the "burden of proof," so to speak, should be less onerous.

It is to be expected that if a supernational federation is formed, the same ideas and arguments utilized today in examining the proper distribution of power and authority as between the various local governments and the national government, will also be invoked in examining the proper distribution of power and authority as between the various national governments and the supernational government. Intense and often acrimonious controversy is to be anticipated. That such controversy is to be expected, however, does not in and of itself imply that supernational government is politically impossible—any more than the analogous controversies of the past rendered the nation-state politically impossible.

Contemporary attitudes are of course highly skeptical of the notion of world government. This skepticism indeed passes over into the realm of prejudice. There are many individuals at the present time—even highly informed, authoritative individuals—who would insist adamantly that there are *no* functions of government which may be handled more efficiently and/or effectively at a higher level of government than that of the nation-state, and hence that no supranational government of any sort should be attempted. It is to be hoped that ultimately this viewpoint will be correctly perceived for what it is: a manifestation of the invalid presumption that a world state must necessarily be an oppressive, totalitarian regime which would respect neither the individual freedom of its citizens nor the national sovereignty of its component nation-states. This book proposes a form of supranational government, the Federal Union of Democratic Nations, which would clearly constitute a state entity, and yet which would incorporate a sufficient number of guarantees of individual liberty and national autonomy to virtually preclude its becoming an instrument of oppression. The basic proposal was set forth in Chapter 2, and the present chapter will conclude with some additional thoughts concerning the practical purposes of a world state in the further development of human civilization.

Prior to developing these additional thoughts, however, it should be emphasized that the fundamental concept of a world state is hardly new or revolutionary. Almost from the beginning of human history, the notion of a universal political entity embracing the entire human population has been slowly and gradually developing and evolving, down through the centuries into the present day. To a large extent the history of the ancient and medieval worlds, in Europe, Asia, and elsewhere, has been the history of empires. These empires were not achieved entirely through means of bloody conquest driven by crass, selfish motivations of personal wealth and power. Bloody conquest might have been needed to bring a new territory into the empire, but to make that territory a stable and productive part of the empire, a large proportion of its population had to be psychologically inducted. That is, they had to believe that their government was on the whole wise and humanitarian, they had to think of themselves as citizens of a great and noble state, and they had to take pride in the civilization and culture of which they were a part. If these attitudes were not achieved, then the territory would have remained a running sore in the side of the empire, a hotbed of resistance and conflict, a liability rather than an asset. By and large, the rulers of the ancient empires made a respectable effort at wise and humane governance. Such governance was required both on utilitarian grounds of maintaining stability and order, and also on grounds of conscience—even the most powerful despots cannot entirely escape the social and humanitarian attitudes instilled within them during childhood by parents and teachers.

This is not to say that any of the ancient empires came anywhere near modern concepts of liberty, toleration, and cooperation. Racial, ethnic, and religious differences bedeviled efforts to achieve internal harmony. Societies were caste and class oriented, and there were only the barest inklings of ideas such as equality and democracy. No systematic means were available either to assess or to influence public opinion. Communications and transport were extremely slow, creating enormous impediments to effective coordination and administration. The economies of the ancient empires were very precarious, and prone to devastation from such natural phenomena as drought and flood. Should such disasters be avoided for a while, building population pressures would cause exhaustion of the fertility of the land, once again leading to famine and pestilence. Aside from these factors, the ancient economies were also pummelled by continuous wars with adjacent realms including competing empires.

Despite all these liabilities and drawbacks, the ancient and medieval empires did undoubtedly—on the whole—advance the cause of human civilization. Human existence within these empires was generally more peaceful, prosperous, secure, and rewarding than it was outside them. The empires established the possibility of very large political entities comprising many millions of inhabitants. They suggested the possibility of a single political entity which would include the entire human population. As a result of these empires, the vision of a universal state gradually became clearer and more tangible in the human imagination.

Just as the individual human child goes through a lengthy process of socialization through which he or she is made increasingly aware of the needs and rights of other people, the same process has been taking place at the social level throughout history. The young child tends to take what he or she wants by force—luckily for others the force mustered by a young child is very slight. But the child is soon taught that the pursuit of self-interest cannot be totally direct and uninhibited—that he or she will do better in the long run if a considerate and cooperative attitude is taken toward others. This same lesson is gradually being learned at the social level through the long and painful processes of history.

The makers of the ancient empires—during the early childhood of humanity—made them primarily in their own direct self-interest, almost entirely by the raw force of conquest. They were originally viewed by the conquerors simply as a means of enhancing their own power, wealth, and prestige. But as human thought and culture advanced—as humanity matured, so to speak—the motivations behind empire-building gradually evolved. Greater emphasis was placed on the potential benefits to the subject peoples of being incorporated into a secure and prosperous political entity. Rather than being perceived solely as a means of advancing the selfish interests of the conquerors, empires were increasingly perceived as means by which the common interests of many peoples could be efficaciously pursued. One such common interest which has been extremely important throughout most of human history has been religion—only very recently, historically speaking, has religion been supplanted to a significant extent by secular ideology.

Allowance must certainly be made for rationalization and hypocrisy in the transformation of empire-building from a manifestation of selfish greed into the benevolent pursuit of social responsibility. Obviously short-run self-interest continued to play a major role in such activity—cynics would say it continued to play the overwhelmingly dominant role. But the social overlay upon the foundation of private self-interest cannot be entirely disregarded as specious and dissimulative. This social overlay had significant practical consequences in the way empires were established and developed throughout their histories. They became significantly less brutal and more enlightened. As a result, by the early modern period, the notion of a progressive, just, and humane universal state was well known in human thinking. A forceful statement of both the utilitarian and moral advantages of a universal league of nations encompassing the entire human population was enunciated by the philosopher Immanuel Kant in 1795.[5]

Obviously the supernational federation being proposed here would be qualitatively different from any empire observed in ancient, medieval, and modern history. Of course, the very concept of the empire is virtually extinct in the modern world. The twentieth century has witnessed the demise of the Ottoman and Austro-Hungarian empires, the dissolution of the colonial empires of Britain and France, the abortive—but very costly—attempt of Nazi Germany to establish an empire on the Eurasian land mass. Essential to the idea of an empire is a high degree of concentration of political power in the center, and the absence of democratic representation of the subject populations of the peripheral regions. Despite sincere efforts at enlightened and benevolent governance, oligarchic concentration of power tends naturally and automatically to produce capricious and oppressive rule. The central characteristics of the empire are inconsistent with contemporary aspirations toward a high degree of local autonomy, and democratic representation of all citizens in the central government. The only commonality between the empire and the proposed world state—a very important commonality, however—is the aspiration toward universality.

This aspiration has become increasingly intense over the past century, and it has produced some notable preliminary steps toward a world state. The primary immediate motivation has been to reduce the likelihood of major war—a motivation which for obvious reasons is always at its most intense in the aftermath of a major war. Thus the end of World War I witnessed the foundation of the League of Nations, and the end of World War II witnessed the foundation of the United Nations.[6] While these two international organizations clearly express the basic human aspiration toward a universal state, and they are certainly important milestones along a path which will hopefully lead eventually to the foundation of a genuine world state, they have nevertheless been serious disappointments. They have not possessed sufficient power and authority to achieve their primary goal of secure world peace. The League of Nations was unable to curb the rampant fascist imperialism of the 1930s which brought on World War II. After World War II, the United Nations was unable to curb the virulent confrontation between the communist and noncommunist nations that generated the Cold War—a protracted period of perilous brinkmanship on the edge of a nuclear World War III.

In a technical sense, neither the League of Nations nor the United Nations qualify as a legitimate state entity. These organizations have not possessed independent authority to tax and to maintain armed forces, to enact and enforce legislation, or to participate meaningfully in the provision of public goods (roads, education, and so on). Representatives to these international organizations have been appointed by national governments rather than being directly elected by the population, thus they possess no little or no independent status and standing—in a word, they have no constituencies of their own. To make matters worse, the principles of decision-making within these organizations have been so specified as to make this decision-making ponderous and ineffective. Nevertheless, despite all their shortcomings and drawbacks, the League of Nations and the United Nations have been important steps forward on the path to viable, meaningful supranational federation. These international organizations manifest a perceived need and an aspiration. They demonstrate a will—what is needed now is merely a workable institutional proposal, along with an adequate respite from the daily dissension and conflict of international human society to permit the contemplation, formulation, and implementation of a supranational state.

Perhaps the incipient demise of the Cold War between the communist and noncommunist nations will provide the necessary respite. Just as the end of World War I was followed by the foundation of the League of Nations and the end of World War II was followed by the foundation of the United Nations, so too the end of the Cold War might now be followed by the foundation of the Federal Union of Democratic Nations. World Wars I and II were of course enormously costly in terms of life, limb, and material. While one certainly cannot directly compare the physical pain, death, and destruction of the two World Wars to the mental pressure and psychological anxiety of the Cold War—nevertheless the Cold War can certainly be described as having been a traumatic human experience. For nearly half a century, there has existed the horrifying possibility of an unimaginably destructive nuclear war. The catastrophe could have been unleashed almost instantaneously, almost without any warning whatsoever. Once unleashed, the consequences would have been nightmarish and irremediable.

Having now been delivered—apparently—from this mind-numbing threat to human life and civilization, perhaps humanity will resolve to undertake a world government. The single most important purpose of such a government, of course, would be to reduce the probability of retrogression to such a condition of strife and dissension among nations that the possibility of nuclear war will again become acute. Aside from this paramount function, there are numerous other less important—but still significant—utilitarian purposes of world government. Some of these purposes will be briefly considered in the final Section C of this chapter.

C. PURPOSES OF A WORLD STATE

In considering the potential functions of a world state, we must keep uppermost in mind that this would be a federal type of state in which the component nation-states would retain their identity and importance. Power, authority, prestige, and citizen loyalty would be shared among the supernational government and the various national governments. The long-run objective of the world federation would be to achieve a condition in which national distinctions would be far less important, both practically and psychologically, than they are at the present time. A major implication of such a condition would be the extreme unlikelihood of large-scale warfare within human civilization. But it must be recognized and fully absorbed that this condition cannot be achieved overnight, and that it must be pursued in a very patient, gradualistic, peaceful, and nonthreatening manner. In the initial stages, the world *with* the Federal Union of Democratic Nations might not seem much different than the world *without* the Federal Union of Democratic Nations. Even so, the foundation of the Federal Union could have a tremendously beneficial impact upon human prospects in the long run. Thus the various practical limitations on the functions and activities of the Federal Union operative during its early period should not be construed as an argument against such a Union on grounds that it would not constitute a sufficient improvement over present conditions to be worthwhile.

The general purposes of a state entity may be categorized as follows: (1) maintenance of security against external threats (self-preservation); (2) peaceful resolution of internal conflicts between citizens and groups; (3) provision of public goods and services, and regulation of the economy; and (4) protection of political and social rights of the citizens. These purposes are pursued today by the various nation-states in the interests of their respective populations. Even if the Federal Union of Democratic Nations were to be established, its component nation-states would continue to pursue these purposes in the interests of their respective populations. However, their activities would be supplemented by those of a supernational state pursuing these same purposes in the interests of the entire world population. Even though some nations will almost certainly decline membership in the Union when it is first established, the aspiration toward universal membership will permit some significant account to be taken of the interests of populations of nonmember nations. This is in contrast to the motivation of each particular nation-state of today which takes extremely little direct account of the interests of the populations of other nations. Let us consider these four categories in turn, under the respective rubrics: external security; internal security; economic participation; protection of rights.

External Security. Perhaps the most fundamental purpose of any state is the protection of its citizens against the threat of foreign invasion, plundering, and conquest. This function is particularly difficult in the case of smaller states lying in close proximity to larger states. The usual counterweight for such states against the military power of their large neighbors is the formation of alliances. Formal and informal alliances of nations have a long and involved history, and they persist into the present day. In one sense, the supernational state would be like a "superalliance." Joining the Federal Union would provide a nation with strong assurances against invasion by nonmember nations. Such assurances would be attractive not merely to small and wealthy nations such as Switzerland and Kuwait; they might also be attractive to larger and powerful nations which are adjacent to still larger and more powerful nations. For example, the French population cannot have totally forgotten what happened to them at the hands of Germany in the first half of the twentieth century; nor can the population of Poland have totally forgotten their forcible incorporation into the Soviet sphere of influence in the late 1940s.

Of course, the *major* means by which the Federal Union would diminish the threat of external aggression would be the inclusion of *all* national participants in the conflicts and wars of the past: France *and* Germany, Poland *and* Russia, Kuwait *and* Iraq, and so on and so forth. But as has often been reiterated, in all probability there will be a substantial number of initial holdouts against membership in the Federal Union, and no doubt at least a few of these holdouts will retain their independence indefinitely—perhaps permanently. Thus the possibility of aggression against member nations by nonmember nations might well never be completely extinguished.

Even if we were to imagine a world in which all nations would be loyal members of the Federal Union of Democratic Nations, and in which the risk of gratuitous aggression by one nation against another would be virtually nonexistent, there might still be a role for the Federal Union to play in maintaining external security. The reference is to the possibility of confrontation and conflict between the human race and intelligent species from other planets. Of course, it is difficult to take seriously the image of warring intergalactic empires which is such a commonplace staple of certain varieties of science fiction. These stories seem to be almost as fantastic and unbelievable as are stories about ghosts and werewolves. To begin with, it is not at all clear whether any practical means of interstellar space travel will ever be devised. Einstein's proposition that the speed of light is an absolute limit may be an insuperable barrier to any significant amount of communication and movement between various solar systems. In any event, it seems plausible that any race of beings—whether human or otherwise—which is sufficiently intelligent to find a practical means of interstellar travel will be of a peaceful and cooperative nature. Such races would presumably have learned that there are more efficient and reliable means of pursuing objectives than conflict and war. This possibility, of course, is the only hope which the human race has if, by some chance, there happens to be a basis of fact underlying the "flying saucer" phenomenon, and human civilization is in fact being monitored by one or more alien species.

According to the astronomers, there are billions of stars within the universe very much like the sun which warms our planet Earth. It seems likely that a large number of these stars have solar systems of planets such as our own. Furthermore, it seems likely that many of these planets are populated by sentient life-forms, and that at least some of these life-forms are as intelligent, if not more intelligent, than the human race. That "somewhere out there" are intelligent non-human species is of course an intriguing concept, but it is not necessarily a practically relevant concept if the tremendous and inconceivable distances between stars will forever preclude any meaningful communication and contact between ourselves and these other intelligent species.

But clearly such communication and contact, while seemingly unlikely, is within the realm of possibility. It is also within the realm of possibility that such communication and contact will not be entirely peaceful and benign. Should the human race be sufficiently unfortunate to have these remote possibilities eventually come to pass, clearly our race's prospects would be somewhat enhanced if we had achieved the level of political unity inherent in a universal world state. Such a state would be able to muster and dispose military force much more quickly than would an assemblage of completely sovereign and independent nation-states. It would obviously be completely unpersuasive to put too much emphasis upon this possibility. To do so would elicit reactions from sensible people akin to those elicited by a lunatic who believes that a world state must instantly be formed to counter the imminent alien invasion of which "flying saucers" are the forerunners. At the present time, the potential role of the Federal Union of Democratic Nations in protecting humanity against the depradations of nonhuman alien species is a very minor consideration. Nevertheless, it is perhaps not a completely negligible argument for supernational federation, especially when taken in conjunction with the more "down to earth" arguments.

Internal Security. At the present stage in human history, clearly the single most important perceived function of a supernational federation would be the reduction of the amount of conflict and warfare within human civilization in the future. There would be both material and psychological benefits of this reduction: in a material sense, it would reduce the amount of deprivation, suffering, and premature death inflicted upon humanity, and in a pyschological sense, it would reduce the amount of apprehension, fear, and stress inflicted upon humanity. The major basis for these benefits is not primarily that the federation would deter aggression by nonmember nations against member nations, nor that it would deter aggression by aliens against the human race. It is rather that the supernational federation would deter conflict and wars among member nations.

This particular conceptualization of the key advantage of supernational federation would be just as attractive to large and powerful nations such as the United States and Russia as it is to smaller, less powerful nations such as Switzerland and Kuwait. More so than small nations, large nations tend naturally to elicit feelings of distrust and hostility in other nations. Large nations tend naturally to become embroiled in large wars with other large nations. Even the most cursory study of history serves to establish the amazing variety and fecundity of human conflicts.[7] Grievances tend to beget violence, which begets still more grievances. The cycle continues and continues—apparently unending. How do these conflicts arise and how do they develop? The reasons for conflict seem to be as numerous as the sands on the beach and the stars in the sky. Their patterns of development are astonishingly complex and varied. At the heart of it all is basic human psychology: individual greed and hostility are manifested at the social level in an "us versus them" mentality in which anything that one's own group does is good and anything which other groups do is bad. But this basic attitude has generated an enormously complex record of human conflict which runs like a broad red stream throughout all history.

The history of conflict and war in human affairs long predates the development of the modern nation-state, and so it would be unreasonable to blame the sovereign nation-state system of the modern world for conflict and war. However, it is certainly arguable that the sovereign nation-state system has contributed to the tremendous destructiveness of modern warfare. The system has been remarkably successful at suppressing dissension and conflict within nations. The result has been very large politically organized populations with massive economic capacity and highly cohesive purposes. When these populations, armed with technologically advanced weaponry, come into conflict in the modern arena of war (a far more extensive area than the "battlefields" of earlier times), the result is a catastrophic level of suffering and destruction unknown in earlier times.

There is a school of thought which proclaims that the destructive potential of modern weaponry—and particularly that of strategic and tactical nuclear weapons—has become so overwhelming that the sovereign nation-state system no longer represents the threat to human welfare that it did in the nineteenth and early twentieth centuries. In the face of the horrifying possibilities of modern war, national leaders will exercise prudence and restraint, and the odds are high that even if the sovereign nation-state system persists indefinitely without fundamental change, never again will an unrestricted world war be experienced by humanity.

In all probability, this viewpoint manifests wishful thinking. In a way, it is reminiscent of the naivety of the idealistic anarchists of the nineteenth century who advocated the abolition of all forms of government above the local level. The common consensus of humanity has been that such an abolition would soon generate a condition of perpetual conflict and war between the host of sovereign cities, towns, and villages. The idealistic anarchists dismissed such visions on the basis that proper education in goodness and virtue would instill in the populations of the localities peaceful and cooperative attitudes. There is no doubt that proper education is vital to the development of the individual human being, and that goodness and virtue should be instilled in the individual to the greatest extent possible. But there are limits to what can be accomplished through proper education. If education is not supplemented by political and social institutions that reinforce goodness and virtue both at the individual level and higher levels, then the level of peace and security that mankind desires is not likely to be achieved.

The notion that mankind will be forever "frightened" into peaceful behavior by the existence of unprecedently destructive weapons is very dubious. The existence of nuclear weapons throughout the second half of the twentieth century did not quickly shut down the virulent ideological confrontation between the communist and non-communist nations. Now that that confrontation seems to be subsiding, it would appear that the instrumental cause of this subsidence was not so much fear of the consequences of nuclear war as it was increasing evidence of the material superiority of the noncommunist economic system. And during the Cold War period, such factors as the extensive civil defense program in the Soviet Union and the Strategic Defense Initiative of the United States suggest that neither side entirely discarded the possibility that a nuclear war might be survivable and even winable. It is also necessary to confront the inevitable mortality of each individual human being. The avoidance of nuclear war would at most permit each individual person to survive for a few more years or a few more decades—but it would not permit indefinite survival. Therefore, from the point of view of each individual person, the benefits of avoiding nuclear war are certainly finite. This suggests that should the person perceive the stakes of a nuclear war to be sufficiently high (i.e., to preserve the accustomed way of life), then war would be regarded as acceptable.

At the present time the human race is breathing a collective sigh of relief that the ideological struggle between communism and noncommunism seems at last to be winding down. This struggle constituted the engine which propelled the nuclear and conventional arms competition which has consumed a tremendous quantity of economic resources over the last four decades, and which has kept humanity perched precariously on the lip of a nuclear volcano. We may certainly rejoice now that the immediate threat is subsiding. But it would be very unwise to become complacent at this stage in human development. New ideological conflicts might develop. Religious differences, which were the bane of civilization for many long centuries prior to the rise of secular ideologies, might come once again to the fore. Perhaps most ominously of all, as we look forward into the future, we perceive great economic stresses emerging. The exhaustion of fossil fuel reserves along with overall environmental degradation, together with steadily increasing population pressure on the finite resources of the earth, could very easily combine to significantly reduce living standards all around the world in the not-too-remote future. In a word, we simply cannot expect the sources of friction and conflict within human civilization to gradually subside and evaporate in the future.

Those sources will remain operative, and they will continue to produce both generalized hostility and specific conflicts of interest between nation-states. Some of these conflicts of interest are likely to become sufficiently intense to warrant contemplation of and preparations for war. What has happened in the past could all too easily happen again in the future. The presence of nuclear weapons might not provide a decisive deterrent. One has to recognize that very frequently wars do not come about because one or both parties deliberately commence them. What might be termed "miscalculated brinkmanship" is often the precipitating factor. The parties issue ultimata to one another in the hope and expectation that confronted with such determination, the other side will submit on some specific demand that might seem relatively minor in and of itself. Both World War I and World War II were launched by miscalculated brinkmanship, and there is no guarantee that miscalculated brinkmanship will not also launch a nuclear World War III.

A supernational federation would create both practical and psychological impediments to wars between member nations. In a practical sense, the supernational federation would possess some standing military forces of its own which would operate as a deterrent, plus it would also have some degree of indirect influence over the military forces of member nations which could be utilized to impede preparations for war. There is also the fact that the existence of a supernational federation would facilitate the development of economic linkages and integration between the various member nations, and this would aggravate the costs of warfare among them. In the final analysis, however, the psychological impediments to internal conflict would no doubt in the long run become much more important and effective than the practical impediments. If the supernational federation achieves a measure of success, and its citizens begin to take a significant degree of pride in it, then an internal war will come to be regarded as a tragic betrayal of human destiny—as something too heinous even to be considered.

A skeptic might point, however, to the extremely important role which civil war has played in human history. There is no question that the creation of an integrated state entity sets the stage for civil war, and there is also no question that some of the civil wars witnessed throughout the modern period have been worse than many international wars. So too it could be with a Federal Union of Democratic Nations. The creation of the Union might create intense aspirations and expectations that would not have come about in its absence. If there are adverse developments which threaten to thwart these aspirations and expectations, the frustration felt by some of its citizens could create serious pressures toward internal warfare.

The primary means by which it is planned to avoid the threat of civil war within the Federal Union of Democratic Nations is the constitutional provision for free secession by any member nation. This would be an absolute, permanent, and inalienable right of each member nation. At any time, and at its own unilateral discretion, any nation could choose to withdraw from the Federal Union. No means of force whatever could be utilized to forestall such a withdrawal. Thus, if a conflict of interest between the supernational federation and any particular nation were to become sufficiently aggravated, that conflict could be simply terminated by means of secession of the nation from the Union.

As a citizen of the United States, the author is well aware of the fact that many U.S. citizens—as well as citizens of other nations—might be dubious that any state entity with such a tolerant policy regarding membership could possibly be successful. It so happens that the history of the United States provides a classic example of a civil war fought to forestall secession from a federation. The U.S. Constitution, ratified in 1788, inaugurated a federal union composed of thirteen states. Unfortunately, the economic evolution of the Northern states and the Southern states diverged significantly during the first half of the nineteenth century. The Southern states became heavily dependent on cotton exports produced by a plantation economy involving slavery. Meanwhile, the Northern states began supplementing their basic yeoman farmer economy with an increasingly important industrial sector. The Southern plantation owners wanted free trade so that they could import cheap manufactured goods from Europe; the Northern factory owners wanted tariffs to protect their "infant industries."

This economic conflict of interest was drastically inflamed by a virulent moral controversy over the institution of slavery.[8] The violent emotions aroused by the ideological conflict over slavery precluded reasonable compromise on the free trade versus tariffs issue. The election of Abraham Lincoln, a critic of slavery and a friend of tariffs, to the U.S. Presidency in 1860, finally precipitated the decision by the Southern states to withdraw from the Union. The Northern states viewed this secession as a treasonous defection, and in 1861 went to war to prevent it. The final military defeat of the Southern forces in 1865, after a prolonged and bloody conflict, brought the Southern states back into the Union. Since then, there have been no further threats by states to secede from the United States.

The U.S. Constitution did not mention secession, either to forbid it or to allow it. It is arguable that had the possibility of secession been considered by the authors of the U.S. Constitution, then whether they forbade it or condoned it, the U.S. Civil War of 1861-65 would not have occurred. Had secession been explicitly forbidden, thus raising the probability that the Northern states would have fought to preserve the Union, then perhaps the Southern states would have been more willing to compromise, and less disposed to contemplating secession. Had secession been explicitly approved, thus raising the probability that the Southern states would secede from the Union, then perhaps the Northern states would have been more willing to compromise.

Of course, both of these speculations are highly conjectural. When the U.S. Constitution was written, the institution of slavery seemed on the verge of extinction. The invention of the cotton gin and the development of the English textile industry gave the institution a new lease on life. The bitter ideological controversy which thereupon arose between defenders and opponents of slavery had never been foreseen by the authors of the U.S. Constitution. But for the sake of argument, suppose these authors had foreseen the possibility of such a bitter and apparently irresolvable conflict arising: would they have more likely forbidden secession or allowed it?

It is quite plausible that they would have allowed it. The United States federation was, at the time of its formation, a voluntary association of states. No state was forced into the Union by means of military conquest. The purpose of the federation was to benefit each and every one of its member states, and this purpose was recognized by each and every one of its member states. So long as this purpose continued to be implemented by the federal government, and so long as this implementation continued to be recognized by the state governments, then none of them would have had an incentive to withdraw from the Union. Therefore an incentive in some states to withdraw from the Union would provide prima facie evidence that the fundamental purpose of the Union was not being implemented by the federal government, and thus the whole basis of the Union would have become null and void. Under this reasoning, the Southern states were legally and morally entitled to withdraw from the Union. This indeed was the general argument advanced by the Southern secessionists at the time of the U.S. Civil War. Generally speaking, contemporary Americans tend to view this argument as did the defenders of the Union during the Civil War: namely as little more than a thin and hollow rationalization, motivated by selfish and short-sighted sectionalism, and by a perverse and irrational determination to preserve the morally offensive system of slavery.

Whatever the underlying motives for the secessionist argument in 1861, as U.S. citizens look forward to the possibility of joining a supranational federation such as the Federal Union of Democratic Nations, and then at some time thereafter to the possibility of witnessing the supranational government embracing an intolerable policy such as, for example, the Crude Redistribution policy discussed above in Chapter 2, then it would be exactly this argument on which the United States would tend to rely in order to justify its own secession from the Federal Union. If the Union Constitution explicitly guarantees the right of secession, it would be less likely that the Federal Union would possess the moral determination to oppose the secession by force. But trouble foreseen may be trouble avoided. If it is made unambiguously clear to the Federal Union government that any attempt to implement such an extremely controversial policy as Crude Redistribution would lead to the secession of many important member nations (without whose membership the policy would be meaningless in any event), then the supranational government would probably refrain from implementing the policy in the first place, and the problem of secession would probably not arise in practice.

The obvious danger in explicitly condoning secession in the Union Constitution is that after the Federal Union starts operating, and its member nations start experiencing various unavoidable short-term stresses and strains, nationalistic chauvinism will quickly surface, and the member nations will commence withdrawing from the Union for a variety of reasons that could plausibly be described as "thin pretexts." Eventually the Federal Union might itself be reduced to a ridiculous little rump state consisting of only a few small nations. Instead of becoming a tower of unified strength and moral authority in human affairs, the Federal Union might end up as nothing more than a laughingstock.

Once again, we must concede that there is no evading the possibility of failure. Each of the specific proposals put forward in this book might be a failure. Pragmatic market socialism might be a failure. The World Economic Equalization Program might be a failure. The Federal Union of Democratic Nations might be a failure. But the fact is that every great undertaking in the history of the human race, including all of those which were afterward deemed to have been marvelous successes, might have been failures. The possibility of failure simply cannot be permitted to forestall every great undertaking if the human race is to have any hope of further progress in the future. So it is with the Federal Union of Democratic Nations. An explicit provision in the Union Constitution authorizing the withdrawal from the Union of member nations dissatisfied with its operations, would greatly augment the possibility of founding a Federal Union of Democratic Nations with a large proportion of the world's nations as charter members.

Once the Federal Union has been established and has commenced its work, then we may hope that it will prove equal to its challenges, and that it will make steady progress toward its higher purposes. It is to be hoped that within a few decades, most if not all nonmember nations, recognizing the advantages of membership, will have entered the Federal Union. Within further decades, it is to be hoped, the provision authorizing secession will have become totally irrelevant, representing nothing more than an obsolescent relic of the dead past. In the United States of America of today, any state leader who proposed that his state should secede from the United States, even if such secession were legally permissible, would surely be deemed by other state leaders and by the state's citizens a candidate for psychiatric examination. It is to be hoped that in the Federal Union of Democratic Nations of tomorrow, any national leader who would propose that his nation should secede from the Federal Union, would be similarly regarded. The hope is, of course, that in the long term the secession possibility will become as unlikely and irrelevant within the Federal Union of Democratic Nations as it is today within most successful nation-states.

Economic Participation. As utilized here, "economic participation" is an umbrella term encompassing a broad range of governmental activities and functions, many of them not directly connected to the basic economy of the supernational federation. These activities and functions may all be described as "economic," however, in the sense that to perform them the supernational government would have to raise revenue by taxation and other means, and to expend revenue in the hiring of personnel and the acquisition of equipment. In general, the supernational federation would definitely take over areas which are clearly handled rather clumsily, inadequately, and ineffectively at the national or lower levels. But at the same time it should also be allowed a certain amount of participation even in areas where adequate performance is arguably possible at the national or lower levels, merely on grounds of enhancing its symbolic importance in human affairs in the long-term interest of promoting psychological unity. If *too* strong a case is needed to justify participation by the supernational state in a certain area of public activity, then its activity might be too minor and vestigial to support its paramount psychological role.

The building and maintenance of highways might be cited as an example of an area of government activity which is arguably handled adequately by national and lower-level governments, but in which the Federal Union should nevertheless become involved as a means of enhancing its visibility and status. Only a small number of highways need be involved, but these would be very substantial and well-constructed continental arteries connecting several nations, and presenting a homogeneous and unified appearance to the traveler. International highways are one aspect of the international transport and communications network, a network which has become highly evolved and effective in the absence of a supernational state. It is not argued that the participation of a supernational federation is necessary to greatly expand and improve this network. But it is certainly argued that this area is a natural one in which a supernational state might become active, and that such activity would appreciably enhance the likelihood that the supernational state would become and remain viable and effective in terms of its larger purposes.

There are other areas in which the participation of the supernational federation is seemingly more supportable simply on utilitarian criteria, although some of these are relatively minor in and of themselves. For example, the work done by Interpol in enforcing the fundamental criminal laws common to practically every nation might be done more efficaciously by an appropriate agency of the Federal Union. Another example of this sort is the data collection and reporting presently done by the World Bank and similar international agencies. The potential contribution of a supernational federation to international police work and data acquisition is perhaps more obvious than its potential contribution to international transport and communications, but police work and data acquisition, in and of themselves, are not as significant as transport and communication. Lest such functions and activities be dismissed as trivial and unimportant, we should recollect that insofar as supernational participation is concerned, it is not merely the direct, short-term utilitarian purposes which should be taken into account, but also the contribution that this participation would make to the long-term objective of promoting psychological unity among the entire human race.

In contrast to the examples mentioned above, there are at least two areas in which the presence of a supernational state will arguably greatly improve the prospects for effective action (relative to the situation under the present sovereign nation-state system), and which are also extremely fundamental and important. These are the interrelated areas of population control and environmental preservation. Under the sovereign nation-state system, vigorous efforts in either of these areas tend to be deterred by feelings of frustration and futility. The problems of excessive population growth and environmental degradation are to a large extent world problems. The benefits to any one nation of attempting to slow population growth and environmental degradation are relatively small—if many or most other nations are pretty much allowing population growth and environmental degradation to proceed unchecked. On the other hand, if a large proportion of the human population were politically united within a supranational federation, and if it were therefore clear that measures taken by the supranational government to slow population growth and improve the physical environment would be more likely to have an appreciable impact upon these problem areas, then there would be more of an incentive to undertake these measures.

Of course, the supranational state would have to be very careful of what it does in these areas lest it come to be regarded as oppressive by an appreciable proportion of the citizens. The problems of population and the environment are not yet sufficiently critical to justify drastic measures. For example, laws dictating limits on the number of children a couple may have would almost certainly be premature. It is certainly to be hoped that such laws will never become necessary throughout all of future human history. At any rate, for the moment, efforts to slow population growth via state action should be limited to such indirect measures as decreasing the informational and cost barriers to contraception, and increasing the financial disincentives to large family sizes. Since human procreation is not directly involved, measures to protect the environment are not as inherently sensitive as are those designed to reduce population growth. Nevertheless, any such measures can and do adversely affect some individuals and groups, and they are thereby rendered controversial. The supranational government should certainly press the cause of environmental preservation, but it must not do so in such an unrestrained manner as to put the continued existence of the supranational federation itself at serious risk.

A more positive area in which the Federal Union would participate is that of space exploration. In this particular area, there are both utilitarian and psychological grounds for the supranational federation to become the primary actor. In a utilitarian sense, concentration of the space exploration effort under the Union would avoid costly duplication of effort; while in a psychological sense, such concentration would enable the Union to assume center stage in a great and noble human undertaking. In contrast to most other areas of government activity, at least there is almost no controversy at all regarding the *objective* of space exploration. Almost every informed human being agrees that space exploration is a worthwhile human endeavor, and that at least *some* effort should be made in this direction. The controversy only arises with respect to *how much* of an effort ought to be made; or more precisely, how much government revenue should be expended on space exploration. Skeptics argue that owing to the tremendous distances involved, any tangible payoff to space exploration is extremely remote and uncertain, and so for the moment, government spending should be devoted almost exclusively to various "down to earth," "closer to home" purposes. Proponents disparage such thinking as limited and unprogressive. Controversy of a sort exists, but it is not as intense and acrimonious as it would be were there fundamental disagreement with respect to the desirability of the objective itself.

Exactly how much the Federal Union of Democratic Nations will be able to accomplish in the above areas, as well as others, cannot be precisely predicted. Even if the basic principle of supernational federation is widely accepted, clearly the conservative viewpoint will tend to resist specific proposals for the extension of activity by the supernational federation. Arguments will be heard that these activities are more effectively performed by lower levels of government, or perhaps by the private sector, and that extending the responsibilities of the supernational government will tend to further expand an already large, unresponsive, and oppressive government bureaucracy.

Any tendency to dismiss such arguments as inane and unprogressive must be resisted. At the beginning of its history, it is much more important that the Federal Union be *maintained,* than that it expand its sphere of activity. The simple fact that it *is,* is more important than what it *does.* Once humanity has become more accustomed to the supernational state and less susceptible to unwarranted fears of totalitarianism and oppression, then perhaps issues of the proper role for this state can be assessed in a more accurate and objective manner. Quite possibly in the long run the Federal Union will become considerably more active and involved than it will be in its early period. But this can only happen if the supernational state does not compromise its viability during its early period through excessive and overenthusiastic activism.

Protection of Rights. The concept of "natural rights" is akin to that of "freedom": it is a noble aspiration and legitimately plays a major role in human thinking—but at the same time it is necessary to be realistic about such rights. We observe that the impersonal forces of nature display no more concern for the natural rights of human beings than they display toward the freedom of human beings. Aside from natural constraints on rights and freedom, we also observe numerous social constraints. The basic problem is that just as excessive freedom on the part of some individuals may reduce the freedom of others to an unacceptably low level, so too excessive regard for the rights of some may entail serious disregard for the rights of others. In the final analysis, there would seem to be considerable substance in the somewhat cynical perception that any given individual has just as many rights as he or she can induce others to recognize—where the means of inducement are mainly coercive although partially persuasive.

It is customary for the constitutions of the modern era to proclaim certain natural rights of the citizen, such as "life, liberty, and the pursuit of happiness." Although many conservatives are skeptical of making economic commitments in political documents, it is proposed here that among the rights guaranteed by the Union Constitution—as part of the overall right to "pursuit of happiness"—would be a right to a "decent standard of living." What constitutes a "decent standard of living" would be left unspecified. The aspiration is that this phrase will eventually denote a prosperous middle-class way of life such as it is presently experienced in the wealthiest industrial nations. It may transpire that the achievement of such a standard of living for the entire world population will never be possible, in which case the phrase may have to denote a subsistence level of life, plus the possible amenity of literacy.

In its pursuance of the World Economic Equalization Program (WEEP), the Federal Union of Democratic Nations would be endeavoring to implement the natural right of each and every citizen to a decent standard of living. The Constitutional provision recognizing this particular right would be an expression of intent toward worldwide equalization of living standards. Such an explicit expression of intent will enhance the likelihood that the WEEP will be successfully pursued to its logical conclusion.

To implement a WEEP sufficiently massive to be successful will be extremely difficult both economically and politically. Next to ideological conflict, the economic gap is the single most formidable obstacle to supernational political unity. Unlike ideological conflict, the economic gap cannot be overcome simply by attitude adjustment—it is a *real* problem rather than merely a *psychological* problem. In all probability, the success or failure of the World Economic Equalization Program will determine whether or not the Federal Union of Democratic Nations will be viable in the long term. As strongly emphasized earlier, this Program must absolutely, positively be guided by the principle of Common Progress rather than by the principle of Crude Redistribution. If the populations of the rich nations arrive at a consensus that the WEEP—if continued—will have the effect of worldwide economic levelling, then they will do everything in their power to shut down the Program, and failing this, they will secede from the Union. In all probability, the departure of the rich nations from the Union would so undermine its effectiveness that its total dissolution would soon follow.

Aside from the right to a decent standard of living (which encompasses food, shelter, medical care, literacy, etc.), the Union Constitution should enumerate certain other rights on which fairly general consensus has been achieved: freedom of speech, press, and political organization, freedom of religious belief and expression, freedom from discrimination on the basis of race, sex, or national origin. The Federal Union of Democratic Nations would endeavor to guarantee that these rights are respected and observed throughout the Union. Although the major focus would be on maintenance of such rights within the Union, some limited efforts might also be made to facilitate their implementation in nonmember nations. One of the primary means by which the Federal Union would demonstrate its benign character would be through its concern and reverence for the natural rights of all human beings.

At the same time, it cannot be overemphasized that the Federal

Union must be realistic and restrained in its efforts to promote natural rights. It must avoid letting its enthusiasm for natural rights evolve into fanaticism. Although indisputably a noble and essential concept in human affairs, the concept of natural rights is also to a considerable extent nebulous and ambiguous. Allegations that certain institutions and activities constitute intolerable violations of natural rights are often quite controversial. Efforts to curb or abolish such institutions and activities—while welcomed by some—might be regarded as misguided and oppressive by many others. The Federal Union must be very patient and very cautious in pursuing the cause of natural rights, because an overenthusiastic pursuit could easily compromise the fundamental viability of the Union. Aspirations toward a utopian condition in human civilization should be avoided, and it should be clearly recognized that progress in the area of natural rights must necessarily be gradual and evolutionary.

To summarize the above, a review of the four fundamental functions of government (external security, internal security, economic participation, and protection of rights) suggests that a supranational state could make an appreciable contribution in all four areas. In general, numerous practical benefits can be perceived in supranational federation. But what is probably still more important is that the existence and functioning of a supranational federation would have a profound long-term effect on the attitudes of people all around the world. This tangible symbol of human solidarity would cultivate psychological feelings of unity and mutual respect. Such feelings would discourage tendencies toward competition and enmity and encourage tendencies toward cooperation and amity.

This is not to imply that the objective is to achieve an ant-like mentality in which every human being would think only of the larger society rather than of himself or herself. Such an objective is not only impossible—it is undesirable and unthinkable. What is rather intended is a relatively modest extension of the typical individual's field of social concern from the national to the supranational level. A citizen of the United States at the present time is not willing to give up everything to assist another citizen of the United States; neither would a citizen of the Federal Union be willing to give up everything to assist another citizen of the Federal Union. But a citizen of the

United States *does* tend to take a basically positive, cooperative, and friendly approach to other citizens of the United States. The objective is to achieve this same basic attitude among all citizens of the Federal Union with respect to all other citizens—even though these citizens would represent a wide diversity of nationalities. With this type of attitude in place, less of humanity's resources would be wastefully employed in preparing for and carrying on conflict and warfare. More of humanity's resources would be productively employed for purposes of material and spiritual wellbeing and progress.

NOTES

1. Some illustrative general references on nationalism include Hans Kohn (1944), Barbara Ward (1966), Karl Deutsch (1966, 1969), K. R. Minogue (1967), Anthony D. Smith (1971), Boyd Shafer (1972), F. H. Hinsley (1973), Eugene Kamenka (1976), Leonard Tivey (1981), John Breuilly (1982), T. V. Sathyamurthy (1983), Edward S. Tiryakian and Ronald Rogowski (1985).

2. As the most horrific episode in modern history, the twelve year period between the accession of Adolf Hitler to power in Germany and the end of World War II has generated a huge literature. A few illustrative references on Adolf Hitler, the Third Reich, and World War II include Alan Bullock (1952), Joachim Fest (1970, 1974), Ramon Knauerhase (1972), Robert Payne (1973), John Toland (1976), Robert G. L. Waite (1976), Milton Mayer (1955), William L. Shirer (1959, 1960, 1984), Helmut Krausnick et al (1968), Albert Speer (1970), Robert Cecil (1972), Eugene Davidson (1972), Walter Laqueue (1976), Norman Rich (1973), David Irving (1977, 1978), B. H. Liddell Hart (1971), Peter Calvocoressi and Guy Wint (1972), Henri Michel (1975), Robert Leckie (1987).

3. Some illustrative references from the large political literature on the concepts of state power and sovereignty include the following: Bertrand de Jouvenal (1949, 1959), F. H. Hinsley (1966), Adolf A. Berle (1967), Alexander Passerin D'Entrèves (1967), W. J. Stankiewicz (1969), Robert G. Wesson (1978), Gene Sharp (1980), William T. Bluhm (1984), Anthony de Jasay (1985), Paul Weiss (1986), James A. Caporaso (1989).

4. Some illustrative references from the political literature on the federal form include Arthur W. Macmahon (1962), Edward McWhinney (1962), Thomas M. Franck (1968), Daniel J. Elazar (1979, 1987), Murray Forsyth (1981, 1987).

5. Kant's essay "Eternal Peace," first published in German in 1795, was

translated into English as an appendix to Carl Joachim Friedrich's book *Inevitable Peace*, published in 1948. Kant's proposal was specifically for a universal federation of republican nations, and it was arguably inspired by the nascent republic of the United States of America, which might provide the necessary catalyst for a quantum advance in international organization. Consider, for example, the following passage (Friedrich, 1948, p. 256): "It can be demonstrated that this idea of *federalization* possesses objective reality, that it can be realized by a gradual extension to all states, leading to eternal peace. For if good fortune brings to pass that a powerful and enlightened people develops a republican form of government which by its nature is inclined toward peace, then such a republic will provide the central core for the federal union of other states. For they can join this republic and can thus make secure among themselves the state of peace according to the idea of a law of nations, and can gradually extend themselves by additional connections of this sort."

6. On the history of the League of Nations see, for example, F. P. Walters (1952), Byron Dexter (1967), D. F. Fleming (1968), George Scott (1973), Elmer Bendiner (1975), F. S. Northedge (1986). Illustrative references from the large literature on the United Nations include John Maclaurin (1951), Stephen S. Fenichell and Phillip Andrews (1954), Leland M. Goodrich and Anne P. Simons (1955), John G. Stoessinger (1965), Alf Ross (1966), David A. Kay (1967), Clark M. Eichelberger (1970), Leon Gordenker (1971), William F. Buckley (1974), Daniel Moynihan (1975), John F. Murphy (1982), Peter J. Fromuth (1988), Amos Yoder (1989).

7. In arguing for the ratification of the proposed United States Constitution—which was to form a politically unified nation-state out of the hitherto loosely confederated original thirteen states—Alexander Hamilton put forward as one of the primary advantages of tighter political integration the avoidance of future armed contests among the states. The following passage from *The Federalist* (Number 6) responds to those who could foresee no obvious wellsprings of conflict between the states:

"A man must be far gone in Utopian speculation who can seriously doubt that, if these states should either be wholly disunited, or only united in partial confederacies, the subdivisions into which they might be thrown would have frequent and violent contests with each other. To presume a want of motives for such contests as an argument against their existence, would be to forget that men are ambitious, vindictive, and rapacious. To look for a continuation of harmony between a number of independent, unconnected sovereignties in the same neighbourhood, would be to disregard the uniform course of human events, and to set at defiance the accumulated experience of ages.

"The causes of hostility among nations are innumerable. There are some which have a general and almost constant operation among the collective bodies of society. Of this description are the love of power or the desire of pre-eminence or dominion—the jealousy of power, or the desire of equality and safety. There are others which have a more circumscribed though an equally operative influence within their spheres. Such are the rivalships and competitions of commerce between commercial nations. And there are others, not less numerous than either of the former, which take their origin entirely in private passions; in the attachments, enmities, interests, hopes, and fears of leading individuals in the communities in which they are members. Men of this class, whether the favorites of a king or of a people, have in too many instances abused the confidence they possess; and assuming the pretext of some public motive, have not scrupled to sacrifice the national tranquillity to personal advantage or personal gratification."

For the most part, Hamilton's ideas concerning the efficacy of political unity are as relevant today to a potential supernational federation as they were in 1787-88 to the potential national federation which ultimately emerged as the United States of America. It would require only a modest amount of updating and revision to transform *The Federalist Papers* into a thoroughly contemporary case for a supernational federation such as the Federal Union of Democratic Nations proposed herein.

8. The dominant role of slavery in bringing on the U.S. Civil War is clearly reflected in the large literature on the institution of American slavery and the origins of the Civil War. Illustrative contemporary contributions to the study of slavery include Eugene Genovese (1969, 1973), David Brion Davis (1966, 1984), and Orlando Patterson (1982). On the ante-bellum slave system in the United States, see Kenneth Stampp (1956), Ann Lane (1971), Eugene Genovese (1974), and Paul David et al (1976). Documentation of the abolitionist antislavery literature is contained in William Pease and Jane Pease (1965), and a history of the abolitionist movement in the pre-war era is provided by Louis Filler (1960). Documents on the Southern proslavery response are provided in Drew Faust (1981). The viewpoint and course of the Southern secessionist movement are examined in J. Jeffery Auer (1963) and William Barney (1972, 1974).

6

SUMMARY AND CONCLUSION

A. THE CASE FOR SUPERNATIONAL FEDERATION

As we peer forward into an unknown future from our present vantage point near the threshold of the third millennium A.D., we may discern intimations of brightest promise, and we may discern intimations of direst peril. Science and technology have achieved practical marvels that would have been unimaginable a few short generations ago. Mankind has explored the land, sea, and sky of the planet earth from pole to pole, and has ventured to the edge of the illimitable vastness of outer space. A level of prosperity has been achieved for ordinary people in the industrially advanced nations that is absolutely unprecedented in the history of human civilization. If the progress of the last several hundred years is extrapolated indefinitely into the future, human civilization may well achieve a level of extent, mastery, and magnificence that will be almost inconceivable to the present generation of humanity.

Unfortunately, this bright and benign future cannot be complacently awaited and anticipated in serene confidence. The same science and technology which has given us jet airplanes, television, computers, and a host of other devices for the improvement of life, has also given us thermonuclear bombs, intercontinental missiles, nuclear-powered ballistic missile submarines, and numerous other instruments of death and destruction whose effectiveness could not have been imagined in earlier ages. The political evolution of humanity has reached a plateau level in which a large number of nation-states, each of which considers itself to be fully sovereign and independent of all others, uneasily share the earth's surface. The sovereign nation-state system has clearly demonstrated its propensity toward conflict and war by means of the two disastrous world wars of the twentieth century. In view of this strong propensity, the present hopes that fear of nuclear armageddon will deter the outbreak of major warfare indefinitely into the future are quite likely to be disappointed.

As for the present economic status of the human race, it must be acknowledged that the highest living standards are enjoyed by a relatively small minority of the earth's population in the United States, the nations of Western Europe, and a few others. The great majority of the earth's population confronts a living standard that would be considered spartan, impoverished, and barely tolerable by the people of the richest nations. The human population of the world has entered a phase of exponential growth, and to make matters worse the rate of population growth is highest in the poorest nations. Excessive population growth has become a severe impediment to economic progress, it is placing a heavy burden on the physical environment, and if continued indefinitely it could lead to a catastrophic ecological breakdown the consequences of which might well be comparable to those of unrestrained nuclear war.

The argument of this book has been that the establishment of a properly designed supernational federation at the present point in world history would substantially improve the probability of a generally favorable evolution of human civilization into the future. Two phrases in this formulation merit special attention: "properly designed" and "improve the probability." With respect to the first, it cannot be overemphasized that at least in its early period the intended supernational federation will not possess the extremely high level of power, authority, and acceptance that is common to the typical nation-state of today. The envisioned supernational federation would be a political compromise, possessing enough power and authority to be indisputably a full-fledged state entity and being sufficiently active in human affairs to capture the attention and the imagination of the human population—but at the same time being subject to a sufficient number of restraints and limitations to allay fears that it will become an instrument for the oppression of member nation-states and individual citizens. The main elements of such a political compromise were elaborated in Chapter 2 above, which described the fundamental institutions and operations of a proposed Federal Union of Democratic Nations.

The second phrase, "improve the probability," expresses the realism and rationality of this proposal toward supernational federation. There is absolutely nothing which we can do—or not do—which would absolutely guarantee a benign future for humanity. In particular, the foundation of a supernational federation along the lines of the Federal Union of Democratic Nations is neither necessary nor sufficient—in a strict logical sense—to assure such a future. Conceivably the future of humanity will be benign into the remote and indefinite future even if no progress whatsoever is ever made beyond the sovereign nation-state system of today. Even without a world state, today's ideological controversy might fade away to insignificance, today's economic disparities might gradually disappear, and the present family of sovereign and independent nation-states might achieve such a high level of mutual respect and consideration as to render a world state needless and superfluous. On the other hand, even if a supernational federation is founded, mankind might encounter severe adversity and complete disaster within a short period of historical time. The formation of a world state might set the stage for a nuclear civil war at some point in the future. It may be that a world state would be no more successful in achieving an adequate degree of population control and environmental preservation than the system of sovereign and independent nation-states would be. Having conceded these points, however, it is fair to state what is by far the more important point in the strongest terms possible: The future prospects for humanity will be substantially better *with* a supernational federation in existence than *without* a supernational federation in existence. A supernational federation *would substantially improve the odds* on a benign course of future human history.

At this point in the historical evolution of human civilization, a world state has become both attainable and desirable. The widespread popular conception of a world state as necessarily ruthless and totalitarian is a serious misconception based largely on the exceptionally troubled historical record of the twentieth century. The twentieth century has seen an excess of ideological conflict and military conflict. As a result, nations have become unduly suspicious and fearful of one another. The concept of a world state has been polluted by visions of brutal "world empires" created through conquest and serving only the purpose of plunder of the weak nations by the strong nations. International relations have been perceived in terms of dog-eat-dog, survival-of-the-fittest, and might-makes-right. But it does not have to be this way. Humanity is learning from its mistakes. Attitudes and viewpoints are evolving. Qualitatively new approaches to the preservation of world peace and the promotion of human progress—approaches which may indeed have been unthinkable in the past—may now be at hand. In particular, conditions may be ripening for mankind to press forward beyond the sovereign nation-state system of today to a fundamentally novel form of international organization: a world state to be known as the Federal Union of Democratic Nations.

The Federal Union of Democratic Nations proposed herein would be a true and authentic state entity with the authority to promulgate and enforce laws, to impose and collect taxes, to raise and maintain permanent military forces. The Union would display the various forms and trappings of state authority: a flag, an anthem, emblems, and a capital city. Formed under a Union Constitution, the Federal Union would comprise the standard three branches of government: a legislative body known as the Union Chamber of Representatives, an executive branch guided by a Union Chief Executive, and a judicial body known as the Union High Court. All three branches would be directly elected by the population: the Union Representatives to five-year terms; the Union Chief Executive to a ten-year term, and Union Justices to 25-year terms. The executive branch of the Federal Union would comprise a number of active ministries, and the Union would become heavily involved in supernational governance. Its numerous activities would range from oversight of a massive worldwide economic development effort to space exploration.

The currently prevalent apprehension about world government is that such a government would tend to become an instrument of oppression. There are two specific scenarios of oppressiveness on which attention has mainly been focused. First, the world government would attempt to impose upon individual nations socioeconomic systems (e.g., communism) to which the vast majority of their populations are bitterly opposed. Second, the world government would endeavor to effect a radical redistribution of wealth and income from the relative handful of richest nations to the numerous and populous poor nations. No doubt there are small kernels of legitimacy underlying these apprehensions, but these small kernels have been so overgrown by unreasoning paranoia as to be practically unrecognizable. Some very straightforward and commonsensical limitations on the power and authority of the supernational federation will suffice to forestall these possibilities to any reasonable degree of certitude.

First and foremost, membership in the Federal Union of Democratic Nations would be completely voluntary, meaning that no nation-state would be required to join the Union, nor would any member nation-state desiring to withdraw from the Union be opposed. In other words, any and all nations taking membership in the Federal Union would retain the permanent, absolute, and inalienable right of unopposed secession at any time. Closely allied to this right would be the right of member nations to maintain military forces which, although formally components of the supernational federation's Union Security Force, would in practice be independent forces subject to the authority of the respective member nations maintaining them. Thus any member nation wishing to secede from the Union would possess the military means to enforce its intention— in the unlikely event that the Union, contrary to explicit Constitutional provision, proposes to forcibly resist the impending secession.

Of course, the right of secession and the right to maintain separate and independent military forces are not customary with respect to the various regional states incorporated into today's nation-states. But we must be flexible and open-minded in considering a future supernational federation. We must accept the fact that in all likelihood the goal of universal membership by all nations in the Federal Union of Democratic Nations will not be achieved for a very long time. Retention of the rights of secession and of maintaining independent military forces are essential as a means of inducing the larger and more powerful nation-states to join the Union. The retention of these rights will allay the unreasonable fears and apprehensions of the populations of these nations against world government. Of course, the hope is that the supernational federation will turn out to be benign and successful, so that in the long run these particular rights of member nations will be rendered obsolete and irrelevant—simply because an overwhelmingly favorable consensus will develop among the populations of the member nations toward continued membership and participation in the Federal Union.

In addition to these fundamental provisions regarding voluntary membership and independent military forces, the institutional structure of the Federal Union of Democratic Nations would incorporate a number of checks and balances militating against oppressive behavior by the Union. The tripartite separation of government authority into legislative, executive, and judicial functions is a traditional device against the development of totalitarian governance, as is the tight budgetary control vested in the legislative branch. A novel provision to the same end is the requirement that any budgets or other legislation proposed in the Union Chamber of Representatives must be passed by a 60-percent majority on the basis of a material vote as well as a population vote. The voting weight of a Union Representative in the population vote would be proportional to the population of his or her own Union District, while that same Union Representative's voting weight in the material vote would be proportional to the Union revenues raised from that District. In particular, this provision would give Union Representatives from richer nations the effective power to veto proposals which are perceived to be contaminated by Crude Redistribution purposes.

The various restrictions and limitations on the power and authority of the supernational federation are essential to make it feasible, to enable its initial formation in a world still very much under the influence of ideas about national independence and sovereignty. It may well be that particularly in the short run the supernational federation will not play as active a role as it perhaps should on objective grounds. Even so, the tremendous symbolic importance of such a state entity in human affairs cannot be underestimated. The existence and operation of a world state would have a profound psychological impact on attitudes and perceptions. As a tangible symbol of solidarity and common purpose among humanity, it would foster attitudes of mutual respect and facilitate cooperative endeavor. The growth of positive attitudes and mutual endeavor will erode propensities toward distrust and hostility, and reduce the likelihood that these emotions will generate tangible conflict and open warfare. It would clearly be unrealistic to expect dramatic changes in the short term. No doubt the early history of the supernational federation will be replete with acrimonious controversy and mutual vilification. But the long-term prospects for peace and friendship will be significantly enhanced through the formation and operation of a supernational federation.

In some obvious technical respects, conditions have become ripe for the foundation of a world state. Modern communications and transportation have totally eliminated the problems of delay and uncertainty which hampered large-scale political entities in bygone times. Individuals on opposite sides of the earth may talk to one another by telephone, and jet airliners convey people from one side of the earth to the other in a matter of hours. International commerce and trade continues to grow and develop, and the economies of even the largest and most self-sufficient nations have become heavily dependent on imports and exports. Multinational corporations are becoming a steadily more important element of the world economy. Numerous international organizations are already in active and successful operation, from the United Nations down to small, private, special purpose agencies. Communications satellites, television, and videotape players bring world news and culture directly into the homes of even the most remote and isolated people. As a result, a very high level of mutual awareness is being achieved among all the people of the world. There is a growing recognition of the unitary nature of the planet Earth and of its human population.

Nevertheless, despite these favorable conditions, at the present time there is no organized, explicit movement toward world government, and among both the intelligentsia and the wider population, attitudes toward the idea of a world state are, on the whole, extremely skeptical and negative. The general presumption on the part of a great many people is that a world state would very likely be a malevolent and oppressive entity which would callously disregard and trample underfoot the natural rights of the great majority of its citizens. There are three principal conditions operative in the contemporary world on which this disturbing vision is mostly based: ideological conflict, economic disparities, and nationalism. Ideological conflict makes people apprehensive that a world state would promote and impose unwanted socioeconomic institutions. Economic disparities make people apprehensive that a world state would reduce their standard of life, either by means of radical redistribution (in the case of people living in the richer nations), or by means of intensifying economic imperialism and exploitation (in the case of people living in the poorer nations). Nationalism promotes generalized attitudes of superiority with respect to one's own nation, and of suspicion and scorn with respect to the people of other nations. Such attitudes tend to amplify apprehensions about a world state based on ideological controversy and economic disparities.

These three impediments to a world state have been carefully considered herein. Following upon some general speculation on possible scenarios toward the foundation of a world state in Section B of Chapter 2, each of the following three chapters dealt with one the three impediments: ideological controversy was the subject of Chapter 3, economic disparities the subject of Chapter 4, and nationalism the subject of Chapter 5. The overall argument advanced in the course of this discussion was that these three impediments, formidable though they undoubtedly are, both individually and in concert, do *not* necessarily preclude the foundation and successful operation of a world state along the lines of the proposed Federal Union of Democratic Nations within the relatively near future.

With respect to the ideological impediment, the epochal transformations now taking place in the communist nations of the world have already significantly reduced the level of ideological conflict, and auspices for further progress are extremely favorable. Already the nations of Eastern Europe, formerly of the communist bloc, can be said to have fully rejoined the mainstream of Western democratic capitalism. The People's Republic of China has effected remarkable economic changes away from central planning and egalitarianism, and although the democratic movement there has been suppressed following the Peking disturbances of 1989, it seems likely that this movement will ultimately prevail. Most dramatic of all has been the rapid transformation of the tightly centralized Union of Soviet Socialist Republics, for many decades the chief proponent and activist for traditional, hard-line communism, into the Commonwealth of Independent States, a loose confederation of republics all of which have proclaimed their determination to thoroughly abrogate the central economic and political institutions of traditional communism just as rapidly as possible. Even Russia—long the center of the U.S.S.R. and hence the center of world communism—has expressed its firm intention to eliminate central economic planning in favor of market allocation, to privatize the entire range of state-owned enterprise, and to adopt Western-style, multi-party political democracy. If this intention is realized, it will represent full and unalloyed ideological capitulation by Russia, and if Russia takes such a path, it is hard to imagine that all the remaining communist nations will not also take this same path in due course. Already international tension is ebbing, military spending is being reduced, and major arms reduction programs have commenced. Optimism about the future seems well justified.

The possibility of full and complete ideological harmonization through total ideological capitulation by the communist East is well known, and hence it has not been greatly elaborated upon herein. Instead, emphasis has been placed on an alternative possibility of full and complete ideological harmonization through the ideological *convergence* of the communist East and the noncommunist West on a common pattern of democratic market socialism, the economic component of which would be pragmatic market socialism. Pragmatic market socialism is a plan of market socialism which would combine the market institutions of contemporary Western capitalism as it operates in the advanced industrial nations (consumer sovereignty, free competition, profit maximization by firms, and so on), with the socialist principle of public ownership of large-scale, established business corporations. The profits produced by the competitive interplay of publicly owned business enterprises would go into a social dividend fund to be distributed to all productively employed citizens on the basis of their respective earned incomes. Such an economic system would in all probability be as efficient as or more efficient than contemporary capitalism, while at the same time it would be significantly more equitable because of the greater equality achieved in the distribution of unearned capital property return. In addition, the economic system of pragmatic market socialism would be entirely compatible with and mutually supportive of the political system of open, multi-party democracy.

Owing to its close economic similarity to contemporary capitalism, which would render it immune to the efficiency problems traditionally ascribed to socialism, pragmatic market socialism is a form of socialism which might well be acceptable to the populations of the noncommunist nations. At the same time, it would be recognized as a genuine form of socialism even by very traditional-minded communist ideologues. As such, it constitutes a viable means by which ideological harmonization could be achieved without need of total ideological capitulation by the communist nations. Such a total ideological capitulation will be difficult to achieve, in view of the fact that is difficult to get human beings to recognize and acknowledge any error whatsoever—let alone total error. According to the proposed ideological convergence scenario, the communist nations would admit to past error in the matters of market orientation versus central planning and pluralistic democracy versus Party oligarchy, while at the same time the noncommunist nations would admit to past error with respect to socialism versus capitalism. This scenario would manifest ideological compromise and mutual concession, in contrast to ideological conquest and unilateral capitulation.

It is certainly quite possible—perhaps probable—that pragmatic market socialism and the convergence scenario will not be necessary. Possibly the transitions which are now well advanced in Russia and the other communist nations will indeed continue smoothly forward to what many people in the West currently see as their logical and inevitable conclusions. But all the same it is very encouraging to reflect on the fact that an alternative to ideological capitulation is available—if needed—to achieve the objective of full and complete ideological harmonization. This alternative gives us even greater cause for optimism that the ideological impediment to world government is nearing its expiration.

Turning to economic disparities as an impediment to world government, it is necessary to acknowledge that this particular impediment is far more substantive and concrete than the ideological impediment. The economic impediment is based on objective differences in human and capital resources between nations, and these differences are far less nebulous and potentially evanescent than are the psychological differences in attitudes and opinions which underpin the ideological impediment. Nevertheless, it is a problem which in all probability can be dealt with decisively—if only humanity can muster the requisite degree of idealism, realism, and determination. What is needed is a massive economic development assistance effort, similar in spirit and operation to the post-World War II Marshall Plan, only on a much larger scale. There would be a major transfer of productive resources, in terms of both physical and human capital, from the rich nations to the poor nations. This transfer would continue only as long as it takes to bring the living standards of the latter nations up to a level reasonably comparable to those of the former nations. This project has been described herein as the World Economic Equalization Program (WEEP). Just as pragmatic market socialism represents a presently unappreciated opportunity for overcoming the ideological impediment to supernational federation, so too the WEEP represents a presently unappreciated opportunity for overcoming the economic impediment.

Attitudes in the rich nations toward economic development assistance have become very skeptical and pessimistic, and many individuals at the present time would be strongly inclined to dismiss the whole idea of a WEEP as an expensive exercise in futility. It has been argued herein that this viewpoint is not derived from any meaningful objective evidence, and instead merely expresses a shallow rationalization for short-sighted selfishness. A WEEP has never been tried, and until it is tried, predictions of its inevitable failure must be entirely speculative. As a matter of fact, some reasonably impressive scientific evidence, in the form of the author's own research on a computer simulation model of a potential WEEP, may be cited in support of the proposition that a WEEP could be remarkably successful in a relatively short period of time. According to the benchmark simulation of this model, dramatic progress in the living standards of the poor nations might be achieved over a planning period of only 35 years—to the point where these standards would be reasonably comparable to those in the rich nations—at the cost of a very minor retardation in the growth rate of living standards in the rich nations. These results are tangible evidence of the feasibility of worldwide economic equalization on the basis of Common Progress. It is not alleged that this evidence is in any way conclusive—in fact, alternative simulations using less favorable parameter values are presented which clearly demonstrate the possible ineffectiveness of a WEEP.

But the point remains that it is morally unacceptable that the people of the rich nations simply *assume* that a major effort at worldwide economic equalization through a WEEP or some similar program would be unsuccessful. The ·winding down of the Cold War is releasing a very large amount of economic resources from military uses. A very high percentage of these resources ought to be reallocated to an unprecedently massive economic development assistance program. Preferably, this effort would be in the form of a World Economic Equalization Program directed by the World Development Authority, an agency of the Federal Union of Democratic Nations. The establishment of a supernational federation with worldwide economic equalization as one of its primary goals during its first decades of operation would substantially augment the probability that the equalization program would be successfully prosecuted to its logical conclusion: the termination of the wide disparities in average living standards between nations which characterize the contemporary world.

Obviously it cannot be predicted with complete certainty that even an unprecedently massive, well designed, energetically prosecuted, and ethically administered World Economic Equalization Program would be a success. Clearly failure is a possibility—not only with respect to a WEEP but also with respect to the Federal Union of Democratic Nations itself. The fact is that any ambitious endeavor runs the risk of failure. But the possibility of failure should not be permitted to extinguish all hope and forestall all action. If these goals of worldwide economic equalization and supernational federation prove beyond the present capacities of humanity to achieve, then the WEEP would be discontinued and the Federal Union would be disbanded. We would have learned from our mistakes, and we would be easy in our consciences.

Continuing on to the nationalistic impediment to world government, we should first of all take note of the fact that this impediment, while logically distinct from the ideological and economic impediments, is in practice closely bound up with them. Depending on the circumstances, the nation-state is perceived as either the principal line of defense against the external imposition of ideologically hateful social systems, or as a principal instrument for the sharing of ideologically superior social systems with the rest of humanity. Throughout the modern era and especially in the twentieth century, ideological fervor and nationalistic patriotism have been intimately related. To the traditional role of the nation-state as the champion of ideologically correct social systems, an increasingly important role has been added as consciousness of the economic gap has intensified throughout the twentieth century: the nation-state as the preserver of economic prosperity and welfare against potential inroads by envious or greedy foreigners. Should worldwide ideological harmonization proceed to the point where people are no longer acutely fearful of being subjected to uncongenial social systems, and should worldwide economic equalization proceed to the point where people are no longer acutely fearful of being subjected to economic despoilation or exploitation, then the nation-state would no longer be so vitally necessary to the preservation of the accustomed way of life, and nationalistic passions would almost assuredly subside significantly. In all probability, they would subside sufficiently to assure the long-term viability of a supernational federation.

Although the typical casual thinking of the present day about the concepts of nationalism and sovereignty normally yields the intuition that they are insuperable obstacles to world government, a more careful and dispassionate consideration of them reveals the weakness and probable invalidity of this intuition. Of the three major historical correlates of nationalism, two might easily work in favor of a world government: in other words, these particular motivations to national pride and patriotism might also serve as motivations to supernational pride and patriotism. The Federal Union of Democratic Nations could be seen as an instrument toward the general reform and progress of worldwide human civilization—as an effective means for the extension to all mankind of such values as personal freedom, political democracy, social equality, and economic prosperity. At the same time, the Federal Union could be perceived as a means for the political unification of an extensive and populous territory, and for the expansion of mankind out into the solar system and beyond. The third correlate of nationalism is where the potential problem for world government lies: the desire for liberation from remote and oppressive governance. But as may be clearly appreciated from the discussion provided herein on the proposed Federal Union of Democratic Nations, a properly designed world government would be neither remote nor oppressive. Therefore, the attitudes and emotions which have been associated with nationalism in the past are by no means uniformly and consistently unfavorable to the foundation and operation of a supranational state in the future.

As for the concept of sovereignty, the fact that the proposed Federal Union of Democratic Nations would be a *federal* form of government, as opposed to a unitary form, indicates that the member nation-states would not fully surrender their sovereignty to it. Even at the present time, there are significant practical constraints on the sovereignty of national governments. National governments which ignore these constraints are liable to be overthrown by internal revolutions, or defeated in wars with other nations. While a nation-state which participates in the Federal Union would indeed have some further constraints imposed on its sovereignty and freedom of action, these disadvantages would be far outweighed by the advantages of membership. And a sufficient degree of independence and autonomy would be retained in certain important areas of government activity that such a state could still be described as sovereign in these areas.

Quite simply, it is a complete misapprehension that participation in a supranational federation would totally eliminate and abrogate the national sovereignty of member-states. Therefore the natural desire on the part of people for a certain reasonable amount of national autonomy, independence, and sovereignty does not by any means preclude the formation of a supranational federation. It only means that the supranational federation would operate under certain constraints on its own autonomy, independence, and sovereignty—just as would the component nation-states. Some of the important constraints have been indicated in the proposal for a Federal Union of Democratic Nations contained herein; certain others may be added as the proposal is subjected to further study and reflection.

There are some important short-term, practical, utilitarian purposes to be served by a supernational federation. Certain aspects of international coordination and regulation, of worldwide data collection and reporting, and so on, would no doubt be more efficiently handled by agencies of a unified supernational government. Space exploration is probably an endeavor where concentration of resources would be beneficial. But it is important to realize that the full potential value of supernational government in human affairs will probably not be attained for a very long time. The foundation of a Federal Union of Democratic Nations would lay a firm foundation on which to gradually build psychological attitudes of solidarity and mutual friendship within humanity. Such attitudes will greatly assist in the preservation of peace and in the undertaking of great mutual endeavors for the overall progress of human civilization: worldwide economic equalization, population control, environmental preservation and enhancement—and possibly, at some distant future point—interstellar expansion.

These are indeed practical, utilitarian purposes of supernational federation—but they are not *short-term* purposes. The supernational federation will not directly and immediately achieve them. The proper psychological attitudes to pursue these objectives energetically probably do not exist among humanity at the present time. In the short term, therefore, a central purpose—if not *the* central purpose—of the supernational federation will simply be to cultivate these proper psychological attitudes. The various constraints and limitations on the supernational federation which are needed to permit its foundation should not be viewed as hamstringing the federation and fatally compromising its potential effectiveness. We must take a long-term view. The foundation of a supernational federation—albeit a weak one in the short run—will establish a natural framework for the further growth and development of positive attitudes within humanity. In the long run, when these positive attitudes have become sufficiently strong and robust, tangible progress will become feasible on many important projects on which little or nothing can apparently be accomplished at the present time.

A consistent effort has been made throughout this book to avoid the taint of utopianism. It has been well emphasized that a supernational federation is neither necessary nor sufficient for a benign future of mankind. The argument has simply been that a supernational federation will *increase the probability* of a benign future. It is perhaps worthwhile to mention at this point that when the expression "benign future" is used, it is not intended to suggest a utopian vision of absolute bliss. It is doubtful that humanity will ever overcome the basic problems of unhappiness, pain, injury, disease, and mortality which devalue and eventually terminate individual human existence. Social problems such as crime, prejudice, violence—even war— probably can never be entirely eradicated. No doubt economic inequality will always be a part of human civilization, and the standard of life experienced by the average person will always be a small fraction of the standard of life experienced by the very wealthy, thus perpetuating feelings of envy, jealously, resentment, and hostility. Finally, there is the fact that human imagination will always outpace human achievement—no matter how favorable conditions become, it is the ineffable capacity of mankind to envision even better conditions.

Conceding all this, the fact remains that from an objective standpoint, the quality of individual human existence is a matter of degree. It seems likely that the human race as a whole has not as yet achieved the highest possible point on the spectrum. As we look forward into the future we see the possibility of further progress along this spectrum—but we also see the possibility of retrogression. Despite the winding down of the Cold War between the communist and noncommunist blocs of nations, the long-term possibility of nuclear war has not been entirely eliminated. Aside from the threat of instantaneous devastation through nuclear war, there is the less dramatic—but possibly just as formidable—threat of eventual population overload on the earth's physical resources. As we contemplate the future prospects for either further progress or possible decline, the question emerges of what, if anything, should be done regarding the political organization of human civilization. In particular, is the sovereign nation-state system of today the best possible basis on which to confront the uncertainties and possibilities of the future?

The answer to this question put forward in this book is that the sovereign nation-state system of today is *not* the best possible basis for this, and that the foundation of a supernational federation to be known as the Federal Union of Democratic Nations would appreciably improve the overall prospects of humanity. It has been argued that with appropriate restrictions and limitations, a Federal Union could be established in the very near future, and that it would thereafter make a very significant contribution to both the material and psychological progress of human civilization. In the material realm, the Union would more effectively accomplish some of the practical functions of government than does the sovereign and independent nation-state system of today. In the psychological realm, the Union is more consistent with the further progress of positive attitudes of mutual respect and support than is the sovereign and independent nation-state system of today.

Considerable stress has been placed on the conservative and evolutionary nature of the Federal Union proposal. Just as the end is not utopian, so too the means are not revolutionary. While it is true that the Federal Union would be a genuine state entity and hence a qualitative step beyond the United Nations of today, at the same time this state entity would be superimposed upon the existing national state entities rather than replacing or subsuming them. Political power and authority would be shared among the supernational state and the various national states, and there would be a number of guarantees against oppression by the supernational state, including the right of member nation-states to secede from the Union at their own discretion, and the right of member nation-states to maintain independent military forces. Thus the foundation of a Federal Union of Democratic Nations would not constitute a radical departure from the conditions of today. It would be an important step forward in terms of setting up solid foundations for the favorable evolution of human civilization in the future—but in and of itself, it would not necessarily accomplish very much in a direct and immediate sense. In this sense, therefore, the Federal Union proposal is indeed fully evolutionary, marginalistic, and incrementalist in nature.

Nevertheless, the symbolic significance of the Federal Union would be enormous. It would constitute a tangible vote of confidence in the future of mankind. Its foundation would be accompanied by a wave of renewed enthusiasm, optimism, and idealism. Even in the short run, these positive attitudes will produce some observable and appreciable practical benefits. But in the long run, the benefits achieved may well exceed anything we are presently capable of imagining.

B. THE QUESTION OF IMPLEMENTATION

On the assumption that mankind is intelligent and rational, there should be a strong positive correlation between the desirability of a certain proposal and its feasibility. The numerous self-inflicted calamities of the twentieth century (World War I, World War II, and so on) have significantly reduced overall confidence in the intelligence and rationality of human beings. As a result, what might be termed the "pure" infeasibility argument against supernational federation is more important at the present time than it would have been back in the nineteenth century, or during the European Enlightenment. This is the argument that *it does not matter* how desirable supernational federation may appear to be—or may even be in reality—because regardless of its objective desirability, it is nevertheless completely impossible because of the enormous and immovable prejudice against the concept among both the intelligentsia and the general public. Owing to this prejudice, no substantial proportion of the population—not even the scholars and intellectuals who ought in principle be most susceptible to creative and progressive thinking—will ever be induced to reflect seriously on the possibility of supernational federation.

As may readily be appreciated, this particular argument evidences at least two important characteristics of the person who articulates it. First, the person harbors an unseemly contempt for the general intelligence and rationality of humanity, in that humanity is perceived incapable of perceiving and acknowledging the truth of the matter with respect to the potential contribution of supernational federation to individual human welfare and the progress of civilization. Second, the person exhibits a fatalistic and passive mentality, in that the person deems himself or herself powerless to resist, alter, and overcome the ignorance and/or encrusted preconceptions which prevent other human beings from appreciating the strength of the case for supernational federation.

Aside from the personal liabilities of people expressing this particular argument against supernational federation, there is the fact that it is faulty on objective grounds. The argument fails to account for the objective fact of political, economic, and social progress throughout the history of human civilization. If humanity were actually as dense and impermeable as the argument implies, this progress could not and would not have been achieved. No doubt inertial conservatism has been, is, and will remain, a very potent force in human affairs. But it is not an utterly irresistible force, and it does not constitute an insuperable obstacle to the formation of the Federal Union of Democratic Nations proposed in this book.

Therefore we should not allow ourselves to be influenced, discouraged, and deterred by unduly negative and defeatist attitudes which proclaim the de facto impossibility of the objective of supernational federation. Our attention should rather be focused on the real issue: the case for supernational federation itself. Is this case adequate to justify the formation of a supernational federation? If we personally believe that the answer to this question is in the affirmative, then we should concentrate on energetically developing and communicating the case for supernational federation, in the trust that if this case is made with sufficient clarity and force, our fellow human beings will eventually perceive its merit.

In the beginning, the objective of those who support the idea of supernational federation should be simply to develop the idea, and to disseminate the idea among the population. The exact tactics that might be followed at some later date in a political election in which the supernational federation proposal is a serious issue is a matter to be handled when the time comes. In any event, if general support for the proposal is strong enough, the exact tactics would not be decisive anyway. Therefore, in the early going it would be a misallocation of intellectual resources to devote a great deal of thought to detailed tactical questions.

The appropriate initial step would be the formation of an interest group, tentatively named the Human Interest Society, dedicated to the study and dissemination of the case for supernational federation. The work of the Society would involve the solicitation of new dues-paying members, the sponsorship of books and pamphlets, and the organization of meetings and discussion groups. Within the general Society there would operate a Human Interest Study Group, consisting of scholars and intellectuals involved in serious analysis of various specific questions and problems pertaining to the core supernational federation proposal, and to the key auxiliary proposals. The results of these analyses would be published in a professional periodical sponsored by the Society, and also in the form of a growing shelf of book-length studies, some published by the Society's own publishing house, and others by various commercial and university presses. The professional output of the Human Interest Study Group would also be summarized in popular polemical form in a series of books and pamphlets of varying length, intended for various audiences. In carrying on this work of study, writing, dissemination, and proselytization, some key principles should be observed, as discussed in the following.

First, the whole campaign should be very low-keyed and conservative in tone. Even in material intended for the least sophisticated minds, excessive enthusiasm and intolerant dogmatism should be strictly avoided. Due respect should always be shown for alternative points of view, and it should often be reiterated that in the final analysis, the question must be judged by each and every citizen on the basis of whatever sensible criteria he or she might choose to apply. Harsh disputation and acrid controversy should be studiously avoided, particularly with individuals who apparently possess inadequate understanding of the supernational federation proposal itself. Such individuals should not be lectured or berated, but simply urged to reserve their judgment until they have had time to learn more about the proposal. Even in circumstances of direct confrontation, advocates of the supernational federation proposal should, to the greatest extent possible, project an attitude of calm, patience, toleration, and good nature.

Among the most important corollaries of the principle of rhetorical and polemical restraint is a continued emphasis upon the tentative and provisional nature of the proposed transition. It should be frequently reiterated that, strictly speaking, the argument of the Human Interest Society is merely that the accumulated evidence suggests the desirability of an experimental formation of a supernational federation. If within a reasonable period of time, say between twenty and thirty years, the results of the experiment were not as favorable as had been hoped, then the various nations should, could, and would return to the sovereign nation-state system with which we are currently familiar. Every effort should be made to remind the undecided that opponents are actually arguing that the case for supernational federation is so feeble that not even an *experiment* with it is worthwhile. If at the same time, the case for supernational federation is being built up and supported by a variety of weighty conceptual and empirical evidence, the dubiousness of this refusal even to experiment with it would become increasingly evident.

A second key principle underpinning the campaign for the enlightenment of the public is that the campaign should be strictly confined to a very specific and clearly defined proposal for supernational federation. There should be no vague and quasi-mystical hints and intimations that this proposal is merely a prelude to various vast and all-encompassing transformations involving the whole of human civilization and the entirety of human nature. It is appropriate to have continuing discussion and debate on what the specific proposal *should be*, but at any point in time there should be no doubt whatever on anyone's part on what the specific proposal *currently is*. One way to facilitate the appropriate focus is to draft at a very early stage, in proper legal form, a *Constitution of the Federal Union of Democratic Nations*.

The fundamental objective of the Human Interest Society in each particular nation would be to secure support through normal democratic channels for national adherence to the Federal Union of Democratic Nations. A practical question concerns how much of its attention and resources the Human Interest Society should devote to the study, promulgation, and dissemination of the two key auxiliary proposals put forward in this book: that worldwide ideological harmonization be achieved through convergence based on the middle ground of pragmatic market socialism, and that worldwide economic equalization be achieved through a massive World Economic

Equalization Program.

An argument that considerable emphasis should be placed on these two auxiliary proposals may be based on the proposition that they are important not only for their own sakes but because of their critical role in establishing conditions conducive to the long-term viability and success of supernational federation. On the other side is the point that emphasis on these auxiliary proposals would complicate the recommended program of the Human Interest Society and disperse its energies and resources. Furthermore, there is the point that some people, who might be favorably disposed toward the core proposal for supernational federation, might at the same time be opposed to one or both of the two key auxiliary proposals.

Of course, real-world developments may have a substantial impact on this question. Although it seems unlikely that the economic gap to be addressed by the World Economic Equalization Program will change very much over the next few decades, the ideological gap to be addressed by pragmatic market socialism is currently evolving at a very rapid pace. At the present time, prospects seem bright for the complete elimination of this gap through total ideological capitulation on the part of the Eastern communist nations within a very few years, or at most within one or two decades. Should these prospects actually be realized, pragmatic market socialism, in and of itself, would no longer possess any relevance whatsoever as far as the central goal of supernational federation is concerned. In this eventuality, pragmatic market socialism should be completely removed from the agenda of the Human Interest Society. Individuals associated with the Society may still desire the implementation of pragmatic market socialism widely throughout the world because of its inherent superiority over contemporary capitalism, and they would certainly be free to work toward this goal. But this work would be conducted through other organizations than the Human Interest Society. A possible name for an interest group specifically dedicated to pragmatic market socialism might be the Pragmatic Progress Society.

Probably the most sensible course would be to deal with these questions, when the time comes, in an empirical way. Among its regular activities, the Human Interest Society would regularly survey both its own members and a random sample of nonmembers, regarding their personal judgments on the various components of the Society's recommended program. The results of these surveys would provide guidance on the emphasis to be applied to the auxiliary proposals. Depending on evolving circumstances, public support might be maximized by greater emphasis on the set of three integrated proposals (for pragmatic market socialism, a World Economic Equalization Program, and supernational federation), or at the opposite extreme, public support might be maximized by sole emphasis on the central proposal for supernational federation contained in the draft Union Constitution. This is one of several important practical questions which must necessarily be left to the future.

It is perhaps worthwhile to emphasize that the Human Interest Society would be merely an interest group, and definitely not a political party. The supernational federation proposal is for a specific social transition to accomplish a specific social purpose. It is not a "general philosophy" (such as conservatism or progressivism) that may be systematically applied to a succession of political issues which arise over the course of time. Every effort should be made to avoid having a single political party become the exclusive standard-bearer for the supernational federation proposal. In the United States, for example, the ideal situation would be to have legislators and executive branch officials from both the Democratic and Republican political parties enlisted in support of the proposal. The emphasis should be on the conversion of individuals, and not on the conversion of political parties. In order to be successful, the idea of supernational federation must eventually achieve support by a large majority of the members of all important political parties.

Two concepts from the sciences are relevant to the proposed campaign of enlightenment under consideration here: critical mass, and logistic dissemination. A critical mass in nuclear physics is defined as a sufficient quantity of fissionable material concentrated at one time and place to commence a chain reaction. With respect to the prospects for supernational federation, a critical mass might be defined as a sufficient amount of printed discussion of supernational federation to arouse the attention and interest of various groups within the general population. There are several distinct groups of particular relevance. One small but extremely influential group consists of professional political scientists, particularly those specializing in international organization. As supernational federation is first and foremost a political proposal, the professional judgment of political scientists will be critical. If all or most political scientists reject the proposal, then almost certainly it would have no chance whatever among the larger population. The political scientists are one component of a larger group that might be variously labeled the professionals, the experts, the scholars, the intellectuals, or some such term. In this group would be included all persons seriously involved in thinking, writing, and teaching: primarily professors, research professionals, consultants, and journalists. Then there are the political leaders, including those serving in public offices and active in political parties. Finally, there is the general public. Within each of these groups, a critical mass of published writing, addressed to the relevant audience, must be achieved in order to arouse interest.

The second concept is that of logistic dissemination. After the critical mass has been achieved within each group of the general population, there will follow a process of dissemination. In biology, there is the process of dissemination of a population throughout a locality, or of an infection throughout a population. In technology, there is the process of dissemination of an innovative product or process. In marketing and political science, there is the process of dissemination of product information or political opinion. In all of these applications of the concept, the dissemination process may be graphically illustrated by a logistic curve: the rate of dissemination is at first slow but gradually increases; a point of inflection is eventually reached at which the curve changes from the convex to the concave form; and thereafter the rate of dissemination decreases as the curve approaches its asymptotic upper limit. For our purposes, we envision a logistic curve, for each segment of the population and for the population as a whole, which expresses the percentage of the group which is in favor of the supernational federation proposal. In order for the proposal to be approved by the democratic political process, the upper asymptote of the logistic curve for the general population must encompass a majority of the population—probably a substantial majority. In order to attain substantial majority support for the supernational federation proposal within the general population, it would probably be necessary to attain substantial majority support for the proposal within almost all sub-groups of the population.

It is proposed that the Human Interest Society keep careful track, by means of the regular surveys already mentioned, of the development of the relevant logistic curves. After a relatively brief period, estimates could be made of the future development of these curves. These estimates, of course, may not augur well. In due course, the points of inflection may be passed, and the indication may become unmistakable that the asymptotic upper limits toward which these curves are tending are well short of the substantial majorities necessary to effect the foundation of a sufficiently comprehensive supernational federation. But while the possibility must be conceded that at some point after the endeavor has been commenced there may come a time when failure must be acknowledged—this possibility by no means constitutes adequate grounds for never undertaking the endeavor in the first place. The implementation of supernational federation, both in its immediate impact and in its long-term consequences, might represent one of the most favorable political developments of modern history. We owe it to ourselves at least to try.

The logistic curves of awareness of and support for the supernational federation proposal among the various sub-groups of the entire population would develop in a roughly simultaneous pattern, but would not be exactly alike. In particular, some would develop slightly earlier than the norm, and others slightly later. The following order seems the most likely: first, the logistic curve for the political scientists; second, that of the intellectuals as a whole; third, that of the general public; fourth and last, that of the political leaders. In other words, the political scientists would lead the intellectuals as a whole; then the intellectuals as a whole would lead the general public; and finally, the general public would lead the political leaders. It is paradoxical that the political "leaders" would come last, but the reason for this is that as those personally responsible for implementing the change, these leaders are naturally the most concerned that the change is widely supported by the rest of the population.

The enlightenment campaign would be a campaign of words and

ideas, but only a very tiny fraction of the general population can be expected to become conversant with the fine details of the case for supranational federation. In order to win over the intellectuals, the case for supranational federation must be developed in great depth and detail, and there must be a large body of professionally competent literature sympathetic to the proposal. This book, obviously, represents an effort to initiate such a literature. But it would clearly be ludicrous to expect any significant part of the general public to read either this book, or any other weighty book on the issue. In literature intended for a mass audience, the case for supranational federation would be sketched out very succinctly, and heavy reliance would be implicitly placed on the number of eminent authorities who are more or less sympathetic to the proposal. Rather than making an explicit appeal to an argument from authority—an argument which is formally deemed unworthy by almost everyone despite its ubiquitous unacknowledged presence and invariably profound impact in practice—it would be emphasized that the support of the supranational federation proposal by many qualified professionals simply indicates that the matter is open to the judgment of everyone, including that of the mythical "average citizen."

Books, journal articles, and professional conferences are the accepted media for the dissemination of an idea throughout the professions, and these would be the media through which the idea of supranational federation would be disseminated throughout the class of intellectuals. Looking beyond this stage to the stage of dissemination of the idea throughout the general public, there would be a larger role for informal meetings and discussions. But just as the principle of low-keyed moderation must be observed in the area of professional dissemination, so too it must be observed in the area of popular dissemination. For example, the regular meetings of the local chapters of the Human Interest Society would be more of a social and recreational nature than of a serious educational nature. Such meetings might be comparable to those of Bible study groups or literary discussion groups: the purpose of the meeting would be primarily to get people together to have a good time, and only secondarily to learn more about a subject of common interest. Then there is the question of attracting the attention of those who have not yet been made aware of the supernational federation proposal. One possibility is that members of the Human Interest Society wear a small and unobtrusive pin on their lapel or shirt pocket. Friends, relatives, or colleagues inquiring about the pin would be presented with a short pamphlet outlining the essentials of the supernational federation proposal, and describing sources of further information.

At a later point in the development of the campaign for popular support, the "gathering" might provide an effective means of spreading a positive awareness of the supernational federation proposal throughout the general public. A gathering, as the name implies, would be a simple assembly of the local membership of the Human Interest Society at some public place, such as a park or a square. This would not be a noisy demonstration with speeches over loudspeakers, chanting, and the waving of placards. Far from it. Demonstrations normally have a pushy and pugnacious air about them: they seem intended more to intimidate various opponents into submission, than to solicit the friendly support of the uncommitted. In contrast to a demonstration, a gathering would be a quiet, peaceful, and good-humored affair. Instead of numerous signs bearing generally irate messages, there might be a single small banner, stretched over a table holding a selection of literature published by the Human Interest Society. Instead of stridently demanding the attention of passers-by, the idea would be to arouse their natural curiosity, so that if they do stop to find out the purpose of the assembly, they will have done so of their own accord. As the movement grows, these gatherings might gradually evolve into substantial affairs involving large numbers of people. But regardless of how big they might become, they must always retain their intended character: that of a peaceful, quiet, and orderly expression of human solidarity and friendship. As such, the gathering would accurately convey the character of the entire movement toward supernational federation.

What are the chances for the formation of a supernational federation within the relatively near future—say, within the lifetimes of the majority of people now living? Obviously, no precise answer can be given to this question. It can certainly be said, however, that if the great majority of the readers of this book decide that the chances for success are so negligible that the proposal of this book is unworthy of further thought and action, then indeed the probability of success would be negligible. This would simply be a self-fulfilling prophecy. What a tragedy it might be if this historic opportunity were wasted, not because success was objectively impossible, but because success was *assumed* to be impossible.

To the argument that "nothing of this sort has ever occurred in human history," the appropriate response is that many things of this sort—i.e., major social and political transitions—have in fact occurred in human history. Moreover, many of these transitions were quite rapid and almost completely unanticipated. We have just witnessed a dramatic example of this in the extraordinary transformation of the Union of Soviet Socialist Republics into the Commonwealth of Independent States. This sudden transformation came as a complete surprise even to the most informed and authoritative specialists on the Soviet Union. Therefore the fact that specialists on international organization at the present time do not anticipate the foundation of a supernational federation as a near-term possibility does not mean that such an event is either impossible or even necessarily improbable.

To the argument that only an extraordinarily and unprecedently severe crisis could bring about the establishment of a world government, the appropriate response is that never before in human history has the human race confronted a situation so fraught with peril, and yet so pregnant with hope, as the situation which currently prevails in the contemporary world. Substantial progress has recently been made, through the ebbing of the Cold War between the communist and noncommunist blocs of nations, toward reducing the immediate threat of all-out nuclear war. Nevertheless, massive nuclear arsenals remain in existence, and even under the most favorable circumstances it will require many years and possibly decades before these arsenals are reduced to truly comfortable levels. The degree of disarmament which will ultimately be feasible is still very uncertain. Despite the best efforts by the nuclear superpowers to slow the rate of nuclear proliferation, in a world of sovereign and independent nation-states each one of which is forced to defend itself, nuclear proliferation is likely to proceed apace. The fact remains that the human race is still perched on the brink of an abyss of unimaginable destruction—if perhaps not so precariously perched now as a few years ago. The threat of nuclear devastation which presently confronts humanity is without precedent in the history of the world. In addition to the nuclear threat, the human population has entered a phase of explosive growth which severely threatens the quality and even the viability of the physical environment. If unchecked, explosive population growth could ultimately have almost as devastating an impact on individual human welfare as would a nuclear war—even though the damage would be done in a much more gradual and undramatic manner. This also is an absolutely unprecedented threat to humanity.

And yet, at the same time, there are myriad positive signs about the future of mankind. Technological marvels of communication and transport, and an ever more abundant international trade, are, for the first time in history, weaving the entire world into a tightly inter-dependent and unified whole. In some parts of the world, the material welfare of the human population has attained heights undreamt of by past generations. The technological and cultural power and energy possessed by the human race as a whole is awesome, almost inconceivable. There is no telling how glorious the future history of the human race might be if this power and energy is unleashed in the right direction. Never in human history has there been such a remarkable contrast between the potential futures that await us—direst disaster on the one hand, brightest triumph on the other. Unprecedented conditions may yield unprecedented events. The foundation of the Federal Union of Democratic Nations might constitute an important step toward avoiding absolute catastrophe, and instead achieving a millenial unleashing of the capacities of mankind.

Another speculation to be advanced against the contention (probably insupportable in any case) that in the entire history of the human race nothing like the proposed transition to supernational federation has ever occurred, is that in the light of historical perspective, the formation of a supernational federation may be deemed by future historians as having been a very marginal and evolutionary transition that was virtually inevitable, given the circumstances of our time. In other words, what we today might be inclined to describe as tremendous and revolutionary transformations might one day be perceived as relatively modest and minor steps on the long and complex path of human development. Throughout this book, the limited and conservative nature and purposes of the Federal Union of Democratic Nations have been continuously emphasized. It is only owing to the widespread misperception of the necessary nature of world government that the foundation of a such a Federal Union would be imagined, by many people at the present time, a major transformation.

In the final analysis, some of the things we do, we do because we *have* to do them. In some cases, the moral imperative to action becomes so strong as to outweigh what appears to be the strong likelihood that the action will prove futile. The foundation of a world state along the lines of the proposed Federal Union of Democratic Nations could well have a tremendously beneficial impact upon the future of human civilization. It could be the instrumentality through which such potential disasters as nuclear armageddon or environmental breakdown are avoided. It could be the instrumentality through which the misery of mass poverty throughout the Third World will be abolished. It could be the instrumentality through which mankind's dreams and aspirations toward interstellar expansion are eventually realized. It could be the instrumentality through which individual human beings will achieve a higher level of moral existence—less vexed and distressed by resentment and hostility toward their fellow human beings, more receptive to attitudes of mutual respect and friendship, and more disposed to actions of mutual cooperation and support.

We cannot know whether success will be achieved. It is certainly possible that even many decades of dedicated effort will fail to establish the appropriate mental and emotional attitudes in the human population that will be necessary to the foundation and successful operation of the Federal Union of Democratic Nations. But we should not let this possibility stay us from the proper course. From our present perspective, supernational federation is a magnificent vision of what might be. It would, in all probability, be a fine and glorious embodiment and manifestation of all the best qualities of humanity. In view of the potentially overwhelming value of the objective, we should—indeed we *must*—turn resolutely toward it.

REFERENCES

Abalkin, Leonid. *The Strategy of Economic Development in the USSR.* Moscow: Progress Publishers, 1987.

Afanasyev, V. G. *The Scientific Management of Society.* Moscow: Progress Publishers, 1971.

Afanasyev, V. G. *Bourgeois Economic Thought: 1930s-70s.* Moscow: Progress Publishers, 1983.

Aggar, Ben. *Western Marxism: An Introduction.* Santa Monica, Cal.: Goodyear Pub. Co., 1979.

Allison, Anthony, editor. *Population Control.* Baltimore: Penguin, 1970.

Alpert, Paul. *Partnership or Confrontation? Poor Lands and Rich.* New York: Free Press, 1973.

Ames, Edward. *Soviet Economic Processes.* Homewood, Illinois: Irwin, 1965.

Anchishkin, A. *The Theory of Growth of a Socialist Economy.* Moscow: Progress Publishers, 1977.

Aron, Raymond. *Peace and War: A Theory of International Relations.* New York: Doubleday, 1973.

Antonov-Ovseyenko, Anton. *The Time of Stalin: Portrait of a Tyranny.* New York: Harper and Row, 1981.

Aragon, Louis. *A History of the U.S.S.R.: From Lenin to Khrushchev.* London: Weidenfeld and Nicolson, 1964.

Arnold, N. Scott. *Marx's Radical Critique of Capitalist Society.* New York: Oxford University Press, 1990.

Auer, J. Jeffery, editor. *Antislavery and Disunion, 1858-1861: Studies in the Rhetoric of Compromise and Conflict.* New York: Harper and Row, 1963.

Bapna, Ashok, editor. *One World, One Future: New International Strategies for Development.* New York: Praeger Special Studies, 1985.

Barber, Benjamin, and Patrick Watson. *The Struggle for Democracy.* Boston: Little, Brown, 1988.

Barbu, Zevedei. *Democracy and Dictatorship.* New York: Grove, 1956.

Barnaby, C. F., editor. *Pugwash: Preventing the Spread of Nuclear Weapons.* New York: Humanities Press, 1969.

Barnaby, Frank, and Ronald Huisken (for the Stockholm International Peace Research Institute). *Arms Uncontrolled.* Cambridge, Mass.: Harvard

University Press, 1975.

Barnet, Richard J. *The Giants: Russia and America.* New York: Simon and Schuster, 1977.

Barney, William J. *The Road to Secession: A New Perspective on the Old South.* New York: Praeger, 1972.

Barney, William J. *The Secessionist Impulse: Alabama and Mississippi in 1860.* Princeton, New Jersey: Princeton University Press, 1974.

Bauer, Peter T. *Economic Analysis and Policy in Underdeveloped Countries.* Durham: North Carolina: Duke University Press, 1957.

Bauer, Peter T. *Indian Economic Policy and Development.* London: George Allen and Unwin, 1961.

Bauer, Peter T. *Dissent on Development.* Cambridge, Mass.: Harvard University Press, 1972.

Bauer, Peter T. *Equality, the Third World, and Economic Delusion.* Cambridge, Mass.: Harvard University Press, 1981.

Bauer, Peter T. *Reality and Rhetoric: Studies in the Economics of Development.* Cambridge, Mass.: Cambridge University Press, 1984.

Bauer, Peter T., and Basil S. Yamey. *The Economics of Under-Developed Countries.* Chicago: University of Chicago Press, 1957.

Bendiner, Elmer. *A Time for Angels: The Tragicomic History of the League of Nations.* New York: Alfred A. Knopf, 1975.

Beres, Louis Rene. *Mimicking Sisyphus: America's Countervailing Nuclear Strategy.* Lexington, Mass.: D. C. Heath, 1983.

Bergson, Abram. "Socialist Economics," in Howard Ellis, ed., *A Survey of Contemporary Economics* (Philadelphia: Blakiston, 1948).

Bergson, Abram. *The Economics of Soviet Planning.* New Haven, Conn.: Yale University Press, 1964.

Bergson, Abram. "Market Socialism Revisited," *Journal of Political Economy* 75(5): 655-673, October 1967.

Berki, R. N. *Socialism.* New York: St. Martin's Press, 1975.

Berle, Adolf A. *Power.* New York: Harcourt, Brace and World, 1967.

Bernstein, Eduard. *Evolutionary Socialism.* Introduction by Sidney Hook. New York: Schocken Books, 1961. Originally published in German in 1899.

Berri, L. Ya., editor. *Planning a Socialist Economy,* two volumes. Moscow: Progress Publishers, 1977.

Bidwell, Shelford, ed. *World War 3: A Military Projection Founded on Today's Facts.* Englewood Cliffs, New Jersey: Prentice-Hall, 1978.

Bluhm, William T. *Force or Freedom? The Paradox in Modern Political Thought.* New Haven, Connecticut: Yale University Press, 1984.

Böhm-Bawerk, Eugen von. *Karl Marx and the Close of His System.* Edited with an introduction by Paul M. Sweezy. New York: Augustus M. Kelley, 1949. Reprinted Philadelphia: Orion Editions, 1984. Originally published in German in 1896.

Bolton, W. F. *The Language of 1984: Orwell's English and Our's*. Knoxville: University of Tennessee Press, 1984.

Bornschier, Volker, Christopher Chase-Dunn, and Richard Robinson. "Cross- National Evidence of the Effects of Foreign Investment and Aid on Economic Growth and Inequality: A Survey of Findings and Re-Analysis," *American Journal of Sociology* 84(3): 658-683, November 1978.

Bowles, Samuel, and Herbert Gintis. *Democracy and Capitalism: Property, Community, and the Contradictions of Modern Social Thought*. New York: Basic Books, 1986.

Bracher, Karl Dietrich. *The German Dictatorship: The Origins, Structure and Effects of National Socialism*. London: Weidenfeld and Nicolson, 1971.

Bradley, John. *World War III: Strategies, Tactics and Weapons*. New York: Crescent Books, 1982.

Bremer, Stuart A., editor. *The Globus Model: Computer Simulation of Worldwide Political and Economic Developments*. Boulder, Colorado: Westview Press, 1987.

Breuilly, John. *Nationalism and the State*. New York: St. Martin's Press, 1982.

Brodie, Bernard, ed. *The Absolute Weapon: Atomic Power and World Order*. New York: Harcourt, Brace and Co., 1946.

Brown, Anthony Cave, and Charles B. MacDonald. *On a Field of Red: The Communist International and the Comming of World War II*. New York: G. B. Putnam's Sons, 1981.

Brzezinski, Zbigniew K. *Ideology and Power in Soviet Politics*. New York: Praeger, 1962.

Brzezinski, Zbigniew K. *The Soviet Bloc: Unity and Conflict*, revised and enlarged edition. Cambridge, Mass.: Harvard University Press, 1967.

Buckley, William F., Jr. *United Nations Journal: A Delegate's Odyssey*. New York: G. P. Putnam's Sons, 1974.

Bull, Hedley. *The Control of the Arms Race: Disarmament and Arms Control in the Missile Age*, second edition. New York: Frederick A. Praeger, 1965.

Bull, Hedley. *The Anarchical Society: A Study of Order in World Politics*. New York: Columbia University Press, 1977.

Bullock, Alan. *Hitler: A Study in Tyranny*. New York: Harper and Row, 1952.

Burns, Emile, editor. *The Marxist Reader*. New York: Avenel, 1982.

Bykov, O., V. Razmerov, and D. Tomashevsky. *The Priorities of Soviet Foreign Policy Today*. Moscow: Progress Publishers, 1981.

Calder, Nigel. *Nuclear Nightmares: An Investigation into Possible Wars*. New York: Viking Press, 1979.

Calvocoressi, Peter, and Guy Wint. *Total War: The Story of World War II*. New York: Pantheon, 1972.

Campbell, Robert W. *The Socialist Economies in Transition: A Primer on Semi-Reformed Systems*. Bloomington: Indiana University Press, 1991.

Capa, Cornell, and J. Mayone Stycos. *Margin of Life: Population and Poverty*. New York: Grossman, 1974.

Caporaso, James A. *The Elusive State: International and Comparative Perspectives*. Newbury Park, California: Sage Publications, 1989.

Carew-Hunt, R. N. "Ideology and Power Politics: Discussion," in Eric P. Hoffman and Frederic J. Fleron, Jr., eds., *The Conduct of Soviet Foreign Policy* (Chicago: Aldine-Atherton, 1971).

Carmichael, Joel. *Stalin's Masterpiece: The 'Show Trials' and Purges of the Thirties*. New York: St. Martin's Press, 1976.

Carr, E. H., and R. W. Davies. *Foundations of a Planned Economy*. London: Macmillan, 1969.

Cassen, R. H. *Does Aid Work?* Oxford: Clarendon Press, 1985.

Cecil, Robert. *The Myth of the Master Race: Alfred Rosenberg and Nazi Ideology*. New York: Dodd Mead and Company, 1972.

Cerami, Charles A., editor. *A Marshall Plan for the 1990s: An International Roundtable on World Economic Development*. New York: Praeger Publishers, 1989.

Chernikov, G. *The Crisis of Capitalism and the Condition of the Working People*. Moscow: Progress Publishers, 1980.

Church, George J. "The Case for a Gobal Marshall Plan," *Time Magazine*, June 12, 1978, pp. 77-78.

Cipolla, Carlo M. *The Economic History of World Population*. Baltimore: Penguin, 1962.

Clark, John Bates. *The Distribution of Wealth: A Theory of Wages, Interest and Profits*. New York: Macmillan, 1899.

Clark, Ronald W. *The Greatest Power on Earth: The International Race for Nuclear Supremacy*. New York: Harper and Row, 1980.

Clarke, Duncan. *Politics of Arms Control: The Role and Effectiveness of the U.S. Arms Control and Disarmament Agency*. New York: Free Press, 1979.

Clarke, Robin. *The Science of War and Peace*. New York: McGraw-Hill, 1972.

Claude, Inis L. *Power and International Relations.* New York: Random House, 1962.

Claude, Inis L. *Swords into Plowshares: The Problems and Progress of International Organization,* fourth edition. New York: Random House, 1971.

Coale, Ansley J., and Edgar M. Hoover. *Population Growth and Economic Development in Low Income Countries.* Princeton, New Jersey: Princeton University Press, 1958.

Cole, George D. H. *A History of Socialist Thought,* five volumes. London: Macmillan, 1953-1960.

Cole, John, and Trevor Buck. *Modern Soviet Economic Performance.* New York: Basil Blackwell, 1987.

Colmans, David, and Frederick Nixson. *Economics of Change in Less Developed Nations.* New York: John Wiley, 1978.

Cook, Robert C. *Human Fertility: The Modern Dilemma.* New York: William Morrow, 1951.

Cousins, Norman. *In Place of Folly.* New York: Harper Bros., 1961.

Cox, Arthur Macy. *Russian Roulette: The Superpower Game.* New York: Times Books, 1982.

Crankshaw, Edward. *The Shadow of the Winter Palace: Russia's Drift to Revolution, 1825-1917.* New York: Viking Press, 1976.

Crankshaw, Edward. *Putting Up with the Russians: Commentary and Criticism, 1947-84.* New York: Viking, 1984.

Crosland, C. A. R. *The Future of Socialism.* New York: Schocken, 1963.

Cruit, Ronald L., and Robert L. Cruit. *Survive the Coming Nuclear War: How To Do It.* New York: Stein and Day, 1982.

Dahlitz, Julie. *Nuclear Arms Control: With Effective International Agreements.* London: George Allen and Unwin, 1983.

Dammann, Erik. *The Future in Our Hands.* Oxford: Pergamon Press, 1979.

David, Paul A., ed. *Reckoning with Slavery: A Critical Study in the Quantitative History of American Negro Slavery.* New York: Oxford University Press, 1976.

Davidson, Eugene. *The Making of Adolf Hitler: The Birth and Rise of Nazism.* New York: Macmillan, 1977.

Davis, David Brion. *The Problem of Slavery in Western Culture.* Ithaca, New York: Cornell University Press, 1966.

Davis, David Brion. *Slavery and Human Progress.* New York: Oxford University Press, 1984.

de Jasay, Anthony. *The State.* New York: Basil Blackwell, 1985.

de Jouvenal, Bertrand. *On Power: Its Nature and the History of Its Growth.* New York: Viking Press, 1949.

de Jouvenal, Bertrand. *Sovereignty: An Inquiry into the Political Good.* Chicago: University of Chicago Press, 1959.

D'Entrèves, Alexander Passerin. *The Notion of the State: An Introduction to Political Theory.* Oxford: Clarendon Press, 1969.

Desai, Meghnad. *Marxian Economics.* Totowa, New Jersey: Rowman and Littlefield, 1979.

Desai, Padma. *The Soviet Economy: Problems and Prospects.* New York: Basil Blackwell, 1987.

Desai, Padma. *Perestroika in Perspective.* Princeton, New Jersey: Princeton University Press, 1989.

Deutsch, Karl W. *Nationalism and Social Communication: An Inquiry into the Foudations of Nationalism,* second edition. Cambridge, Mass.: MIT Press, 1966.

Deutsch, Karl W. *Nationalism and Its Alternatives.* New York: Alfred Knopf, 1969.

Deutscher, Isaac. *Stalin: A Political Biography,* second edition. New York: Oxford University Press, 1967.

Dexter, Byron. *The Years of Opportunity: The League of Nations, 1920-1926.* New York: Viking Press, 1967.

Dilloway, James. *Is World Order Evolving? An Adventure into Human Potential.* Oxford: Pergamon Press, 1986.

Donovan, Robert J. *The Second Victory: The Marshall Plan and the Postwar Revival of Europe.* New York: Madison Books, 1987.

Dorn, James A., editor. "Development Economics after 40 Years: Essays in Honor of Peter Bauer," *Cato Journal* 7(1): 1-254, Spring/Summer 1987.

Dyker, David A. *The Soviet Economy.* New York: St. Martin's Press, 1976.

Easterlin, Richard A., editor. *Population and Economic Change in Developing Countries.* Chicago: University of Chicago Press, 1980.

Eddy, W. H. C. *Understanding Marxism.* Totowa, New Jersey: Rowman and Littlefield, 1979.

Ehrlich, Paul R. *The Population Bomb.* New York: Ballentine, 1968.

Ehrlich, Paul R., Carl Sagan, Donald Kennedy, and Walter Orr Roberts. *The Cold and the Dark: The World after Nuclear War.* New York: W. W. Norton, 1984.

Eichelberger, Clark M. *UN: The First Twenty-Five Years.* New York: Harper and Row, 1970.

Elazar, Daniel J., editor. *Federalism and Political Integration.* Ramat Gan, Israel: Turtledove Publishers, 1979.

Elazar, Daniel J. *Exploring Federalism.* Tuscaloosa, Alabama: University of Alabama Press, 1987.

Emmanuel, Arghiri. *Unequal Exchange: A Study of the Imperialism of*

Trade. New York: Monthly Review Press, 1972.

Endres, Michael E. *On Defusing the Population Bomb.* New York: John Wiley, 1975.

Epstein, William. *The Last Chance: Nuclear Proliferation and Arms Control.* New York: Free Press, 1976.

Erlich, Alexander. *The Soviet Industrialization Debate, 1924-1928.* Cambridge, Mass.: Harvard University Press, 1960.

Estrin, Saul. *Self-Management: Economic Theory and Yugoslav Practice.* Cambridge: Cambridge University Press, 1983.

Etzioni, Amitai. *The Hard Way to Peace: A New Strategy.* New York: Collier Books, 1962.

Falk, Richard A. *A Global Approach to National Policy.* Cambridge, Mass.: Harvard University Press, 1975.

Falk, Richard A. *A Study of Future Worlds.* New York: Free Press, 1977.

Faramazyan, R. *Disarmament and the Economy.* Moscow: Progress Publishers, 1981.

Faust, Drew Gilpin, ed. *The Ideology of Slavery: Proslavery Thought in the Antebellum South, 1830-1860.* Baton Rouge: Louisiana State University Press, 1981.

Fedorenko, Nikolai P., et al. *Soviet Economic Reform: Progress and Problems.* Moscow: Progress Publishers, 1972.

Fedorenko, Nikolai P. *Optimal Functioning System for a Socialist Economy.* Moscow: Progress Publishers, 1974.

Fedoseyev, P. N., et al. *Karl Marx: A Biography.* Moscow: Progress Publishers, 1973.

Feiwel, George R. *The Soviet Quest for Economic Efficiency: Issues, Controversies, and Reforms,* revised edition. New York: Praeger, 1972.

Fenichell, Stephen S., and Philip Andrews. *The United Nations: Blueprint for Peace.* Philadelphia: John C. Winston, 1954.

Ferro, Marc. *The Russian Revolution of February 1917.* Englewood Cliffs, New Jersey: Prentice-Hall, 1972.

Fest, Joachim C. *The Face of the Third Reich: Portraits of the Nazi Leadership.* New York: Pantheon Books, 1970.

Fest, Joachim C. *Hitler.* New York: Harcourt Brace Jovanovich, 1974.

Filler, Louis. *The Crusade against Slavery: 1830-1860.* New York: Harper and Bros., 1960.

Fischer, Louis. *Russia's Road from Peace to War: Soviet Foreign Relations, 1917-1941.* New York: Harper and Row, 1969.

Fisher, Tadd. *Our Overcrowded World.* New York: Parents' Magazine Press, 1969.

Fisher, Walter D. "Oskar Ryszard Lange, 1904-1965," *Econometrica* 34(4):

733-738, October 1966.

Fishlow, Albert, et al. *Rich Nations and Poor Nations in the World Economy.* New York: McGraw-Hill, 1978.

Fleming, D. F. *The United States and the League of Nations, 1918-1920.* New York: Russell and Russell, 1968. First published in 1932.

Forsyth, Murray. *Unions of States: The Theory and Practice of Confederation.* Leicester: Leicester University Press, 1981.

Forsyth, Murray. *Federalism and Nationalism.* New York: St. Martin's Press, 1987.

Franck, Thomas M., editor. *Why Federations Fail: An Inquiry into the Requisites for Successful Federalism.* New York: New York University Press, 1968.

Frank, Pat. *How to Survive the H-Bomb—and Why.* New York: Lippincott, 1962.

Fraser, Dean. *The People Problem.* Bloomington: Indiana University Press, 1971.

Freedman, Lawrence. *The Price of Peace: Living with the Nuclear Dilemma.* New York: Henry Holt and Company, 1986.

Freris, Andrew. *The Soviet Industrial Enterprise: Theory and Practice.* New York: St. Martin's Press, 1984.

Friedman, Milton. *Capitalism and Freedom.* Chicago: University of Chicago Press, 1962.

Friedman, Milton, and Rose Friedman. *Free to Choose.* New York: Harcourt Brace Jovanovich, 1979.

Friedrich, Carl Joachim. *Inevitable Peace.* New York: Greenwood Press, 1969. First published in 1948.

Fromuth, Peter J. *A Successor Vision: The United Nations of Tomorrow.* Lanham, Maryland: University Press of America, 1988.

Gaddis, John Lewis. *The United States and the Origins of the Cold War, 1941-1947.* New York: Columbia University Press, 1972.

Gaucher, Roland. *Opposition in the U.S.S.R., 1917-1967.* New York: Funk and Wagnalls, 1969.

Genovese, Eugene D. *The World the Slaveholders Made.* New York: Pantheon Books, 1969.

Genovese, Eugene D., editor. *The Slave Economies,* two volumes. New York: John Wiley, 1973.

Genovese, Eugene D. *Roll, Jordon, Roll: The World the Slaves Made.* New York: Pantheon Books, 1974.

Ghosh, Pradip K., editor. *New International Economic Orders: A Third World Perspective.* Westport, Connecticut: Greenwood Press, 1984.

Ghosh, Pradip K., editor. *Population, Environment and Resources, and*

Third World Development. Westport, Connecticut: Greenwood Press, 1984.

Glezerman, G. *Socialist Society: Scientific Principles of Development.* Moscow: Progress Publishers, 1971.

Goldblat, Jozef, editor (for the Stockholm International Peace Research Institute). *Non-Proliferation: The Why and the Wherefore.* Philadelphia: Taylor and Francis, 1985.

Goodman, Eliot R. *The Soviet Design for a World State.* New York: Columbia University Press, 1960.

Goodrich, Leland M., and Anne P. Simons. *The United Nations and the Maintenance of International Peace and Security.* Washington, D.C.: Brookings Institution, 1955.

Goodspeed, Stephen S. *The Nature and Function of International Organization,* second edition. New York: Oxford University Press, 1967.

Gordenker, Leon, editor. *The United Nations in International Politics.* Princeton, New Jersey: Princeton University Press, 1971.

Gordon, David. *Resurrecting Marx: The Analytical Marxists on Freedom, Exploitation, and Justice.* New Brunswick, New Jersey: Transactions Books, 1990.

Gouverneur, Jacques. *Contemporary Capitalism and Marxist Economics.* Totowa, New Jersey: Barnes and Noble, 1983.

Gregory, Paul R., and Robert C. Stuart. *Soviet Economic Structure and Performance,* fourth edition. New York: Harper and Row, 1990.

Grey, Ian. *Stalin: Man of History.* Garden City, New York: Doubleday and Co., 1979.

Griffin, Keith B. *International Inequality and World Poverty.* New York: Holmes and Meier, 1978.

Griffin, Keith B., and John Gurley. "Radical Analyses of Imperialism, the Third World, and the Transition to Socialism," *Journal of Economic Literature* 23(3): 1089-1143, September 1985.

Grigryan, L., and Y. Dolgopolov. *Fundamentals of Soviet State Law.* Moscow: Progress Publishers, 1971.

Gruchy, Allan G. *Comparative Economic Systems,* second edition. Boston: Houghton Mifflin, 1977.

Haas, Michael. *International Conflict.* Indianapolis: Bobbs-Merrill, 1974.

Hagen, Everett. *The Economics of Development.* Homewood, Ill.: Richard D. Irwin, 1968.

Halm, George N. *Economic Systems: A Comparative Analysis.* New York: Holt, Rinehart and Winston, 1960.

Hamilton, Alexander, John Jay, and James Madison. *The Federalist.* First published 1787-88.

Hammond, Thomas T. "Moscow and Communist Takeovers," *Problems of Communism* 25(1): 48-67, January-February 1976.

Hanrieder, Wolfram F., editor. *Arms Control and Security: Current Issues.* Boulder, Colorado: Westview Press, 1979.

Harrington, Michael. *The Twilight of Capitalism.* New York: Basic Books, 1980.

Hauser, Philip M., ed. *The Population Dilemma.* Englewood Cliffs, New Jersey: Prentice-Hall, 1963.

Hayek, Friedrich, editor and contributor. *Collectivist Economic Planning: Critical Studies on the Possibilities of Socialism.* London: George Routledge and Sons, 1935. Reprinted Augustus M. Kelley, 1975. (Hayek's contributions: "The Nature and History of the Problem," "The Present State of the Debate.")

Hayek, Friedrich. "Socialist Calculation: The 'Competitive Solution,'" *Economica* 7 (New Series): 125-149, May 1940.

Hayek, Friedrich. *The Road to Serfdom.* Chicago: University of Chicago Press, 1944.

Hayek, Friedrich. *The Fatal Conceit: The Errors of Socialism.* Edited by W. W. Bartley III. Chicago: University of Chicago Press, 1988.

Heller, Michel, and Aleksandr Nekrich. *Utopia in Power: A History of the USSR from 1917 to the Present.* London: Hutchinson, 1986.

Hertzler, J. O. *The Crisis in World Population.* Lincoln, Nebraska: University of Nebraska Press, 1956.

Hewett, Edward A. *Reforming the Soviet Economy: Equality versus Efficiency.* Washington: Brookings Institution, 1988.

Hickman, Bert G., editor. *Global International Economic Models.* Amsterdam: North-Holland, 1983.

Hilsman, Roger. *The Crouching Future: International Politics and U.S. Foreign Policy, A Forecast.* Garden City, New York: Doubleday and Co., 1975.

Himes, Joseph S. *Conflict and Conflict Management.* Athens, Georgia: University of Georgia Press, 1980.

Hinsley, F. H. *Sovereignty.* New York: Basic Books, 1966.

Hinsley, F. H. *Nationalism and the International System.* Dobbs Ferry, New York: Oceana Publications, 1973.

Hitler, Adolf. *Mein Kampf.* Boston: Houghton Mifflin, 1943. Originally published in German, 1925 (Volume I) and 1927 (Volume II).

Holesovsky, Vaclav. *Economic Systems: Analysis and Comparison.* New York: McGraw-Hill, 1977.

Hook, Sidney. *Political Power and Personal Freedom.* Criterion Books, 1959.

Howe, Irving, editor. *Essential Works of Socialism*. New Haven: Yale University Press, 1976.

Howe, Irving, editor. *1984 Revisited: Totalitarianism in Our Century*. New York: Harper and Row, 1983.

Hyams, Edward. *The Millenium Postponed: Socialism from Sir Thomas More to Mao Tse-tung*. New York: Taplinger, 1974.

Hynes, Samuel, editor. *Twentieth Century Interpretations of 1984: A Collection of Critical Essays*. Englewood Cliffs: New Jersey: Prentice-Hall, 1971.

Inkeles, Alex. *Public Opinion in Soviet Russia: A Study in Mass Persuasion*. Cambridge, Mass.: Harvard University Press, 1950.

Inkeles, Alex. *Social Change in Soviet Russia*. Cambridge, Mass.: Harvard University Press, 1968.

Inozemtsev, N. *Contemporary Capitalism: New Developments and Contradictions*. Moscow: Progress Publishers, 1974.

Ireland, Norman J. *The Economics of Labor-Managed Enterprises*. New York: St. Martin's Press, 1982.

Irving, David. *The War Path: Hitler's Germany, 1933-39*. New York: Viking, 1978.

Irving, David. *Hitler's War*, 2 volumes. New York: Viking, 1977.

Jacob, Phillip E., and Alexine L. Atherton. *The Dynamics of International Organization: The Making of World Order*. Homewood, Ill.: Dorsey Press, 1965.

Jacobs, Dan N., editor. *From Marx to Mao and Marchais: Documents on the Development of Communist Variations*. New York: Longman, 1979.

Jalee, Pierre. *The Pillage of the Third World*. New York: Monthly Review Press, 1968.

Jalee, Pierre. *The Third World in World Economy*. New York: Monthly Review Press, 1969.

Jaworskyj, Michael, editor. *Soviet Political Thought: An Anthology*. Baltimore: Johns Hopkins University Press, 1967.

Jepma, C. J. *North-South Co-Operation in Retrospect and Prospect*. New York: Routledge, 1988.

Johnson, F. Ernest, editor. *Foundations of Democracy*. New York: Harper and Row, 1947.

Jones, Anthony, editor. *Perestroika and the Economy: New Thinking in Soviet Economics*. Armonk, New York: M. E. Sharpe, 1989.

Jones, Anthony, and William Moskoff, editors. *The Great Market Debate in Soviet Economics*. Armonk, New York: M. E. Sharpe, 1991.

Kahn, Herman. *On Thermonuclear War*. Princeton, New Jersey: Princeton University Press, 1960.

Kahn, Herman. *Thinking about the Unthinkable.* New York: Avon, 1962.

Kamenka, Eugene, editor. *Nationalism: The Nature and Evolution of an Idea.* New York: St. Martin's Press, 1976.

Kangas, Georgia Lee. *Population and Survival: The Challenge in Five Countries.* New York: Praeger Publishers, 1984.

Kant, Immanuel. "Eternal Peace." In Carl Joachim Friedrich, *Inevitable Peace* (New York: Greenwood Press, 1969). Kant's essay first published in German in 1795.

Kapur, Ashok. *International Nuclear Proliferation: Multilateral Diplomacy and Regional Aspects.* New York: Praeger, 1979.

Kaser, Michael. *Soviet Economics.* New York: McGraw-Hill, 1970.

Kashlev, Yu. *After 14,000 Wars.* Moscow: Progress Publishers, 1979.

Katkoff, Vladimir. *The Soviet Economy, 1940-1965.* Westport, Connecticut: Greenwood Press, 1973.

Kay, David A., editor. *The United Nations Political System.* New York: John Wiley and Sons, 1967.

Keep, John L. H. *The Russian Revolution: A Study in Mass Mobilization.* New York: W. W. Norton, 1976.

Kelley, Allen C. "Economic Consequences of Population Change in the Third World," *Journal of Economic Literature* 26(4): 1685-1728, Dec. 1988.

Khachaturov, T. *The Economy of the Soviet Union Today.* Moscow: Progress Publishers, 1977.

King, Timothy, et al. *Population Policies and Economic Development.* Baltimore: Johns Hopkins University Press, 1974.

Klochkovsky, L. L. *Economic Neocolonialism.* Moscow: Progress Publishers, 1975.

Knapp, Wilfred F. *A History of War and Peace: 1939-1965.* London: Oxford University Press, 1967.

Knauerhase, Ramon. *An Introduction to National Socialism, 1920 to 1939.* Columbus, Ohio: Charles E. Merrill, 1972.

Koenig, William J. *Weapons of World War 3.* London: Bison Books Ltd., 1981.

Kohler, Foy D. *Understanding the Russians: A Citizen's Primer.* New York: Harper and Row, 1970.

Kohn, Hans. *The Idea of Nationalism.* New York: Macmillan, 1944.

Kortunov, V. *A Third World War? Threats: Real and Imaginary.* Moscow: Progress Publishers, 1982.

Kozlov, G. A., editor. *Political Economy: Capitalism.* Moscow: Progress Publishers, 1977.

Krausnick, Helmut, Hans Buchheim, Martin Broszat, and Hans-Adolf

Jacobsen. *Anatomy of the SS State*. New York: Walker and Company, 1968.

Kravis, I. B., A. W. Heston, and R. Summers. "Real GDP per Capita for More than One Hundred Countries," *Economic Journal* 88(350): 215-242, June 1978.

Krutogolov, M. A. *Talks on Soviet Democracy*. Moscow: Progress Publishers, 1980.

Laird, Roy. *The Soviet Paradigm*. New York: Free Press, 1970.

Lane, Ann J. *The Debate over Slavery: Stanley Elkins and His Critics*. Urbana: University of Illinois Press, 1971.

Landauer, Carl. *European Socialism*, two volumes. Berkeley, California: University of California Press, 1960.

Landauer, Carl. *Contemporary Economic Systems: A Comparative Approach*. Philadelphia: J. B. Lippincott Co., 1964.

Lange, Oskar. "On the Economic Theory of Socialism," *Review of Economic Studies* 4(1): 53-71, October 1936, and 4(2): 123-142, February 1937. Issued in book form with contributions by Benjamin Lippincott, ed., and Fred M. Taylor: University of Minnesota Press, 1938. Reprinted by McGraw-Hill, 1964.

Laqueur, Walter, editor. *Fascism: A Reader's Guide*. Berkeley and Los Angeles: University of California Press, 1976.

Laudicina, Paul A. *World Poverty and Development: A Survey of American Opinion*. Washington: Overseas Development Council, 1973.

Laurence, William L. *The Hell Bomb*. New York: Alfred Knopf, 1951.

Lazuthin, Y. *Socialism and Wealth*. Moscow: Progress Publishers, 1974.

Lebedev, Nikolai. *The USSR in World Politics*. Moscow: Progress Publishers, 1982.

Leckie, Robert. *Delivered from Evil: The Saga of World War II*. New York: Harper and Row, 1987.

Leeman, Wayne A. *Centralized and Decentralized Economic Systems*. Chicago: Rand McNally, 1977.

Leonhard, Wolfgang. *Three Faces of Marxism: The Political Concepts of Soviet Ideology, Maoism, and Humanist Marxism*. New York: G. P. Putnam's Sons, 1979.

Leontyev, L. *A Short Course of Political Economy*. Moscow: Progress Publishers, 1968.

Liddell Hart, B. H. *History of the Second World War*. New York: G. P. Putnam, 1971.

Lindsay, Jack. *The Crisis in Marxism*. Totowa, New Jersey: Barnes and Noble, 1981.

Lincoln, W. Bruce. *Passage through Armageddon: The Russians in War and*

Revolution, 1914-1918. New York: Simon and Schuster, 1986.

Lincoln, W. Bruce. *Red Victory: A History of the Russian Civil War*. New York: Simon and Schuster, 1989.

Lively, Jack. *Democracy*. New York: St. Martin's Press, 1975.

Loup, Jacques. *Can the Third World Survive?* Baltimore: Johns Hopkins University Press, 1983.

Lozoya, Jorge, and Rosario Green, editors. *International Trade, Industrialization, and the New International Economic Order*. New York: Pergamon Press, 1981.

MacBean, Alasdair I., and U. N. Balasubramanyan. *Meeting the Third World Challenge*. New York: St. Martin's Press, 1976.

Maclaurin, John. *The United Nations and Power Politics*. New York: Harper and Brothers, 1951.

Macmahon, Arthur W. *Federalism: Mature and Emergent*. New York: Russell and Russell, 1962.

Mandel, Ernest. *Marxist Economic Theory*, two volumes. New York: Monthly Review Press, 1970.

Mangone, Gerald J. *The Idea and Practice of World Government*. New York: Columbia University Press, 1951.

Markey, Edward J., and Douglas C. Waller. *Nuclear Peril: The Politics of Proliferation*. Cambridge, Massachusetts: Ballinger, 1982.

Martin, Joseph. *A Guide to Marxism*. New York: St. Martin's Press, 1980.

Martin, Laurence. *Arms and Strategy: The World Power Structure Today*. New York: David McKay, 1973.

Marx, Karl. *Capital: A Critique of Political Economy*, three volumes. Moscow: Progress Publishers, 1959. Originally published in German: Vol. I (1867), Vol. II (1885), Vol. III (1894).

Mayer, Milton. *They Thought They Were Free: The Germans, 1933-45*. Chicago: University of Chicago Press, 1955.

Mayo, Herbert B. *An Introduction to Democratic Theory*. New York: Oxford University Press, 1960.

McKenzie, Kermit E. *Comintern and World Revolution, 1928-1943: The Shaping of Doctrine*. New York: Columbia University Press, 1964.

McLellan, David. *Karl Marx: His Life and Thought*. New York: Harper and Row, 1974.

McLellan, David. *Marxism after Marx: An Introduction*. New York: Harper and Row, 1979.

McWhinney, Edward. *Comparative Federalism: States' Rights and National Power*. Toronto: University of Toronto Press, 1962.

Meadows, Dennis L., et al. *The Limits to Growth*. New York: Signet, 1972.

Mehring, Franz. *Karl Marx: The Story of His Life*. London: George Allen and Unwin, 1948.

Melman, Seymour. *The Peace Race*. New York: Ballentine, 1961.

Mendlovitz, Saul H., compiler and editor. *Legal and Political Problems of World Order*, preliminary edition. New York: Fund for Education concerning World Peace through World Law, 1962.

Messenger, Charles. *Armies of World War 3*. Greenwich, Conn.: Bison Books, 1984.

Meyer, Alfred G. *Marxism: The Unity of Theory and Practice*. Cambridge, Massachusetts: Harvard University Press, 1970.

Michel, Henri. *The Second World War*, 2 volumes. New York: Praeger Publishers, 1975.

Mileikovsky, A. G., editor. *Present-Day Non-Marxist Political Economy: A Critical Analysis*. Moscow: Progress Publishers, 1975.

Milenkovitch, Deborah D. "Is Market Socialism Efficient?" In Andrew Zimbalist, ed., *Comparative Economic Systems: An Assessment of Knowledge, Theory and Method* (Boston: Kluwer-Nijhoff, 1984).

Mill, John Stuart. *On Liberty, The Subjection of Women, Chapters on Socialism*. Cambridge: Cambridge University Press, 1989. "Chapters on Socialism" first published in 1879.

Millis, Walter, and James Real. *The Abolition of War*. New York: Macmillan, 1963.

Mills, C. Wright. *The Power Elite*. New York: Oxford University Press, 1956.

Mills, C. Wright. *The Causes of World War Three*. New York: Ballentine, 1958.

Minogue, K. R. *Nationalism*. New York: Basic Books, 1967.

Mises, Ludwig von. "Economic Calculation in the Socialist Commonwealth," in Friedrich Hayek, ed., *Collectivist Economc Planning* (London: George Routledge and Sons, 1935). Originally published in German in 1920.

Mises, Ludwig von. *Bureaucracy*. New Haven, Connecticut: Yale University Press, 1943.

Mises, Ludwig von. *Socialism: An Economic and Sociological Analysis*, revised English edition. New Haven, Connecticut: Yale University Press, 1951. Reprinted Indianapolis: Liberty Classics, 1981. First published in German in 1922.

Mises, Ludwig von. *The Anti-Capitalist Mentality*. New York: Van Nostrand, 1956.

Moore, Barrington, Jr. *Terror and Progress: USSR*. Cambridge, Mass.: Harvard University Press, 1954.

Mosley, Paul. "Aid, Savings and Growth Revisited," *Oxford Bulletin of*

Economics and Statistics 42(2): 79-96, May 1980.

Mosley, Paul. *Overseas Aid: Its Defense and Reform.* Brighton: Wheatsheaf, 1987.

Mosley, Paul, John Hudson, and Sara Horrell. "Aid, the Public Sector and the Market in Less Developed Countries," *Economic Journal* 97(387): 616-641, September 1987.

Moynihan, Daniel Patrick. *A Dangerous Place.* Boston: Little, Brown and Company, 1975.

Murdock, William W. *The Poverty of Nations: The Political Economy of Hunger and Population.* Baltimore: Johns Hopkins University Press, 1980.

Murphy, John F. *The United Nations and the Control of International Violence: A Legal and Political Analysis.* Totowa, New Jersey: Allenheld Osmun, 1982.

Mushkat, Mario'n. *The Third World and Peace: Some Aspects of the Interrelationship of Underdevelopment and International Security.* New York: St. Martin's Press, 1982.

Myrdal, Gunnar. *The Challenge of World Poverty: A World Anti-Poverty Program in Outline.* New York: Pantheon, 1970.

Nelson, William N. *On Justifying Democracy.* London: Routledge and Kegan Paul, 1980.

Neuberger, Egon, and William J. Duffy. *Comparative Economic Systems: A Decision-Making Approach.* Boston: Allyn and Bacon, 1976.

Newhouse, John. *Cold Dawn: The Story of SALT.* New York: Holt, Rinehart and Winston, 1973.

Ng, Larry K. Y., editor. *The Population Crisis.* Bloomington: Indiana University Press, 1965.

Nicol, Davidson, Luis Echeverria, and Aurelio Peccei, editors. *Regionalism and the New International Economic Order.* New York: Pergamon Press, 1981.

Northedge, F. S. *The League of Nations: Its Life and Times, 1920-1946.* New York: Holmes and Meier, 1986.

Nove, Alec. *The Soviet Economy.* New York: Praeger, 1961.

Nove, Alec. *The Economics of Feasible Socialism.* London: George Allen and Unwin, 1983.

Oakley, Allen. *Marx's Critique of Political Economy: Intellectual Sources and Evolution,* 2 volumes. Boston: Routledge and Kegan Paul, 1984, 1985.

O'Ballance, Edgar. *Tracks of the Bear: Soviet Imprints in the Seventies.* Novato, Cal.: Presidio Press, 1982.

Office of Technology Assessment, U.S. Congress. *The Effects of Nuclear*

War. Washington: U.S. Government Printing Office, 1979.

Ohlin, Goran. *Population Control and Economic Development*. Paris: Organization for Economic Cooperation and Development, 1967.

Ohlin, Goran. "International Politics of Underdevelopment." In Gustav Ranis, ed., *The Gap between Rich and Poor Nations* (New York: St. Martin's Press, 1972).

Olsevich, Y. Y., and S. A. Khavina, "Critique of Right-Wing Revisionist Conceptions of the Socialist Economy," Chapter 12 in *Right-Wing Revisionism Today* (Moscow: Progress Publishers, 1976).

Olson, William C., and Fred K. Sondermann, eds. *The Theory and Practice of International Relations*, second edition. Englewood Cliffs: New Jersey: Prentice-Hall, 1966.

Orwell, George. *1984*. New York: Harcourt, Brace and Co., 1949.

Overstreet, Harry, and Bonaro Overstreet. *What We Must Know about Communism*. New York: W. W. Norton, 1958.

Papanek, Gustav F. "The Effect of Aid and Other Resource Transfers on Savings and Growth in Less Developed Countries," *Economic Journal* 82(327): 934-950, September 1972.

Papanek, Gustav S. "Aid, Foreign Private Investment, Saving and Growth in Less Developed Countries," *Journal of Political Economy* 81(1): 120-130, January-February 1973.

Patterson, Orlando. *Slavery and Social Death: A Comparative Study*. Cambridge, Mass.: Harvard University Press, 1982.

Pauling, Linus. *No More War!* New York: Dodd, Mead and Co., 1958.

Payne, Robert. *Marx*. New York: Simon and Schuster, 1968.

Payne, Robert. *The Life and Death of Adolf Hitler*. New York: Praeger, 1973.

Pearson, Lester B., chairman. *Partners in Development: Report of the Commission on International Development*. New York: Praeger, 1969.

Pease, William H., and Jane H. Pease, editors. *The Antislavery Argument*. Indianapolis: Bobbs-Merrill, 1965.

Pendell, Elmer. *Population on the Loose*. New York: Wilfred Funk, 1951.

Perfilyev, M. *Socialist Democracy and Bourgeois Sovietology*. Moscow: Progress Publishers, no date.

Pevsner, Ya. *State-Monopoly Capitalism and the Labour Theory of Value*. Moscow: Progress Publishers, 1982.

Pickersgill, Gary M., and Joyce E. Pickersgill. *Contemporary Economic Systems: A Comparative View*, second edition. St. Paul, Minnesota: West Pub. Co., 1985.

Pilat, Joseph F., editor. *The Nonproliferation Predicament*. New Brunswick, New Jersey: Transactions Books, 1985.

Pipes, Richard, editor. *Revolutionary Russia*. Cambridge, Mass.: Harvard

University Press, 1968.

Ponomarev, B. N., A. Gromyko, and V. Khvostov. *History of Soviet Foreign Policy, 1917-1945.* Moscow: Progress Publishers, 1969.

Ponomarev, B. N., et al. *A Short History of the Communist Party of the Soviet Union.* Moscow: Progress Publishers, 1970.

Prostyakov, Igor. *The Mechanism of Soviet Economy: Problems, Quests, Solutions.* Moscow: Progress Publishers, 1987.

Pryor, Frederick L. "The Economics of Production Cooperatives," *Annals of Public and Cooperative Economy* 54(2): 133-173, June 1983.

Quester, George. *The Politics of Nuclear Proliferation.* Baltimore: Johns Hopkins University Press, 1973.

Raddatz, Fritz J. *Karl Marx: A Political Biography.* Boston: Little, Brown and Co., 1978.

Radkey, Oliver Henry. *The Sickle under the Hammer: The Russian Socialist Revolutionaries in the Early Months of Soviet Rule.* New York: Columbia University Press, 1963.

Rakove, Milton L., editor. *Arms and Foreign Policy in the Nuclear Age.* New York: Oxford University Press, 1972.

Ranis, Gustav, editor. *The Gap between the Rich and Poor Nations.* New York: St. Martin's Press, 1972.

Rejai, M. *Democracy: The Contemporary Theories.* New York: Atherton, 1967.

Reubens, Edwin P. "International Migration Models and Policies," *American Economic Review* 73(2): 178-182, May 1983.

Rhodes, Edward. *Power and Madness: The Logic of Nuclear Coercion.* New York: Columbia University Press, 1989.

Rhodes, Robert I., editor. *Imperialism and Underdevelopment: A Reader.* New York: Monthly Review Press, 1970.

Rich, Norman. *Hitler's War Aims: Ideology, the Nazi State, and the Course of Expansion.* New York: Norton, 1973.

Riddell, Roger C. *Foreign Aid Reconsidered.* Baltimore: Johns Hopkins University Press, 1987.

Roemer, John E. *Analytical Foundations of Marxian Economic Theory.* Cambridge: Cambridge University Press, 1981.

Roemer, John E. *A General Theory of Exploitation and Class.* Cambridge, Massachusetts: Harvard University Press, 1982.

Roemer, John E. *Free to Lose.* Cambridge, Massachusetts: Harvard University Press, 1988.

Ross, Alf. *The United Nations: Peace and Progress.* Totowa, New Jersey: Bedminster Press, 1966.

Rubin, Jacob. *Your Hundred Billion Dollars: The Complete Story of*

American Foreign Aid. Philadelphia: Chilton, 1964.

Rummel, R. J. *Understanding Conflict and War,* Volume II: *The Conflict Helix.* New York: Wiley, 1976.

Rush, Myron. *Political Succession in the U.S.S.R.* New York: Columbia University Press, 1965.

Russell, Bertrand. *Has Man a Future?* New York: Simon and Schuster, 1962.

Russett, Bruce. *The Prisoners of Insecurity: Deterrence, Arms Races, and Arms Control.* San Francisco: Freeman, 1983.

Ryndina, M., and G. Chernikov, editors. *The Political Economy of Capitalism.* Moscow: Progress Publishers, 1974.

Salisbury, Harrison E. *Black Night, White Snow: Russia's Revolutions, 1905-1917.* Garden City, New York: Doubleday and Co., 1978.

Samuelson, Paul A. "Understanding the Marxian Notion of Exploitation: A Summary of the So-Called Transformation Problem," *Journal of Economic Literature* 9(2): 399-431, June 1971.

Sartori, Giovanni. *Democratic Theory.* New York: Praeger, 1962.

Sathyamurthy, T. V. *Nationalism in the Contemporary World: Political and Sociological Perspectives.* Totowa, New Jersey: Allenheld, Osmun, 1983.

Sau, Ranjit. *Unequal Exchange: Imperialism and Development.* Calcutta: Oxford University Press, 1978.

Sauvy, Alfred. *Fertility and Survival.* New York: Collier Books, 1963.

Scheer, Robert. *With Enough Shovels: Reagan, Bush and Nuclear War.* New York: Random House, 1982.

Schell, Jonathon. *The Fate of the Earth.* New York: Alfred A. Knopf, 1982.

Schelling, Thomas C., and Morton H. Halperin. *Strategy and Arms Control.* New York: Twentieth Century Fund, 1961.

Schnitzer, Martin C. *Comparative Economic Systems,* fourth edition. Cincinnati: South-Western Pub. Co., 1987.

Schwartz, Fred. *The Three Faces of Revolution.* Washington, D.C.: Capitol Hill Press, 1972.

Scott, George. *The Rise and Fall of the League of Nations.* New York: Macmillan, 1973.

Seigel, Jerrold E. *Marx's Fate: The Shape of a Life.* Princeton, New Jersey: Princeton University Press, 1978.

Shafer, Boyd. *Faces of Nationalism.* New York: Harcourt Brace Jovanovich, 1972.

Shaffer, Harry G., editor. *The Soviet System in Theory and Practice: Western and Soviet Views,* second edition. New York: Frederick Ungar, 1984.

Shahnazarov, G. *Socialist Democracy.* Moscow: Progress Publishers, 1974.

Sharp, Gene. *Social Power and Political Freedom*. Boston: Porter Sargent, 1980.

Shaw, George Bernard. *The Intelligent Woman's Guide to Socialism and Capitalism*. New York: Brentano's, 1928.

Shemyatenkov, V. *The Enigma of Capital: A Marxist Viewpoint*. Moscow: Progress Publishers, 1981.

Sherman, Howard J. *Radical Political Economy*. New York: Basic Books, 1972.

Sherman, Howard J. *Foundations of Radical Political Economy*. Armonk, New York: M. E. Sharpe, 1987.

Shirer, William L. *The Rise and Fall of the Third Reich: A History of Nazi Germany*, 2 volumes. New York: Simon and Schuster, 1959, 1960.

Shirer, William L. *Berlin Diary: An Inside Account on Nazi Germany*. New York: Bonanza, 1984.

Shoham, Shlomo Giora, and Francis Rosenstiel, editors. *And He Loved Big Brother: Man, State and Society in Question*. London: Macmillan, 1985.

Shue, Henry, editor. *Nuclear Deterrence and Moral Restraint*. Cambridge: Cambridge University Press, 1989.

Shultz, T. Paul. *Economics of Population*. Reading, Massachusetts: Addison-Wesley, 1981.

Shvyrkov, Yu. M. *Centralized Planning of the Economy*. Moscow: Progress Publishers, 1980.

Simirenko, Alex, editor. *Social Thought in the Soviet Union*. Chicago: Quadrangle Books, 1969.

Simon, Julian L. *The Economics of Population Growth*. Princeton, New Jersey: Princeton University Press, 1977.

Simon, Julian L. *The Ultimate Resource*. Princeton, New Jersey: Princeton University Press, 1981.

Singh, Jyote Shanker. *A New International Economic Order: Toward a Fair Redistribution of the World's Resources*. New York: Praeger, 1977.

Smith, Anthony D. *Theories of Nationalism*. London: Duckworth, 1971.

Smith, Gerald. *Doubletalk: The Story of the First Strategic Arms Limitation Talks*. Garden City, New York: Doubleday, 1980.

Smith, Hedrick. *The Russians*. New York: Quadrangle/New York Times Book Co., 1976.

Smirnov, A. D., V. V. Golosev, and V. F. Maximova, editors. *The Teaching of Political Economy: A Critique of Non-Marxian Theories*. Moscow: Progress Publishers, 1984.

Snyder, Jed C., and Samuel F. Wells, Jr., editors. *Limiting Nuclear Proliferation*. Cambridge, Massachusetts: Ballinger, 1985.

Sobolev, A. I., et al. *Outline History of the Communist International*.

Moscow: Progress Publishers, 1971.

Spanier, John W., and Joseph L. Nogee. *The Politics of Disarmament: A Study in Soviet-American Gamesmanship*. New York: Frederick A. Praeger, 1962.

Speer, Albert. *Inside the Third Reich: Memoirs*. New York: Macmillan Publishing Co., 1970.

Spulber, Nicholas. *The Soviet Economy: Structure, Principles and Problems*. New York: W. W. Norton, 1962.

Spulber, Nicholas, editor. *Foundations of Soviet Strategy for Economic Growth*. Bloomington: Indiana University Press, 1964.

Stampp, Kenneth M. *The Peculiar Institution: Slavery in the Ante-Bellum South*. New York: Alfred A. Knopf, 1956.

Stamps, Norman L. *Why Democracies Fail*. South Bend, Indiana: University of Notre Dame Press, 1957.

Stankiewicz, W. J., editor. *In Defense of Sovereignty*. New York: Oxford University Press, 1969.

Stauber, Leland G. "The Implications of Market Socialism in the United States," *Polity* 8(1): 38-62, Fall 1975.

Stauber, Leland G. "A Proposal for a Democratic Market Economy," *Journal of Comparative Economics* 2(4): 382-389, December 1978.

Stauber, Leland G. *A New Program for Democratic Socialism*. Carbondale, Illinois: Four Willows Press, 1987.

Steinherr, Alfred. "The Labor-Managed Firm: A Survey of the Economics Literature," *Annals of Public and Cooperative Economy* 49(2): 129-148, April-June 1978.

Steinhoff, William. *George Orwell and the Origins of 1984*. Ann Arbor: University of Michigan Press, 1975.

Stern, Nicholas. "The Economics of Development: A Survey," *Economic Journal* 99(397): 597-685, September 1989.

Stoessinger, John G. *The United Nations and the Superpowers*. New York: Random House, 1965.

Stoessinger, John G. *The Might of Nations: World Politics in Our Time*. New York: Harper and Row, 1965.

Stoneman, Colin. "Foreign Capital and Economic Growth," *World Development* 2(1): 11-26, January 1975.

Stonier, Tom. *Nuclear Disaster*. Cleveland: World, 1963.

Sullivan, David S., and Martin J. Sattler, editors. *Change and the Future International System*. New York: Columbia University Press, 1972.

Talbott, Strobe. *Endgame: The Inside Story of Salt II*. New York: Harper and Row, 1979.

Talbott, Strobe. *Deadly Gambits: The Reagan Administration and the*

Stalemate in Nuclear Arms Control. New York: Alfred A. Knopf, 1984.

Talbott, Strobe. *The Master of the Game: Paul Nitze and the Nuclear Peace.* New York: Alfred A. Knopf, 1988.

Tiryakian, Edward A., and Ronald Rogowski, editors. *New Nationalisms of the Developed West: Toward Explanation.* Boston: Allen and Unwin, 1985.

Tivey, Leonard, editor. *The Nation-State: The Formation of Modern Politics.* New York: St. Martin's Press, 1981.

Todaro, Michael P. *Economic Development in the Third World,* second edition. New York: Longman, 1981.

Toland, John. *Adolf Hitler.* Garden City, New York: Doubleday, 1976.

Topornin, B., and E. Machulsky. *Socialism and Democracy: A Reply to Opportunists.* Moscow: Progress Publishers, 1974.

Towster, Julian. *Political Power in the U.S.S.R.: 1917-1947.* New York: Oxford University Press, 1948.

Treadgold, Donald. *Twentieth Century Russia,* second edition. Chicago: Rand McNally and Co., 1964.

Tucker, Robert C., ed. *Stalinism: Essays in Historical Interpretation.* New York: W. W. Norton, 1977.

Tyler, William G. *Issues and Prospects for the New International Economic Order.* Lexington, Massachusetts: D. C. Heath, 1977.

Ulam, Adam. "Ideology and Power Politics: Discussion," in Erik P. Hoffman and Frederic J. Fleron, eds., *The Conduct of Soviet Foreign Policy* (Chicago: Aldine-Atherton, 1971).

Ulam, Adam. *In the Name of the People: Prophets and Conspirators in Prerevolutionary Russia.* New York: Viking Press, 1976.

Ulam, Adam B. *The Unfinished Revolution: Marxism and Communism in the Modern World,* revised ed. Boulder, Colorado: Westview Press, 1979.

Ulam, Adam B. *Russia's Failed Revolutions: From the Decembrists to the Dissidents.* New York: Basic Books, 1981.

United Nations. *Nuclear Weapons: Report of the Secretary-General of the United Nations.* Brookline, Massachusetts: Autumn Press, 1980.

Usachev, Igor. *A World without Arms?* Moscow: Progress Publishers, 1984.

Vakhrushev, Vasily. *Neocolonialism: Methods and Maneuvers.* Moscow: Progress Publishers, 1973.

Vanek, Jaroslav. *The General Theory of Labor-Managed Market Economies.* Ithaca, New York: Cornell University Press, 1970.

Vanek, Jaroslav. *The Participatory Economy.* Ithaca, New York: Cornell University Press, 1971.

Vanek, Jaroslav. *The Labor-Managed Economy: Essays.* Ithaca, New York: Cornell University Press, 1977.

Varga, Y. *Politico-Economic Problems of Capitalism*. Moscow: Progress Publishers, 1968.

Waite, Robert G. L. *The Psychopathic God: Adolf Hitler*. New York: Basic Books, 1977.

Walters, F. P. *A History of the League of Nations*. New York: Oxford University Press, 1952.

Ward, Barbara. *Nationalism and Ideology*. New York: W. W. Norton, 1966.

Ward, Barbara. *The Widening Gap: Development in the 1970's*. New York: Columbia University Press, 1971.

Weede, Erich. "Extended Deterrence by Superpower Alliances," *Journal of Conflict Resolution* 7: 231-253, June 1983.

Weiss, Paul. *Toward a Perfected State*. Albany: State University of New York Press, 1986.

Weizsacker, Carl Friedrich von. *The Politics of Peril: Economics, Society and the Prevention of War*. New York: Seabury Press, 1978.

Welch, William. *American Images of Soviet Foreign Policy: An Inquiry into Recent Appraisals from the Academic Community*. New Haven: Yale University Press, 1970.

Wells, H. G. *The Work, Wealth and Happiness of Mankind*. Garden City, New York: Doubleday, Doran and Company, 1931.

Werth, Alexander. *Russia at War, 1941-1945*. New York: E. P. Dutton, 1964.

Werth, Alexander. *Russia: Hopes and Fears*. New York: Simon and Schuster, 1969.

Wesson, Robert G. *State Systems: International Pluralism, Politics, and Culture*. New York: Free Press, 1978.

Wentz, Walter B. *Nuclear Proliferation*. Washington, D.C.: Public Affairs Press, 1968.

Wheeler-Bennett, John W., and Anthony Nicholls. *The Semblance of Peace: The Political Settlement after the Second World War*. New York: St. Martin's Press, 1972.

Wiles, Peter J. D. *The Political Economy of Communism*. Cambridge, Mass.: Harvard University Press, 1962.

Wiles, Peter J. D. *Economic Institutions Compared*. New York: Wiley, 1977.

Wilson, Edmund. *To the Finland Station*. New York: Doubleday, 1947.

World Bank. *World Development Report 1985*. New York: Oxford University Press, 1985.

Wright, Quincy, William M. Evan, and Morton Deutsch, editors. *Preventing World War III: Some Proposals*. New York: Simon and Schuster, 1962.

Yager, Joseph A., editor. *Nonproliferation and U.S. Foreign Policy*. Washington, D.C.: Brookings Institution, 1980.

Yakovlev, A. N., editor. *Capitalism at the End of the Century*. Moscow:

Progress Publishers, 1987.

Yefremov, A. Y. *Nuclear Disarmament*. Moscow: Progress Publishers, 1979.

Yoder, Amos. *The Evolution of the United Nations System*. New York: Taylor and Francis, 1989.

York, Herbert. *Race to Oblivion: A Participant's View of the Arms Race*. New York: Simon and Schuster, 1970.

York, Herbert F. *Making Weapons, Talking Peace: A Physicist's Odyssey from Hiroshima to Geneva*. New York: Basic Books, 1987.

Yun, Oleg. *Improvement of Soviet Economic Planning*. Moscow: Progress Publishers, 1988.

Yunker, James A. "Capital Management under Market Socialism," *Review of Social Economy* 32(2): 196-210, October 1974.

Yunker, James A. "A Survey of Market Socialist Forms," *Annals of Public and Cooperative Economy* 46(2): 131-162, April-June 1975.

Yunker, James A. "A World Economic Equalization Program: Results of a Simulation," *Journal of Developing Areas* 10(2): 159-179, January 1976.

Yunker, James A. "On the Potential Efficiency of Market Socialism," *ACES Bulletin* (Association for Comparative Economic Studies) 18(2): 25-52, Summer 1976.

Yunker, James A. "The Social Dividend under Market Socialism," *Annals of Public and Cooperative Economy* 48(1): 91-133, January-March 1977.

Yunker, James A. "Investment Propensities under Capitalism and Market Socialism," *Rivista di Scienze Economiche e Commerziali* 25(10): 842-855, October 1978.

Yunker, James A. "The Microeconomic Efficiency Argument for Socialism Revisited," *Journal of Economic Issues* 13(1): 73-112, March 1979.

Yunker, James A. "Ideological Harmonization as a Means of Promoting Authentic Detente: A False Hope?" *Co-Existence* 19(2): 158-176, October 1982.

Yunker, James A. "The People's Capitalism Thesis: A Skeptical Evaluation," *ACES Bulletin* (Association for Comparative Economic Studies) 24(4): 1-47, Winter 1982.

Yunker, James A. "Practical Considerations in Designing a Supernational Federation," *World Futures* 21(3/4): 159-218, 1985.

Yunker, James A. "A Market Socialist Critique of Capitalism's Dynamic Performance," *Journal of Economic Issues* 20(1): 63-86, March 1986.

Yunker, James A. "Would Democracy Survive under Market Socialism?" *Polity* 18(4): 678-695, Summer 1986.

Yunker, James A. "Is Property Income Unearned? A Survey of Some Relevant Theoretical and Empirical Evidence," working paper, Center for Business and Economic Research, Western Illinois University, 1987.

Yunker, James A. "Risk-Taking as a Justification for Property Income," *Journal of Comparative Economics* 12(1): 74-88, March 1988.

Yunker, James A. "A New Perspective on Market Socialism," *Comparative Economic Studies* 30(2): 69-116, Summer 1988.

Yunker, James A. "A World Economic Equalization Program: Refinements and Sensitivity Analysis," *World Development* 16(8), August 1988.

Yunker, James A. "An Economic Model of the East-West Confrontation," *Conflict Management and Peace Science* 10(2): 1-20, 1989.

Yunker, James A. "Ludwig von Mises on the 'Artificial Market,'" *Comparative Economic Studies* 32(1): 108-140, Spring 1990.

Yunker, James A. "The Equity-Efficiency Tradeoff under Capitalism and Market Socialism," *Eastern Economic Journal* 17(1): 31-44, January 1991.

Yunker, James A. *Socialism in the Free Market: The Case for Pragnatic Market Socialism.* New York: Praeger Publishers, 1992.

Yunker, James A. "New Prospects for East-West Ideological Harmonization," *Coexistence*, forthcoming Fall 1992.

Zimbalist, Andrew, and Howard J. Sherman. *Comparing Economic Systems: A Political-Economic Approach.* Orlando, Fla.: Academic Press, 1984.

Zuckerman, Edward. *The Day after World War III.* New York: Viking Press, 1979.

INDEX